"*Underestimated* is an absolute delight—a brilliant, kind, and disarming guide for anyone who has spent precious time playing small or second-guessing themselves. Marantz invites you on a wisdom-soaked journey of self-discovery, helping you face your fears while keeping you laughing out loud, all while empowering you to embrace your unique purpose and finally show up for yourself. A must-read!"

Dr. Alison Cook, bestselling author of *I Shouldn't Feel This Way* and *The Best of You*

"Mary has that rare gift of words to say exactly what she wants to say in a way that is equal parts funny and smart, poetic and razor-sharp. This is the best of what happens when EQ meets IQ. If you are fed up with fear having the final say in your life, I dare you to read just the first few pages of this book. You won't be able to stop when you do!"

Jon Acuff, *New York Times* bestselling author of *Soundtracks: The Surprising Solution to Overthinking*

"While you're waiting until you feel 'ready' for your dreams, pick up *Underestimated*. Mary will show you that you already have exactly what you need and there's no time like the present!"

Jess Ekstrom, founder of Mic Drop Workshop and author of *Chasing the Bright Side*

"*Underestimated* delivers a knockout punch to playing small. Chapter by chapter, Marantz goes toe-to-toe with all the different faces of fear that keep people stuck, and emerges on the other side as a trustworthy guide for all of us. Mary is the real deal. This book will change lives!"

Steven Pressfield, *New York Times* bestselling author of *The War of Art*

"Mary Marantz is one of my favorite voices to listen to when I need to get out of my head and stop sabotaging my own potential. Her stories and wise words in *Underestimated* made me want to break my own lifelong patterns of people-pleasing and hiding behind perfectionism. As soon as I closed the book, I started mapping out the next steps in a project I've been procrastinating on."

Laura Tremaine, podcaster and author of *The Life Council: 10 Friends Every Woman Needs*

"Once again, Mary meets us in hard spaces with wisdom, wit, and hard-won truths of how to make long-shelved dreams into reality. Her never-minced exhortations always meet us with empathy, and her passion to call us into our next, authentic best seeps from every page. When you don't believe you can do it, Mary reminds you—you can."

Mattie Jackson, bestselling author and host of *In Joy Life* podcast

"*Underestimated* is the handbook for how to quit playing small that I *wish* I would have had twenty years ago because it seriously would have changed everything! This book is sharp, funny, and heartfelt, as well as truly practical. Mary Marantz has packed a lifetime of grit and hard-won wisdom into these pages, and we are all better for it. I can't wait to share this book with everyone I know!"

Jason VanRuler, bestselling author of *Get Past Your Past*

"WARNING: If you want to keep playing small and putting off the dream another year longer, do not open this book! Mary Marantz is a wonderful combination of power and grace, and in this book she has done all the heavy lifting for us to make sure we don't have a single excuse left for not getting started. *Underestimated* will make you laugh, make you cry, make you think, and challenge all your 'I'm my own worst enemy' ways . . . often on the same page. Read this EXCELLENT book!"

Graham Cochrane, *USA Today* bestselling author of *Rebel: Find Yourself by Not Following the Crowd*

"If you've ever struggled with fear, doubt, insecurity, or impostor syndrome, this book is for you. In *Underestimated*, Mary Marantz gives you the encouragement you need to get back up and try again, and she gives you the kick in the pants you need to stop making excuses and playing small. This book will fire you up and make you believe that you can do that new hard thing you've been wanting to do—because guess what? You can. I'm so thankful for Mary and this powerful book."

Christy Wright, bestselling author of *Take Back Your Time*

underestimated

Books by Mary Marantz
_____

Dirt
Slow Growth Equals Strong Roots
Underestimated

underestimated

The Surprisingly Simple Shift
to Quit Playing Small, Name the Fear,
and Move Forward Anyway

MARY MARANTZ

a division of Baker Publishing Group
Grand Rapids, Michigan

© 2025 by Mary Marantz

Published by Revell
a division of Baker Publishing Group
Grand Rapids, Michigan
RevellBooks.com

Printed in the United States of America

All rights reserved. No part of this publication may be reproduced, stored in a retrieval system, or transmitted in any form or by any means—for example, electronic, photocopy, recording—without the prior written permission of the publisher. The only exception is brief quotations in printed reviews.

Library of Congress Cataloging-in-Publication Data
Names: Marantz, Mary, author.
Title: Underestimated : the surprisingly simple shift to quit playing small, name the fear, and move forward anyway / Mary Marantz.
Description: Grand Rapids, Michigan : Revell, a division of Baker Publishing Group, [2025] | Includes bibliographical references.
Identifiers: LCCN 2024044839 | ISBN 9780800738495 (cloth) | ISBN 9781493448562 (ebook)
Subjects: LCSH: Self-actualization (Psychology) | Success. | Resilience (Personality trait)
Classification: LCC BF637.S4 M22847 2025 | DDC 158.1—dc23/eng/20241211
LC record available at https://lccn.loc.gov/2024044839

Excerpts from *Dirt* by Mary Marantz, Copyright © 2020, are used by permission of Revell, a division of Baker Publishing Group.

Excerpts from *Slow Growth Equals Strong Roots* by Mary Marantz, Copyright © 2022, are used by permission of Revell, a division of Baker Publishing Group.

Published in association with Illuminate Literary Agency, www.illuminateliterary.com.

Interior design by William Overbeeke
Illustrations by Hannah Boers

Baker Publishing Group publications use paper produced from sustainable forestry practices and postconsumer waste whenever possible.

25 26 27 28 29 30 31   7 6 5 4 3 2 1

"Beautiful people do not just happen."
—Elisabeth Kübler-Ross

Hard-story people are *my* kind of people.

Here's to the kind ones, the quiet ones, the ones so often overlooked.

Pain, like progressively finer grits of sandpaper, has worn off your hard edges, making you a soft, safe place to land for others. But your muddy story also means you just can't believe . . . someone like *you* will ever matter.

For all those who have ever felt *Underestimated*—first by the world, but even worse by yourself—these words are both a love letter to you and a field guide as we fight our way forward *together*. More than anything, as we begin, know this:

**A lifetime of being overlooked . . .
has now turned you into someone who *sees*.**

contents

Foreword by Sharon McMahon 11

1. Starting Over Is a Rolling Boulder 15

2. Fear Is a Broken Script 30

3. Self-Sabotage Is a Shot Glass 39

✦ **THE SHIFT:**
Ironically, We Quit Playing Small by Starting Small 52

4. Second-Guessing Is a Missing Handbook 54

5. "Not Enough" Is a Blank Space 67

✦ **SCENIC OVERLOOK #1:**
Resilience Is a Long Road Ahead 78

6. Impostor Syndrome Is a Sheet of Thin Ice 80

7. Overthinking Is an Orange Safety Cone 97

8. Procrastination Is a Double-Edged Sword   119

9. People-Pleasing Is a Lonely Intersection   142

10. Perfectionism Is Hiding with Better PR   158

✦ SCENIC OVERLOOK #2:
   Grief Is a Story Not Yet Lived   172

11. Failure Is a Bankrupt Identity   174

12. Criticism Is an Inside Job   190

13. Distraction Is a Clock That's Ticking   219

14. Success Is a Slippery Slope   237

✦ THE SUMMIT:
   Finish Lines Are a Full-Circle Moment   252

Acknowledgments   255

Notes   259

foreword

REBECCA BROWN MITCHELL STEPPED off the train, covered from head to toe in black taffeta fabric. Her teenage daughter followed behind and glanced warily around at this unfamiliar town perched on the banks of a churning river: Eagle Rock, Idaho. In 1882, Eagle Rock was barely more than saloons and shanties, and certainly no place for a single woman and her daughter. Rebecca was forty-eight years old, her hair now graying, her jaw set into the firm resolve of a woman who has seen the valley and is determined to summit the mountain in front of her.

No part of her external circumstances would lead one to believe that Rebecca was about to change the course of history. Not her finances—she was poor. Not her personal life—she had lost two husbands, one to death and his brother to a failed marriage. Not her education—she had little.

And yet, Rebecca, like my friend Mary Marantz, knew that she was meant for more. When Rebecca disembarked in the town that would someday change its name to Idaho Falls, necessity forced her to knock on doors until someone loaned her a shed behind a saloon to sleep in.

But audacity—the courage to fulfill her purpose despite her circumstances—propelled her forward the next day. Rebecca began knocking on doors once again, this time telling the inhabitants of the shanty town that she was starting a school in her single-room dwelling with no heat. *Who does she think she is?* people whispered to each other over coffee. *You can't just get off the train and start a school.*

Oh, but friends, you can.

Rebecca did. And then she went on to be a founder of the Idaho Falls Public Schools and the Idaho Falls Public Library, and she became the first woman to serve as chaplain in a legislature anywhere in the world. Her work was instrumental in the constitutional amendment that helped the women of Idaho be among the first in the country to be granted suffrage.

You can't bubble-wrap purpose, you'll soon see in the pages of *Underestimated*. And while Rebecca lived before the advent of plastic pockets of air meant to keep things safe from harm, she beautifully illustrates the time-tested principles Mary imparts in this inspiring, heartfelt book. Rebecca knew, and soon you will too, that avoiding criticism at all costs is not your purpose in life. That shrink-wrapping yourself into a tidy, tiny package will not protect you, it will only suffocate you.

Mary writes from personal experience, but you will recognize yourself on page after page. It didn't matter where my finger landed in this manuscript, there was something that I felt was not just written for me but could have been written *about* me. "If you wait for the world's approval or co-signature before you do a thing," Mary says, "I promise you that you'll be waiting a very long time. Just smile when they snark. One day soon they'll be asking how you did it."

From Mary I have learned that whether you set out to walk in your purpose or you stay home and play it small, tongues will wag. People will judge either way. From Rebecca I have learned that history smiles kindly on the doers, not the critics. And so, we might as well have the audacity to try. We might as well have the courage to let other people watch us fail, knowing that the odds of arriving at our destination are far greater if we keep putting one foot in front of the other. "Creating nothing," Mary says in this book, "isn't preferable to creating failure."

I can tell you from personal experience how terrifying it is to take the first step. How we listen to the repetitive lies that fear whispers. The lies of "you'll start tomorrow" or "someone has already done that and no one cares if you do it too." The lies that are meant to help maintain the status quo, the ones that tell us we'll always be underestimated and nothing we do will ever really matter. Mary shows us how to shift, incrementally at first, to creating forward momentum that takes fear out of the driver's seat.

The book you're about to read isn't written by some unrelatable guru or filled with empty platitudes about self-improvement. Mary, I can personally attest, is the real deal. I knew before we were friends that her mind is sharp and her eyes are kind. But now I know with certainty that her heart is true and her spirit is gentle. Mary has been through the valley, and her wisdom is hard-won.

This book is a guide through the wilderness of being underestimated. And there is no one better than Mary Marantz to lead us to the mountaintop.

I'll see you there.

Sharon McMahon, #1 *New York Times* bestselling author of *The Small and the Mighty*

1

starting over is a rolling boulder

For some of us, it just takes a little longer.

For the life of us, we can't seem to understand why other people can just decide on a thing and then go do it right away.

They implement.
They execute.
They achieve.

Without so much as a second thought or a look back over their shoulder, they simply shrug it off Elle Woods style and keep right on trucking. *"What, like it's hard?"*

And while they do it, we're over here mad at ourselves for all the stutters and stops and once again starting over from the bottom... this myth of a boulder rolled all the way back down the mountain. Sometimes (okay, *all* of the time) we're our own worst enemies.

We shrink.
We self-sabotage.
We play small.

We repeat the lesson until it is learned (only we *never* seem to learn it).

The way we speak to ourselves? We would never speak that way to anyone else. The doubts and the fears and the venom we spit inside the flickering, neon-lit corridors of our own well-rounded, wounded, raw-nerve-ending minds still shocks even us sometimes. How quickly it can all short-circuit. We look up startled from this busy work of our own hands forever pulling at all these loose threads, this expert task of our own unraveling, and wonder who could actually hate us enough to keep ripping us apart that way.

Believe us. NO ONE is tougher on us . . . than *us*.

From my very scientific observations, from a safe distance and as far as I can tell, these other people do not overthink the thing. They do not game out the approximately 1,001 Gerard Butler–level doomsday scenarios for how it all might go wrong that I have playing on constant repeat in my head—this projector reel of catastrophizing once again springing to life at the mere mention of finally getting started on the dream. Personally, I like to keep all of mine categorized and cross-referenced in at least triplicate form: (a) alphabetically, (b) in chronological order of impending disaster date (*obviously*, that one's a staple), and (c) a color-coded sliding scale of "oh you will NEVER be able to come back from THAT" running all the way up to Threat Level Midnight. It's your basic five-tiered risk assessment for total self-esteem annihilation.

Hey, maybe that could be Gerard's next movie in the franchise: *Confidence Has Fallen*.

These other people though, they just . . . START a thing. And then, *get this*, they actually FINISH it. And, as if that wasn't enough, they then immediately turn right around and leverage that win into the next win into the next one, and so on. Virtuous cycle, baby! Wins beget more wins. Momentum begets more momentum. Up and up and up their stock rises. They ride that linear straight-line graph like

> Believe us.
> NO ONE
> is tougher
> on us . . .
> than *us*.

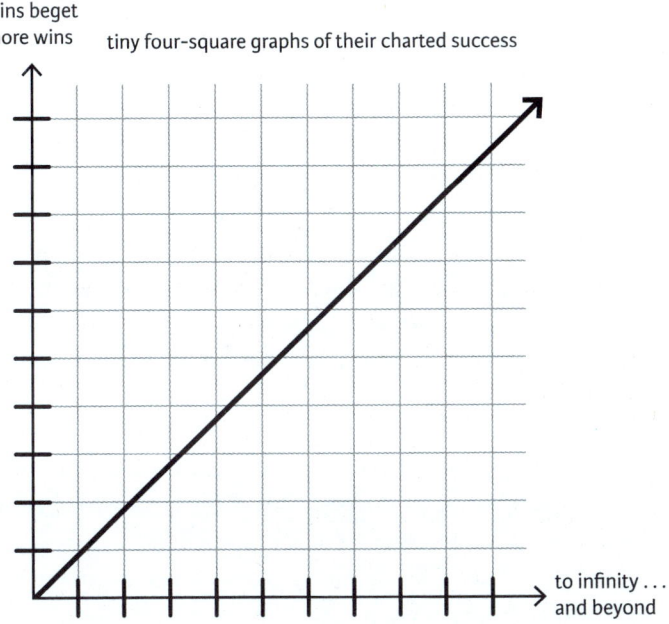

a bucking bull market, all the way up and decidedly to the right, until the tiny four-square graphs of their charted success disappear right off the edge of the paper to a future we dare not dream of, these economies of scale running all the way to infinity . . . and beyond.

These people do not shrink, self-sabotage, second-guess, play small, or assume everyone else is more qualified than they are. They have no time for the hem, the haw, the hang back, or even the hesitate. They never get tripped up. And they never once fall flat on their faces.

They decide to start and then they see it all the way through without stopping. They just keep *going and going and going* until it's done, banging that drum all the way to the end like some sort of deranged Energizer Bunny. Whose only real internal power, it turns out, is not having to first wallow in self-loathing and existential crisis for months on end before they get started, like I always do. *Huh. Who knew?*

Meanwhile, we find ourselves back down at the bottom, staring up at this mountain still in front of us as we once again begin the long, slow climb. We push and we push, we grind our way up the steep incline, the soles of our well-worn Chuck Taylors searching for any kind of relief they can find in the treacherous terrain. Oh, make no mistake. We're GOOD at the grind. We *thrive* in the grind. If there was an award for long-suffering, we would take first prize every time.

It's the breakthrough we struggle with.

It's those mountain-top moments and wide-open, spacious views—the ones that tell us it's finally safe now for us to rest—that make us want to run and hide. No, for us, we prefer to push all the way up to the top until we are almost within arm's-length reach of that small, wooden, staked sign in the ground at the summit—the one that says "Arrived" and "You Are Here"—to let us know just how close we came this time. We teeter there for a minute on the brink of getting everything we ever wanted. And then we let playing small push us right back over the edge. Like Wile E. Coyote about to get his comeuppance—just before the bottom drops out and it all falls off the proverbial cliff—we freeze when we make eye contact with everyone watching at home.

And for just one moment suspended in time . . . *we* are the kind of people who defy gravity.

We are within breathing-room distance of our breakthrough. We can taste the rarefied air. The echoes of a thousand "almost" moments crack in the atmosphere and rumble down the mountainside, like an icy finger running its way along our rocky backbone, tapping us on the shoulder, and pointing up ahead to all the summits we have still yet to climb. Both our legs and our lungs are burning. Our arms are shaking to the point of failure. We see a repeating pattern of punishment now stretching out in front of us. This soul-crushing future where we are doomed to carry the weight of the world on our shoulders over and over until the day we die.

We come so close to finally being able to lay it all down.

And then at the last minute, that shred of a moment before we reach our tipping point . . . we *blink*.

We lose our grip. And we lose our way.

And the boulder rolls all the way back down the mountain.

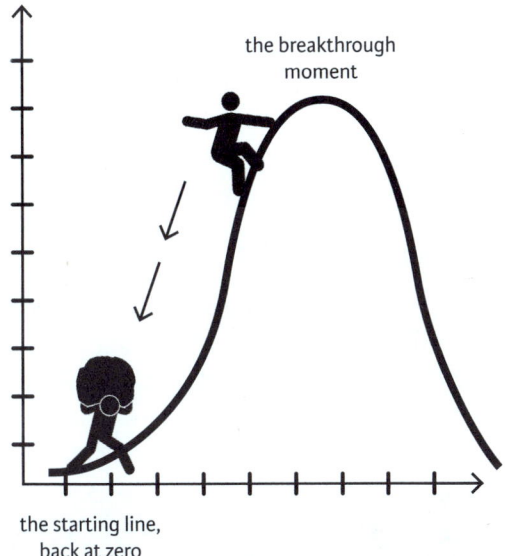

Like I said, sometimes (okay, all the time) we're our own worst enemies.

And yet.

And yet, we forget that we don't all start at the same starting line in life.

Day by day, some of us are out here unraveling a lifetime of limiting beliefs turned lead weights tied up around our ankles. Forgive us if we get tripped up. We're doing the work. It's just that *our* work involves healing decades-old traumas, moving away from wild-eyed scarcity to finally believing once and for all we've stumbled our way into safety. It's sorting through the generations-deep tangle of beliefs about what we are capable of. And what happens to a person when they finally get MORE.

Forgive us if it takes a little longer. It's just that our whole life we've believed the lie that "more" would one day be our downfall.

So, little by little, day by day, we are learning to trust ourselves. And in the process, we are changing patterns that will in turn change our family trees.

So yeah, that's going to take a while. But make no mistake about it. We're not weak. We're not fragile. We're not delicate.

We're out here doing the heavy lifting of breaking generational chains.

So, it's okay if it takes us a little longer.

Deep breath here. Find your footing.

A different sort of climb starts now.

A Reveille for the Underestimated

I suppose now is as good a time as any for us to talk about that word *underestimated*, fraught though it is.

I say "fraught" because for a word that is supposed to describe something or someone as being deemed *less* important than they actually are . . . ironically, for some of us this word has become the single most important thing about us.

I grew up in a single-wide trailer in rural West Virginia before eventually going on to Yale for law school.

So, it would be safe to say . . . I speak fluent Underdog Story.

Give me your Rudys, your Goonies, your Molly Ringwalds in a homemade pink polka-dot prom dress still not good enough for the "snooties." While we're at it, I'll take a ring full of Rockys, every Daniel LaRusso and Mr. Miyagi, and the entire roster of a 1980s miracle team that loved to play hockey. *These* are my people.

In my first book, *Dirt*, I wrote about this feeling of looking at my life, even from a very young age, and somehow knowing I was meant for . . . *more*. I knew that one day all of it was going to make sense. The muddy, the hard, the broken, the beautiful . . . the caved-in ceiling where it rained just as hard on the inside as it did on the outside until the particleboard floor began to crumble beneath our feet. Until the only things left holding that shaky foundation together were the remnants of some threadbare, dirt-caked, brown shag carpeting . . . and each other. Even then, I somehow knew. "One day God would put words to it. And then I'd see. My story wouldn't be wasted."[1]

And yet, I also talk about being so convinced I would fail out of college, despite being among the top of my high school class, that I almost didn't apply. How the sickly-sweet smell of mildew mixed with dollar store vanilla perfume followed me everywhere I went. How it still follows me to this day. I wrote about how words have the power to speak life or death and how these labels we wear can either become a lifeline... or a lifelong curse.

So, I know what it is to be both simultaneously driven by this unshakable sense you're being called up to something greater, to know in your bones you were somehow meant for more... and, at the very same time, still doubt that a person like *you* will ever get there.

And then, as if we don't spend enough time counting ourselves out, there is a whole world out there always more than willing to underestimate us on our behalf.

For most of our lives, we have been the ones left out on purpose when the invitations were made. We don't seem, at first glance, to be one of the shiny, *shiny* perfect people, so we get passed over again and again. There has always been someone louder, someone more outgoing, someone more popular with the crowds. We are the last ones anyone would ever think would go on and do big things.

We are the kind ones, the quiet ones, the ones so often overlooked.

We are the tender hearts, the gentle spirits, the old souls so often missed despite all these see-through layers of thin skin. The ones who never take up too much oxygen in the room.

They mistake our kindness for weakness. They mistake our humility for not really mattering. They mistake our silence as us not having anything particularly interesting or important to say.

And in doing that, the mistake they *really* make is that they MISS it...

The quiet one who is actually a prolific writer.
The misfit who etches beauty from pain with every brushstroke.
The hidden one who sings a new song, and it calls heaven closer.
The humble one who is, in fact, a brilliant business owner.
The unassuming one who dances, and every gesture forms a posture of prayer.
The one who has a teacher's heart that *changes* the trajectory of other people's lives.

The overlooked one who shrinks into corners at cocktail parties but opens their mouth to speak from the stage, and it's as if the whole room floods with golden light.

It's so easy for other people to look right through us and miss the pure magic we hold inside.

And years of accumulation of other people's doubts have now blurred and bled into one another, at once auto-tuned and amplified, until they've become the singular voice of reason in our own heads.

Every day it tells us, *It would be safer not to show up.*

For some of us, the weight of those doubts crushes us right where we are. Keeps us standing in one place. We are forever ready to give up before we even begin. Day by day, faced with the choice between creating nothing and creating failure . . . we choose *nothing*. We hide in plain sight. We wait on perfect. We contort because it is easier than to be criticized. And yet another year goes by. The clock goes on ticking. And the world is worse for our absence.

> Another year goes by. The clock goes on ticking. And the world is worse for our absence.

For others of us though, in a true Jeff Goldblum–worthy "Life, uh . . . finds a way" adapt-or-find-yourself-extinct moment of clarity, we take those petrified doubts, inject them with every ounce of survival wired right into our DNA, and hatch an entirely new species of success altogether.

We take their underestimation, and we wear it like an eternal badge of honor.

Now we are the keepers of every perceived slight. The oracles of the uninvited. Patron saints of the underdogs. These modern-day alchemists who take other people's doubts and turn them into our own determination.*

For those of us among the Sacred Order of the Underestimated, we have become experts in our own internal combustion. We found a way to take other people's words and shove them down, bottle them

---

*I heard this line from my *favorite* instructor, Robin Arzon, one day on the Peloton, and I haven't been able to stop thinking about it.

up for future use as an accelerant of explosive proportions to show everyone who ever doubted us just exactly how far we've come. We figured out somewhere along the way how to harness the decomposing, off-gassing, hot piles of rejection rotting in the backyard corners of our minds . . . and turn it into jet fuel.

Or, as the sweatshirt I once found on Etsy so succinctly put it, "Underestimate me, that'll be fun."

And at first glance it *is* fun, isn't it? This dedicating our entire lives to proving other people wrong.

Spoiler alert: The hero gets everything they ever wanted. Oh, you thought you should bet against me? You thought I couldn't do it? *Big mistake. Huge.* Cue the Rodeo Drive shopping-spree montage.

So why then does it feel like we are the ones always left holding the boulder when it all comes crashing down?

That's because in our most honest moments, when it's just us and the darkness settled in, we know we have made an external enemy of anyone who would ever doubt us because it's easier than having to deal with what's on the inside. If you think we're mad at other people for underestimating us . . . you should see how much we hate ourselves.

What's on the inside.

At this I picture a Pandora's Box—inside is a glass menagerie of all our most fragile doubts, our most shattered self-sabotaging, the sharpest shards of all our second-guessing, perfectionism, overthinking, overapologizing, and generally taking ourselves out of the race before it has even begun. They are all stuffed down and hidden, temporarily kept captive even, in this gold music box we keep proudly displayed on the mantel and take down at least once a day to spit polish until it shines. We've been told that it's one of those music boxes with a tiny ballerina inside, her feet grotesquely fused directly into the metal spring meant to keep her forever spinning out. It's in there now to remind us how we must always be on our toes, and how if we ever let anything drop, including the act, we will just cease to exist altogether.

But we don't dare ever look inside to confirm this.

Because once you lift that lid there's no going back.

> If you think we're mad at other people for underestimating us... you should see how much we hate ourselves.

Here's what they don't tell you about Pandora's Box. We know it as the latch that was lifted and let a swarm of evils loose on the world. But did you know that at the very last second, when it was all but too late, the box was slammed shut, leaving only one thing remaining inside: *hope*.

Philosophers have argued for years about whether this silver lining of hope was intended as a "divine gift... a lifeline, a spark that can see us through the darkest of nights"[2] in a world with so much trouble. Or whether that kind of hope—the hope that says you will always get everything you ever wanted if you will only just keep pushing harder—was intended as a curse itself, "offering the illusion of comfort while keeping us in perpetual longing, and when our dreams shatter, plunging us [back] into despair."[3]

Anyone who has spent a lifetime playing small knows what it's like to be suspended in a perpetual state of longing. We know what it's like to act as if it's all on us. We know the curse we walk around with—carrying both the heavy weight of our wildest expectations and the even heavier regret of all our many deep disappointments—knowing full well that we only wound up back here, back down at the bottom, because *we* are the ones who once again dropped the ball.

Sisyphus and his elusive boulder roll all the way back down the mountain to offer us this cautionary tale. We think that's a story solely about having to spend an eternity carrying very heavy things in order to get to where we're going. But the truth is, the real curse was always a lifetime spent putting our hope in the wrong things, perpetually starting over thinking *this* time it will be different, only to get to the end of our lives and realize these decades of heavy lifting were, in fact, meaningless all along.

They say the definition of insanity is doing the same thing over and over again and expecting different results.*

For you and me, our hope does not rest in pushing and pushing until we get everything we ever wanted. It's going back to the beginning, busting the lid off of things, and healing everything that made us think we had to push so hard in the first place.

In *Dirt*, I talk about this dream I once had where the trailer I grew up in was sinking:

> In a panic, afraid of losing it all, I found a garbage bag and began to fill it with things. Ratty stuffed animals and musty old clothes. My hands couldn't move fast enough to take it all with me. It was just then I heard a voice telling me that there was still time for me. That it wasn't too late.
>
> *But I first had to be willing to lay that junk down.* This baggage I had been trying so hard to hold on to. These scraps of my life that no longer stood for what I thought they had. This supposed evidence of something always lacking, a scarcity mindset that now no longer served....
>
> It was a rhapsody and a reveille of a wake-up call that came to me once in a dream. It told me there is freedom in laying down these heavy things we were never meant to carry.[4]

For a lifetime, being underestimated and trying to prove other people wrong has been one of the most important things about you.

But now, the blast of a new refrain fills the air.

The sharp, brass notes flood your veins like a fight song and tell you it's time to RISE, this time not to prove something but because you have something to say.

It is a reveille of a wake-up call that will no longer be silenced.

A screaming alarm going off in every waking cell of your body.

It repeats over and over until you finally refuse to ignore it.

With an ever-rising, urgent crescendo, it at last opens your eyes.

The person underestimating you the most . . . just might be YOU.

---

*Often attributed to Albert Einstein.

What Happens to Us Out on That Mountain?

In my experience, there are two types of people standing at the base of this mountain.

There are those of us who feel like we've spent years getting *so* close to our breakthrough moment, only to find ourselves once again back at the bottom staring up from the starting line. A stopwatch forever resetting to zero, it's there now to remind us how many times we've been lapped on the climb.

And then there are those of us who have never even gotten the courage to start in the first place. Those of us whose walking shoes are still a bright manufacturer's white, with pristine, unscuffed soles and a TJMaxx sticker that has yet to rub off. These are the ones who have never even taken the first step, let alone made it to that first scenic overlook you come to somewhere around mile marker #5.

Here, I will pause to allow you to (a) determine which one you are, and (b) decide which one is worse. Is it a life full of getting your hopes up over and over, only to once again be disappointed? Or is it a life of not even showing up at all?

In either case, we are what I like to call The Ones Afraid to Start (Again).

So, what exactly happens to us out there on that mountain?

It's all-or-nothing thinking.

And it talks to us differently, depending on our type.

For those of us who never even start, all-or-nothing thinking likes to whisper:

> You can't start this perfectly today, so it's better to put it off until tomorrow.
>
> You can't finish this in one sitting, so you should wait until you have more time.
>
> Ninety-nine percent may as well be ZERO. Anything less than A+ means that you failed.
>
> If you can't do this "right" the first time, it will prove you're not good enough.

This won't be the BEST one of these that's ever existed, so what's the point?

Life is so busy right now, better to wait until everything else has calmed down.

All-or-nothing thinking loves to tell us there is this elusive "someday" just a little way up ahead in the distance when all the conditions to begin will be perfect.

And today is *not* that day.

But what about those of us who keep starting over? Those of us who do muster up the courage to begin the long, slow climb. The ones with more than their fair share of scuffs on their *souls* and a long weary road that has left them worse for the wear. What happens to us on that mountain? We already know.

We *blink*. We lose our grip, and we lose our way.

But what's *behind* the blink?

For us, all-or-nothing thinking shows up differently . . . it shows up like a *cycle*, not a *stop sign*.

When I talk to people who tell me they fall into the "Ones Afraid to Start Again" camp, they all say some version of the same thing: *I always start out so strong.*

As Heather, one of my coaching clients, put it, "It's like I get this surge of energy where I have all this confidence. I know I can do it, I have the gifts and the abilities, I can SEE everything it could be. But the further I go up the mountain, the heavier the boulder gets . . . because it turns out I'm carrying all my junk with me too."

In fact, most of my coaching clients who identify as "keep starting over" people tell me that the biggest thing that happens to make them blink is something happens to confirm their worst fear.

My client Kristen said it this way: "When I see the slightest HINT of something that confirms a lie I was already thinking about myself—mostly that no one cares what I have to say or that I will be criticized if I try—that's when I blink and drop the boulder. It's like I'm looking for the permission to bow out."

For Brittany, it was more of a fear that all of this will be a waste anyway. "What if I'm heading in the wrong direction? What if I miss the REAL thing I should be going after? Am I even on the right mountain? Will this all be a waste because I was climbing after the wrong thing?"

But I think it was Liz, a fellow hard-story person and client of mine, who said it in the most heartbreaking way of all: "We try so hard to push through with resiliency and sheer grit, but I was literally not taught ANYTHING growing up other than to survive to live the next day. So, the second there are any kind of hurdles, we revert to that littlest version of us, once again hearing the same lies someone once spoke over us from the very beginning, 'See, I told you! You can't do this. You'll *never* be able to do this. You're not good enough. You just don't have what it takes.'"

All-or-nothing thinking keeps those of us who keep starting over in this *Motivation/Defeat Cycle*. It looks something like this:

Start off feeling motivated, confident, and able to SEE what it could be.
Try to do every single step "right" so the results are never disappointing.
Inevitably come up short anyway, and it confirms "I guess I'm not that great after all."
Doubt creeps in and says none of this will ever matter or actually help anyone.
Get overwhelmed. Get defeated. Give up. Go radio silent.
Remember why I started in the first place and get a whole new surge of energy.

And the cycle starts all over again.

It turns out Liz was onto something when she talked about resiliency.

She went on to say, "Resiliency—this deep knowing of where I'm MEANT to go and that I was made for something more—that is

THE MOTIVATION/DEFEAT CYCLE

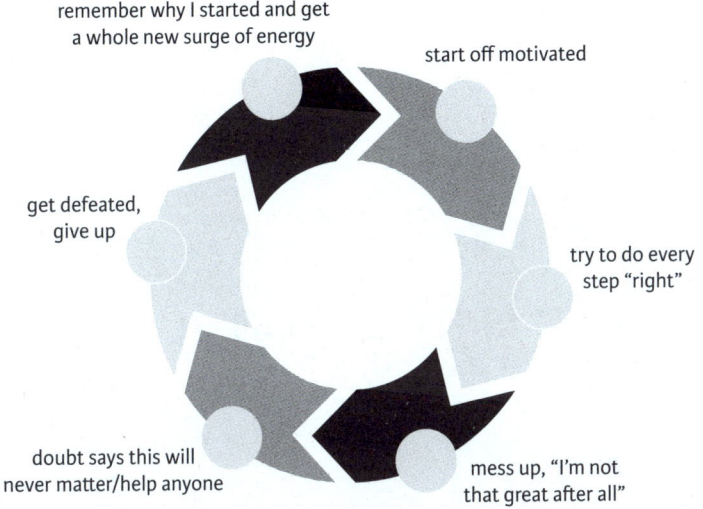

what's pushing me up the mountain. While fear is what keeps pushing me down. It's just this constant push and pull between the two."

So, for those of us who keep starting over, how do we break that cycle? How do we stop swinging from these two extremes of being ALL IN on something we care about . . . only to shut down to NOTHING at the first sign of disappointment?

And for those of us afraid to start at all, how do we let go of that all-or-nothing thinking that says everything has to be perfect before we can even begin?

In either case, it starts with us being willing to face that fear out there on the mountain head-on.

And it turns out "All-or-Nothing" is just one of the *many* names fear answers to.

2

fear is a broken script

I WAS FIVE YEARS OLD the first time I knew I wanted to write a book.

Most kids in 1985 were probably far more concerned with watching the latest episode of *Punky Brewster* or deciding which Care Bear they wanted for Christmas,* rather than feeling particularly called to pen the next great American novel.

But I was a decidedly *different* sort of kid.

Just to give you an idea of how different I was, I spent less time thinking about which Care Bear I wanted to *own* come Christmas morning and far more time thinking about which Care Bear I would *turn into* if I was ever somehow sucked into the 19-inch television set in our living room and instantly converted into two-dimensional cartoon form. It was a dinky little set with oversized knobs and faux-wood paneling, so you would be right to assume that it probably didn't have the requisite power all on its own to pull off something as complicated and volatile as human-to-cartoon-bear nuclear particle acceleration. Especially without the obligatory amounts of plutonium

---

*Let us be clear, I also cared about both those things.

and the necessary 1.21 gigawatts of power. But this was a set that was also being directly beamed into from the giant, NASA-sized satellite dish we paid good money to have installed in the overgrown yard outside our single-wide trailer—a 1980s status symbol if ever there was one—so I'm just saying, *anything* was possible.

I decided right away that it would have been far more desirable to be the type of person who would become Cheer Bear—the pink, bubbly, fun one with a brightly colored rainbow on her belly—the one everyone loved because she was always so happy everywhere she went. But alas, I knew right from the beginning that I was doomed to become plain old boring-brown Tenderheart Bear, who always shows up wearing his heart on the outside. Why? Because Tenderheart Bear was the *leader*.

I just need to give us a minute to unpack all that.

I was *five*.

And I somehow already intuitively knew a few key things about how the world works: (a) The world rewards the bubbly, fun, happy people, it is far better to be one of them; (b) I was clearly *not* that; (c) even back then I knew I was a natural-born leader,† and I also somehow knew enough to know *the heavy burden that would be*, because (d) the best leaders wear their hearts on the outside... where that also means they run the very real risk of getting hurt.

I can't emphasize this enough. I didn't *set out* to be a Tenderheart Bear because I found out he was the leader and I was some power-hungry five-year-old bent on world domination.

I *reluctantly* came to that realization.

At five years old, I already knew some things about how my life was going to go.

I was always going to be the tenderhearted one. Not the loud one, not the popular one, not the pretty one, not the happy one. The gentle one. The reluctant leader. The one whose gift was looking ordinary on the outside so I could help other people shine.

Care Bear stare style.

Like I said, I was a *decidedly* different sort of kid.

---

†True story: I was elected president of my kindergarten class.

The kind of kid who walked around the yard thinking in narrative. "She walked through the yard and picked up the teddy bear, its worn fur only further evidence that it had once been fiercely loved."

I was five years old the first time I knew I wanted to write a book. But I was *forty* the year my first book, *Dirt*, finally came out.

So, what took up residence in the space between? *Fear.*

I spent the next thirty-five years of my life delaying the dream—overthinking, getting stuck, believing that it had to be perfect before I could even start.

Which is why I feel confident sharing this with you now . . .

Fear Is a Really *Boring* Liar

"It's all been done."

"It's all been done better."

"It's all been done by somebody the world *actually* wants to pay attention to."

"I can't start until it's perfect."

"I can't start until *I* am perfect."

"I can't start until I know every single step in the staircase and have been given the complete start-to-finish blueprint."

"What if I start and I can't stay consistent with it?"

"What if I start and the critics come?"

"What if they say, 'Who does she think she is?'"

"What if I don't actually have what it takes?"

"What if I try and fail?"

"What if I prove that the people who said I would never amount to anything were right about me all along?"

"Who is ever going to care about this?"

"What if my voice doesn't matter?"

"What if *I* don't really matter?"

"What if it's *already* too late?"

Chances are, if you and I were playing "Fear Is a Punk" bingo right then, your hot pink dauber would have just run out of ink. Fear has probably hit you with almost all of these at one point or another... up, down, sideways, and diagonally.

Like I said, fear is a really *boring* liar.

But here are a few other things I've learned about fear in the last three and a half decades.

Fear attacks creatives because it's jealous that it is not creative at all.

The day this thought first zipped through my head, I realized these are the kinds of moments writers live for. Those crystallizing moments of clarity where somewhere in the deep recesses of your limbic brain— tucked somewhere amidst the rows and rows of dusty file cabinets* absolutely filled to the brim with 1990s pop culture references, a plethora of Journey and Aerosmith lyrics, and the memorized word-for-word script of every *Gilmore Girls* episode ever made†—a synapse unexpectedly fires and you suddenly connect two dots in a way that you haven't quite ever seen them connected before.

This is the high every writer is chasing.

Sure, we know that fear is the enemy of creativity. It loves nothing more than to derail you from creating anything new or putting good things out into the world.

But what if the real reason fear is so prone to attacking creatives is because it's jealous that it *itself* is not creative at all?

Think about it.

Fear is one of the most unoriginal forces out there. Just look at all those same old, tired, broken scripts it uses on all of us. There is a reason they all sound so familiar. There is a reason it probably felt like I was reading your bingo card just then. The same scripts fear uses on you it also uses on me.

Fear does not tap into the divine, into the infinite source. It is not tethered to muse or melody or the original force of all creation. In fact, short of being able to throw its voice, fear is not really imbued

---

*I owe this limbic brain filing cabinet imagery to my friend Ally Fallon from her wonderful book *The Power of Writing It Down*. We will revisit this concept in chapter 7.

†If you're a fan of the show, you *know* how big that is.

with any inherent gifts at all. So, it must spend all eternity trying to derail those of us who are.

Fear attacks you at the crosshair intersection where your gifts meet your story.

Go ahead. Drop a pin. Fear will attack you at this exact location.

Fear wants to attack you at the precise GPS coordinates for where you would have the most impact. That means it loves to attack you at the crosshair intersection where your gifts meet your story, because this is the place that has the power to change lives. Fear knows attacking just our gifts is not enough. Like my friend Kim Butler says, "Our greatest points of impact will come from our deepest places of empathy." And that requires our story. So, fear has to find a way to take us out at each axis.

> Fear attacks you at the crosshair intersection where your gifts meet your story.

If you have the gift of words, fear will tell you your voice doesn't matter, how your voice has *never* mattered. If you have the gift of helping people, it will tell you how selfish you are to start this work, how selfish you have *always* been. If you have the gift of being a visionary—being able to look at someone and know both where they are and where they are headed, seeing people for both who they are and who they are becoming—it will make sure you spend your whole life feeling invisible and unseen. And if you have a powerful story, it will make sure to tell you that it disqualifies you before you even begin.

The worst part?

We *believe* fear when it tells us these things. Which brings me to my next point.

The reason fear is so good at tricking you is because it uses your own voice.

It makes sense. If fear had the voice of Morgan Freeman talking to us solely in Mad Libs one-liners from the *Shawshank Redemption* monologue—"I hope I can make it across the border. I hope to see my friend and shake his hand. I hope the Pacific Ocean is as blue as it's been in my dreams. I hope."[1]—it would be pretty easy to spot fear coming a mile away. Sure, we'd probably still end up listening because . . . well, *it's Morgan Freeman*. We might even believe him when he says things like, "Let me tell you something, my friend. Hope is a dangerous thing. Hope can drive a man insane."

But we would at least be *aware* we were under the influence of outside forces.

And it would give us a fighting chance to muster up our best Tim Robbins as Andy Dufresne and say back to fear, "I guess it comes down to a simple choice, really. Get busy living or get busy dying."

But instead, fear has learned to mask its voice—to throw it across the room and land it squarely in the middle of your own internal monologue—speaking to you as if you are speaking to yourself.

And why wouldn't it? The truth is, we're already speaking some pretty harsh words to ourselves when fear finds us. Remember the venom we spit inside the flickering neon-lit corridors of our raw-nerve-ending minds?

What perfect camouflage that is for fear to slip right in.

And, for our part, we go right along with it.

There's a reason so many of the names we give fear include that word *self*: self-doubt, self-sabotage, self-loathing, self-pity.

They say the fish don't know the water is toxic because they're already so submerged in it. It's the same thing with our thoughts and fear.

So, it turns out, one of our biggest weapons in battling back these attacks is going to start with us just being kinder to ourselves. That way we know when we hear words we would never speak to someone we love, which now includes how you speak to *yourself*.

One of the trickiest lies fear will tell you is "later would be better."

Fear will tell you that you have too much going on right now. That the next few weeks (turned years) will be too hectic. It will tell you that this elusive place called "someday" up in the distance will somehow magically have more time, more money, more quiet, more focus, more discipline. Fear doesn't shout "NEVER," it simply whispers "not yet."

To paraphrase Steven Pressfield,* the reason this particular lie makes such an effective trap is because it's not saying, "I'm never going to start this dream." It just says, "I'll start tomorrow."[2]

In a similar way, another of my favorite quotes I remind myself of says, "If fear can't make you quit, it will make you busy."†

Fear operates in a currency of wasted minutes turned wasted years. And the more of your minutes it can get you to trade away—believing that it's not really a forfeiture, just a delay—the more of your life it will own.

It will own you with its distractions.

It will own you with its delays.

It will own you with the lie that someday would be better than today.

Fear is not your friend. Start anyway. Start now.

Fear wouldn't bother you unless it knew how much this work matters.

Fear attacks you in direct proportion to how much you're *meant* to do this work. The more you are doing the work you are MOST called to do, the louder fear will get.

See, fear is not a very *creative* guy ... but he IS a *busy* guy.

Fear has tons of people to go torment. So, like any good productive overachiever, it has learned to prioritize.‡ And part of that prioritizing means not really concerning itself too much with the ones who are already playing it safe. They are in maintenance fear mode, at best. A

---

*Steven Pressfield wrote in-depth about what he calls The Resistance and the tricks it uses on us in his formidable book *The War of Art*, which I recommend to every one of my writing course students. Consider this me now recommending it to you as well.

†This is an adaptation of a saying commonly attributed to Corrie ten Boom, "If the devil can't make you sin, he'll make you busy."

‡Here I want you to picture nothing short of Jim Carrey as The Grinch reading off his checklist: "Wallow in self-pity, stare into the abyss, dinner with me (I can't cancel that again!), wrestle with my own self-loathing."

little all-or-nothing thinking sprinkled in every now and then, and they are all set.

But show up and start to build something that might actually help people? Show up and do the work you were most created to do? You'd better expect fear to arrive in full force, teeth bared and snarling.

We can *use* that to our advantage.

From here on out, rather than using the fact that fear has shown up as an excuse to bow out of doing this work, we can look to it as a sign we're right where we're supposed to be.

Fear wouldn't bother us unless it *knew* how much this work matters.

Fear is not a very *creative* guy . . . but he IS a *busy* guy.

We Have to Flip the Script

If that's what we're up against, here's how we battle back.

The *easiest* way to fight back FEAR when it shows up? It's to flip it for this script:

"Wow, I must really CARE about this thing if I feel this afraid."

Honestly, some of the least original, least REAL deal people I've ever met act as if they're not afraid at all and this thing they're doing is no big deal. That's because to them it *is* no big deal. They have no skin in the game, they're not invested. They don't know what it is to bleed on the page for original work you are proud of. They are just putting together a glorified book report of other people's ideas. So, *really*, what is there to be afraid of?

For us, it's *different*.

When fear shows up, it tells us we care about whether this thing we're creating is good or bad—whether it's useful, excellent, actually helps people, moves the conversation forward, and adds something that hasn't already been said a thousand times before. It tells us we care about whether our work delivers on the promised transformation. Fear lets us know that we've showed up to build this thing with our heart on the outside, where we run the very real risk of getting hurt.

Because we don't know how to do it any other way.

Fear is one of the most boring, predictable forces out there.

So, how about we use it to *predict* when we're on the right track?

Here's what I know. Fear shows up the MOST in my life when I finally start to do the work I was most created to do. *It's not the opposite.* So rather than taking it as a sign that I'm not meant to do this, I relax a little and exhale.

"Good, I must really CARE about what I'm putting out into the world."

And *those* are the kind of tender hearts we need more of.

WE'VE TALKED about the mountain.

And those moments when we teeter there on the edge.

The pages to come are going to bring us up to a different sort of brink, right up to this threshold point of no return. It is this place where, from here on out, we become people who NAME the fear... and *move forward anyway.*

The gifts and the story you've been given are not an accident. And there is a reason it has started to get so uncomfortable to go on keeping them hidden.

Instead of always listening to that tired, unoriginal voice of fear, what if from here on out you start to honor that small, still voice from somewhere deep inside? It is a voice that sounds more like the real you than fear ever could.

It's a voice that now whispers, *"Maybe it's time."*

Fear just showed up in full force? Good.

You're about to do work that matters.

3

self-sabotage is a shot glass

I SAW A POST ONCE on one of those "success" social media accounts. You know the kind. They are the ones always posting up some sort of deep, meaningful graphic complete with a lion's head superimposed in low opacity over a Lamborghini. "ROAR UNTIL YOU GET EVERYTHING YOU CAME FOR" the all-caps font shouts at us from the surface-level safety of the screen. Sometimes, they'll even excavate a layer deeper than that, a real revelation in wordplay about how "THE LION WILL ONE DAY LIE DOWN WITH THE LAMBO." Either way. Super inspiring stuff. *Life-changing, really.*

This was not that.

I suppose here is where I first have to admit to you that I follow these kinds of accounts as one of my guilty pleasures. Some people have *The Kardashians* or, y'know, *The Bachelor in Purgatory* (where you might not get picked, but you're still not going home). Me? I prefer pithy one-liner life lessons delivered to me over the wing of a private jet while some tech bro in sunglasses descends the stairs going

39

absolutely nowhere. Those and the scripty power quotes full of timeless wisdom scrawled over black-and-white photos of Albert Einstein that were *definitely* never said by him. These are what I live for.

But again, this was *not* that.

Mixed in among all those high-octane posts about apex predators and performance-enhancing vehicles was a simple post about capacity and what we believe we are capable of.

It was a quick scroll-by, and it's been a few years since I saw it, but the basic gist of the quote was this: If you think you have the capacity of a shot glass, then every time you get a little bit more than that, you will *subconsciously shrink yourself down until you can fit back into the tiny containers you believe you belong in.*

It said our goal should be to expand our capacity. Expand it until it feels more like an infinity pool. (*Of course* it had to be an infinity pool on an account like this.)

Still.

It was the clearest explanation of self-sabotage I had ever seen.

For those of us who feel like we keep playing small and starting over, we have to begin by first determining just what, exactly, that threshold is.

When it comes to what we think we can handle, just how much *is* too much before we start to shrink ourselves back down to shot glass size?

Is it anything above barely-get-by (because anything more than that feels selfish)?

Is it anything that makes other people feel small or intimidated?

Is it anything that would require us to be a beginner again?

Is it anything that doesn't come prepackaged with a paint-by-numbers instruction manual and would require us to figure out some things all on our own?

Or, going a layer deeper here, for some of us it just might be anything that starts to feel a little too much like ... *peace.*

(I'm just going to let that one hang in the air there over our heads for another second longer while we allow the echo of it to really sink in and rattle our rib cages.)

CAPACITY:
HOW MUCH WE TRUST OURSELVES

what this dream will actually require

what we trust ourselves to handle

What's ironic here is that most of us think the reason we keep playing small is because we don't want to give up the protection of our comfort zones (that part's true). And isn't that us actually pursuing *more* peace? Isn't our refusing to blow up our entire lives and risk everything that's already working, just on the off chance we might be able to one day make good on the dream, actually a master class in *choosing* peace over ambition?

Not necessarily.

Most likely, that is us mistaking what is *familiar* for what is *safe*.

Here we tend to divide into two general, broadly defined camps, where in either case the outcome—mistaking what is familiar for what is safe—still holds true.

For some of us, our familiar is pleasant enough. Day-to-day life is good, we have all we need, everyone is generally healthy, and when we count up all of our blessings, we can't really complain. This is the group that falls into the camp "Good [enough] is the enemy of Great."[1] Our pleasant familiar becomes a full-time prison we're afraid to break out of.

For *others* of us though, our familiar doesn't feel like peace at all. We have spent so much of our lives in chaos and instability that we have been conditioned to think of them as the baseline factory settings we must always return to.

Or, as our flickering, exposed, raw-nerve-ending neurons so often misinterpret it, like a bad geometry proof gone awry:

1. Chaos is familiar.
2. Familiar is comfortable.
3. Somewhere along the line we mistook being comfortable for being safe.
4. If A=B and B=C and C=D, then A=D.
5. Therefore, by the law of transitive property, chaos must equal safe.

Which is why, often without even realizing it, we find ourselves returning to chaos again and again.

Lindsay C. Gibson, a clinical psychologist and the author of *Who You Were Meant to Be*, provides us the context that backs this up:

The most primitive parts of our brain tell us that safety lies in familiarity. We gravitate to situations we have had experience with because we know how to deal with them. As children, we don't recognize our parents' limitations, because seeing our parents as immature or flawed is frightening. Unfortunately, by denying the painful truth about our parents, we aren't able to recognize similarly hurtful people in future relationships. *Denial makes us repeat the same situation over and over because we never see it coming the next time.*[2]

Psychologist Annie Tanasugarn takes it a step further: "There are several key behavioral patterns seen when a person has a 'need' for chaos. At the root of this pattern are unmet needs to feel safe, seen, heard and valued. In an attempt to numb these unmet needs, a person can begin actively (but often subconsciously) seeking out the very relationships or situations they swore off and swore never again."[3]

And for the life of us, we can't understand why we keep starting over.

For some of us, the shot glass we shrink ourselves down to fit into can look a lot like living on the financial edge where money is always a source of stress, because that is the kind of home environment we grew up in. For others, it can look like allowing other people to twist you up into tiny, tethered knots with their criticism, because you grew up in a very critical household. It can look like finding ways to hide in plain sight, because disappearing into the background was the only way you stayed safe as a child. For many others, it can be a life of stuffing down any hopes or dreams you can't go a day without thinking about, because you were taught when you were little that not asking for too much or not being a bother to anyone else was how you earned love. Your shot glass whispers to you over and over again: *Stay quiet, don't expect too much . . . and you'll never be rejected again.*

In her phenomenal book *The Best of You*, which is about breaking free from painful patterns and mending our past, Dr. Alison Cook says this work starts by asking the following three questions:

What happened [to you]?*
What faulty messages did you pick up?
What unhealed wounds are still lodged in your body?[4]

She adds, "Left untended, these wounds can impede your ability to live from a calm, centered place internally. Instead, you operate out of survival mode."[5]

Here's what I know about those of us in that second camp.

Survival mode sees peace as the enemy.

Survival mode sees peace as a threat to its very, well, *survival*. It knows that if we start pursuing too much calm, too much margin, too much rest, too much healthy, responsible, well-adjusted adult behavior, we might just downshift our way right out of fight-or-flight mode altogether. Peace is an existential threat to survival mode. So, any time life starts to get a little too stable, a little too centered, a little too *boring*, survival mode finds ways to press its thumbs right into our wide-open wounds and send us roaring back into chaos any chance it gets.

> Peace is an existential threat to survival mode.

---

*She credits this first question to Oprah's book *What Happened to You?*

It makes me think of Stephen Covey and his Time Management Matrix in *The 7 Habits of Highly Effective People*.[6] Picture a four-square grid with "important" and "not important" stacked along the side and "urgent" and "not urgent" running across the top. Covey tells us that the place we should spend *most* of our time is in the second quadrant of "important, but not yet urgent," taking care of things *before* they feel like they're on fire.

Survival mode *hates* quadrant two.

Survival mode wants us running around with our hair on fire for so long that it burns into the whorls and ridges of our very identity, leaving these raw, bloody fingerprints all across our lives. It wants us crawling back into these self-sabotaging, shot-glass-sized prisons any time we get a little breathing room, any time we get a little "more." It wants us perpetually starting over. It wants us living in a constant cycle of chaos and instability for so long that it becomes a very part of who we are.

Until it becomes familiar.

Until it becomes comfortable.

Until it becomes safe.

Until we don't even know who we are anymore without the struggle.

There Is a Grown-Up in the Room

What no one talks enough about is just how lonely survival mode is. In *The Best of You*, Alison Cook tells us,

> Trauma more simply defined is an *unwitnessed pain*. Painful events bring on a cascade of complex emotions such as fear, shock, anger, and a sense of vulnerability. Stress chemicals, like cortisol, are released, affecting the brain, body, and responses to other people. If the pain isn't acknowledged and healed through loving connection, a wound is created that can fester for years.
>
> Children are particularly vulnerable to the impact of trauma because they don't have the capacity to process complex, emotionally charged situations. When left alone with any sort of pain, children will infuse events with meaning that is often self-shaming.[7]

At this, a thousand memories come flooding back all at once, playing one over another—bleeding and blurring into each other until you can't tell where one ends and the other begins—like one film reel with far too many soundtracks.

But in the end, there is this one that always crystallizes above the rest.

A tiny me. Alone with the hurt. Bare legs and a broken heart. Crying and crying on the kitchen floor until I can't breathe. And no one is coming to save me. There is hardly a day that goes by now where I don't think about what I would give, as a grown-up woman, to be able to bend down, pick up that littlest version of me, and rock her gently in my arms. To pat her back and feel the thin flannel of her little nightgown, press my cheek into her cheek and feel her hot tears trace the depths of the laugh lines on my forty-four-year-old face. I would give anything to hold her little hand to my heart until it starts keeping time with the beat of her own drum—a backbeat, driving rhythm thudding out the apology we have both so longed to hear: "I'm sorry this happened to you"—and whisper over and over gently to her there until the sobs subside.

I often wake in the middle of the night from that nightmare even now, this scene playing out again and again in the most wounded recesses of my mind. And in the 3 a.m. darkness I put a cool hand on my own grown-up forehead, and I repeat the words I would whisper over her: "You are okay. You are safe. You are loved."*

What happened to you?
What faulty messages did you pick up?
What unhealed wounds are still lodged in your body?

Not long after first seeing that capacity post, I got to sit down with Dr. Alison Cook on my podcast, *The Mary Marantz Show*.

And I told her about the shot glass.

---

*I first heard these three phrases in a video from Mel Robbins and I say them to myself all the time now.

> "There IS a grown-up in the room who can be trusted. That grown-up is you."

I asked her how we were supposed to ever break out of these tiny containers we keep putting ourselves in if most of the time we don't even realize we're doing it. If we're doing it subconsciously.

There is not an ounce of hyperbole in this next part when I tell you: Her answer is *changing* my life.

She said the way you start to stretch and build your capacity is by *making (and keeping) small but important commitments to yourself each day.*[8]

Going back to her book *The Best of You*, we pulled up and talked about this quote:

> If you didn't experience security growing up as a child, you may feel a sense of chaos internally. But you can teach yourself what safety feels like by building trust with yourself. Start by making—and keeping—small commitments to yourself each day. Choose something basic that also feels important to you... and commit to it for one week....
>
> As you build consistency into your days and weeks, you start to trust yourself. You can do small things each day to create a sense of order and predictability.... Remind yourself that learning to honor yourself in small and big ways is key to reestablishing a sense of safety.[9]

She then looked me straight in the eye and said, "As you do this you are teaching yourself that there IS a grown-up in the room who can be trusted. That grown-up is you."

I burst into tears on the spot.

A Fear More Haunting Than Failure

A lot of people hear a word like "capacity" and they instantly think of *bandwidth*. As in, "I don't have the capacity to take on that task or add another single thing to my calendar right now."

And this is certainly *one* reason why people play small. They can get into a scarcity mindset around whether or not they'll have enough time, enough money, enough margin, enough energy, enough focus, or whether they'll be able to start something new and actually stay consistent with it. So maybe it's best not to start right now at all. There's that all-or-nothing thinking come back to haunt us.

But capacity, true to its infinity-pool version of itself, is actually something far more expansive than this.

I went to law school, so I am a big fan of working definitions. For our purposes here, I want us to think about capacity as this: *the amount we trust ourselves to steward well.*

Whether that's time, money, success, responsibilities, attention, applause—or some of the more potentially negative situations too, like criticism, pressure, pruning, setbacks, disappointments, a season of anonymity—whatever the case, *capacity is the amount we are able to hold space for and navigate well as we respond to it with wisdom.*

In other words, capacity expands in direct proportion to our ability to become the grown-up in the room who can be trusted.

Back to bursting into tears on the spot.

That line hit me like a pinprick to a water balloon because I know what it is to have something about your childhood make you go on doubting yourself well into your grown-up years.

In *Dirt* I wrote:

> Growing up without a lot does something to your brain. I can't explain it. Maybe it has something to do with the prefrontal cortex still developing. Or maybe it's negative neural pathways grown closer over time at the repetition and replaying of bad thoughts turned bad generational patterns. I don't know, maybe it's just inhaling all the mildew.
> Whatever it is, it makes you *expect* to fail before you've even tried. . . .
> There are a lot of different ways to describe this feeling. You can call it fear of failure, being your own worst critic, being too hard on yourself, self-doubt, lack of confidence, low self-esteem, insecurity, a poverty mentality, or just a plain old pervasive sense that no matter what you do, you will *never* be enough.
> *Pretty fun, right?*[10]

But the truth is, that's just the start of it.

For some of us, there is a specter of fear far more haunting than failure. It is the apparition of success.

We are the ones who have spent our whole lives believing the lie that "more" would one day be our downfall.

Greedy, selfish, narcissistic, vain, vapid, self-centered, shallow. These are the words I hear my students use when I ask them how "more" might change them for the worse.

The more eyes on what we're doing, the more criticism will come.

The more success we find, the more chance of making it all about us.

The more money we make, the more the likelihood of losing it all.

But here's the other side of this: More can also feel like a betrayal of the very people and places that once raised you.

Growing up, my family made no secret of how they felt about those with "more."

Dad would sit at our kitchen table rubbing his chainsaw-grease-stained hands together, the well-inked evidence of a lifetime spent logging in the treacherous West Virginia woods now leaving black marks all up and down my own permanent record.

"Kid." (JR Bess *always* called me Kid.)

"Kid, let me tell ya." (And he always started all of his *most* serious sentences with *let me tell ya*.)

"Kid, let me tell ya. There's good people. And then there's RICH people. And the two are *rarely* the same."

With him, it was always an us versus them. An otherization of people born into a world he had no desire to understand. The

> There is a specter of fear far more haunting than failure. It is the apparition of success.

outsiders. The people who didn't belong. The ones who clearly weren't from around here.

In my father's worldview, good hardworking people showed up with some *dirt* on their hands. In his "if you didn't struggle for it, you probably don't deserve it" economy, it turned out we had our own version of the haves and have-nots.

We had integrity, character, work ethic, and grit.

And "they" had *not*.

Some of us grew up with a really ... *complicated* ... relationship with "more."

We were simultaneously pressured to excel and achieve, to break all the barriers of the "firsts" in our family tree, to make both our parents and our hometowns proud ... but to never go so far out into the world that they no longer recognize us. It was a delicate tightrope to walk, indeed. An underdog story threaded through the eye of a needle where our hero never once gets too big for their britches or does anything to act higher than their raising. Everyone loves the spotlight we're standing in, so long as the shine reflects well on them. Just make sure you watch out for that first perceived misstep. The sudden drop is a real doozy on the way down.

More feels fraught with its own worst-case scenarios.

More feels like you are being set up from the very beginning to fail.

More feels like you are a bad case study in the making.

Oh, you heard about the Joneses, right? Everything was going so great for them, we were all just trying to keep up ... until they got just a little bit more. And THAT, as it turns out, was their undoing.

Like Icarus with his waxen wings flittering just a little too close to the sun, the subtext pulls all of its own punch lines.

"See, it's when you try to climb too high, *that's* when you get burned."

Our shot glass echoes with the scarcity mindsets of every generation who came before and tells us the past is doomed to repeat itself.

Kid, let me tell ya. This is the way it is, this is the way it was, this is the way it always will be.

So, we go ahead and wire that poverty mentality right into our DNA. It whispers to us how we will never be more than the muddiest parts of our story. How we cannot be trusted with more than barely-get-by. How we should never be left to our own devices.

And no matter how hard we try . . . we will always wind up right back where we started.

We Like to Sip Our Self-Sabotage

The shot glass really is the perfect symbol of our self-sabotaging. Not only because it represents the tiny little containers we try to put ourselves back into rather than risk taking up even one inch of space too much in this ever-shrinking world . . . but also because it reminds us how *we do this to ourselves a little bit at a time.*

Oh sure, sometimes our self-sabotage is a fire hose. We gulp down our own self-destruction, wide-eyed and willing, a torrent of bad decisions tearing through our lives. And we can't swallow it down fast enough. It's a rip current when the dam breaks, pulling us out farther and farther into the deep end until we're in way over our heads. Another poor soul lost to the depths of the drink.

But most of the time, we like to sip our self-sabotage.

We prefer it in little doses. We think we can keep it under control that way. Just enough to take the edge off, but never so much that other people start to take notice. We're social saboteurs. A little light self-deprecation among friends never hurt anybody. But when we get back home, there's a fifth of dysfunction waiting for us on the top shelf. A fireball label with a very short fuse. Until bit by bit—the little match girl burning herself down to her very end and setting all these little fires everywhere—we look up one day and all that is left are the charred remains of the life we once dreamed of.

Hear me out.

Maybe the reason you keep starting over is not because you're not meant to do it. Maybe it's just because something in your story taught you that it's not safe to trust anyone . . . including *yourself*.

"Play small" you hear that familiar *hiss* say. Shrink yourself up a little tighter. Disappear altogether if you can. Apologize for taking up any space at all. The world can't hurt you if it can't find you.

There is this version of you that you became in order to survive. Be kind to her. She was doing the best she could with what she had at the time.

Be gentle with her.

Make friends with her.

But also maybe introduce her to this new version you are becoming. There is a grown-up in the room who can be trusted.

That grown-up . . . is *you*.

the shift

ironically, we quit playing small by starting small

I once read an article that said the best ideas are a switch, not a dial.[11]

They don't just turn the volume up on what we were already thinking. They find a way to flip that very thinking on its head.

The most common accepted wisdom is that if we want to Quit Playing Small, we have to become the kind of people who always GO BIG. Just leap without looking and the net will appear.

And don't get me wrong, I am a huge fan of the Go Big moment. From getting into Yale for law school to publishing my first book to a coast-to-coast speaking tour... I have spent years chasing down some very BIG dreams.

But do you want to know what happened the very next day, the day after "our hero gets everything they ever wanted"?

I went right back to doubting myself and playing small.

That's because all those things felt like something that had happened *to* me... but they didn't sink down into the very core of *who I am*. They didn't have a chance to become part of my day-to-day identity.

What I have learned over these last twenty years or so of building big dreams is that life is rarely changed overnight. Instead, it is changed by small degrees at a time. Like a compass used for navigation, these small shifts of course correction really make a big difference in where you end up. In other words, it's not what we do *one* day but what we do *every* day that changes our entire trajectory and our uphill climb the most. And the shifts that have changed me the most in my life were when I focused more on who I was *becoming* than what I was *achieving*.

Our surprisingly simple shift, then, is this: We think to quit playing small we have to always GO BIG, but *ironically*, some of the most important work we'll do to quit playing small . . . is actually by STARTING small.

Let's take a look at how that plays out with self-sabotaging.

the shift

Self-sabotaging has told you to shrink yourself back into the tiny containers you belong in because you can't be trusted with more. Instead, set small but important commitments to yourself (and actually keep them!) to stretch your capacity for self-trust and show yourself there is a grown-up in the room who can be trusted. That grown-up is you.

In the next chapters, we'll look at each of the faces of fear to see how to fight that particular brand of playing small with another small, surprisingly simple shift.

You'll notice I said "simple," which of course doesn't always mean it will be EASY.

But I promise you this . . . it *will* be worth it.

4

second-guessing is a missing handbook

THERE IS A BLANK SPACE on my bookshelf.

It sits gathering dust—this one-quarter-inch coating of my once thinly layered epidermis turned a shedding of old skins that never quite seemed to fit, mixed in with two parts golden retriever fur and endless piles of laundry lint. It gathers there, stale on the shelf, a testament to how quickly our days turn into years, until at last I can draw my name in cursive in all the missing gaps. Tracing, always retracing. The curved, twisting lines that brought me here often cut back on themselves sharply in unexpected places and then turn to reluctantly begin again. I am forever trying to put my finger on just where, exactly, it all went wrong.

And I know I'm not alone.

Every hard-story person I know in real life has told me at one point in time or another that they feel like they missed out on being given the handbook for life.

In my head, this handbook looks like the ultimate Scout's survival guide. It's that 1970s faded olive-green color of an old-school national park logo, the rough, weather-worn, textured linen typical of this exact kind of hard-won, hardbound wisdom no longer in need of its once-embellished covers. It's blank on the front, a veritable stealth-wealth of information, so that only those in the know will ever be able to reveal what's inside. It has been passed down now for generations, a gradual *Succession* of accumulated knowledge (worth far more, it turns out, than even accumulated wealth). And it has been dog-eared and underlined and added to with notes in the margins throughout the years, so that each new generation has it easier than the last.

Somewhere in our minds, we imagine every other kid in America sitting around the dinner table one night when this wealth of wisdom is just dropped in their laps.

"Chad, pass the mashed potatoes. And, oh by the way, make sure you understand compound interest."

Never once wanting to seem pushy or presumptuous enough to tell anyone else how to raise their kids, these families keep it to themselves. Those in the know keep on knowing. While the rest of us continue to stay out of the loop. And thus, the virtuous/vicious cycle of the haves and have-nots continues.

In our minds, this wisdom is passed down in these hushed, knowing whispers from one set of stable, secure, never-once-even-bounced-a-check parents to their progeny, and their progeny's prodigies, and so on all the way down the lineage until it ultimately culminates in the glaring exception that at last disproves the rule: It turns out, money really *does* grow on some (family) trees.

Whatever it is, however it is passed down, we just know that we *for sure* didn't get it.

So, what's in this handbook we feel like we're missing, you ask?

Oh, just everything you need to be a fully functioning, successful, self-actualized, whole human being living up to your highest potential. *No big deal.*

It is a step-by-step instruction manual for a life well lived. How to be happy. How to build wealth. How to invest in stocks and real estate and turn it all into one big tax write-off that also somehow pays for your vacation home. It contains the exact and precise coordinates for all the legal loopholes that will set your kids up for success, starting well before they're born and lasting for generations. There are entire chapters on running your home like a well-oiled machine: laundry schedules, Whole Foods grocery lists (for the kind of good nutrition that only good money can buy), and color-coded cleaning calendars so you never, *ever* end up with a quarter inch of dust on your shelves.

And then there's the outward appearance. How to dress appropriately for every situation and never once show up wearing the wrong thing. The proper optimal nighttime skincare routine that gives you the ultimate daytime glow. And don't even get me started on the missing secret formula, found scrawled in the margins on page 47, for how to finally get the shiny, *shiny*, perfect Pantene hair once only reserved for the likes of J.Crew catalog models and the most elite of the Martha's Vineyard summer set.

Definitely not for the eyes of this gap-toothed, skinned-knees, wild-thing, untamed, working-class girl from West Virginia . . . the one with such unruly hair.

In two words, I imagine it to be . . . inherited wisdom.

THE MISSING HANDBOOK

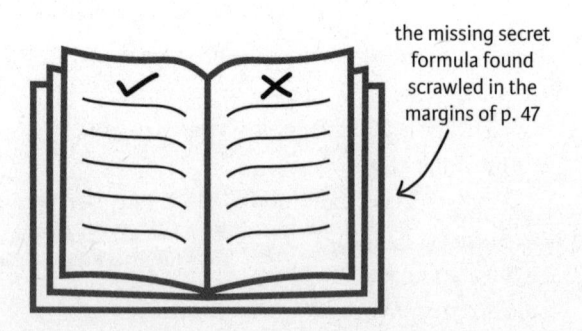

the missing secret formula found scrawled in the margins of p. 47

all the rules, knowledge, wisdom, and information we feel like we never got (and everyone else did)

And this particular set of insider secrets was never passed down to me.

Let me be clear, I inherited plenty of other good things from my family. Things like work ethic, integrity, grit, a lifelong study in prolific storytelling, and a streak of stubborn that runs right through my backbone like an iron lightning rod where every vertebra should be. But what I didn't get... was the handbook.

For those of us who feel like we've been stumbling through life without this handbook, our days have become an exercise in frantically feeling our way around every next corner. Here I want you to picture nothing short of a blindfolded Miss Sandy Bullock in *Bird Box*, rowing us out to the middle of nowhere as a thick fog settles in. For people like *us*, we have become the experts in avoidance, these highly skilled survivalists who have learned to hide in plain sight as if our life depends on it.

We walk into the demands of each new day—made all the more daunting by having to be the *first* in our family tree to figure it out—look our tired mirror reflections in the eye, and repeat those same words that Sandra once said:

"Listen to me, I am only going to say this once. We are going on the trip now. It is going to be *rough*.... You have to do every single thing I say, or we will not make it. Understand?"[1]

We're not really sure where we're going. And we definitely don't know the best way to get there. But still, we bravely soldier on.

> Handbook people always get there in the shortest amount of time.

This handbook that everyone else received apparently also comes with a map and a compass, a true north for constant course correction, and, *for all I know*, a lifetime subscription to Waze always poised at the ready to send them an alert in some posh British accent anytime there is a convenient shortcut up ahead.

Handbook people do not get lost. They never have trouble finding their way. And they *always* get there in the shortest amount of time.

Their point A to point B looks like this:

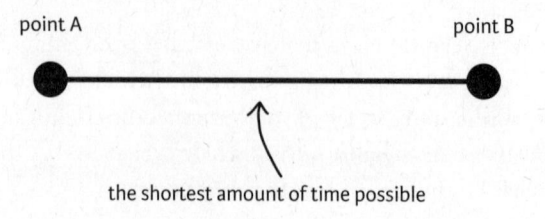

point A ●————————————● point B

↑
the shortest amount of time possible

Mine looks more like this:

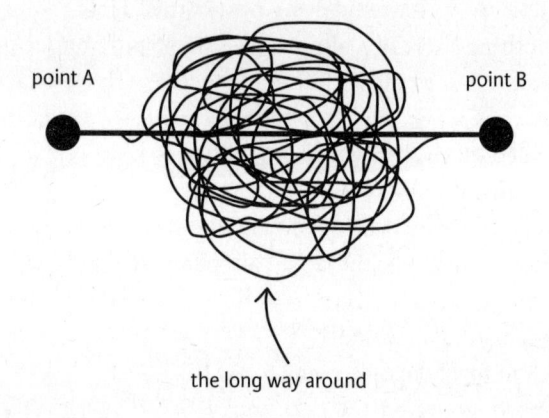

point A ●——〰〰〰〰〰——● point B

↑
the long way around

Natalie Maines and the rest of The Chicks have a song that is a favorite of mine called "The Long Way Around." If my life had a GPS input, this would be it.

Calculating . . . Calculating . . . Eliminating any route that is a straight shot to the desired destination. Warning: This will add YEARS to the arrival time. Proceed anyway?

Proceed.

If second-guessing ourselves had an origin story, this missing handbook would be it.

It's Actually Far More Heartbreaking Than That

Some people may be tempted to hear something like this and think, "So what's the big deal if you didn't learn this when you were little?

You're a GROWN-UP now. How about you *handle* it? Here, *let me google that for you.*
But the truth is, it cuts so much deeper than that.
When I talk to people about what this "missing handbook" feeling has done in their lives, the answers are actually far more heartbreaking than anything we've talked about so far.
In writing this book, I polled social media and asked people, "If you feel like you were never given the handbook for life growing up, what are some surprising ways that has stuck with you, even as an adult?"
They didn't hold back.

I was never taught boundaries.
I was never taught to regulate my emotions.
I don't know how to ask for and receive love.
I never learned to believe that I could overcome challenges, so I don't even try.
I was never taught that it was okay to say no and not give in to every emotional demand of the grown-ups around me.
I still bend over backward to people-please and second-guess my own feelings.
I still find it hard to disagree with someone. I just shut down and go silent.
When I realize everything I never learned, I wonder what else I'm missing.
I always feel like my instincts are off.
I feel like there's someone more qualified than me who got all the information.
It feels like SHAME! When it comes to not knowing things I think I should by now, I feel such shame around that.

This missing handbook makes us feel like we're walking around in the world without all the pertinent parts.

Like Edward Scissorhands dropped down right in the middle of some color-coded, pastel, suburban hell—where the name of the game was always about conformity, keeping up with your neighbors, and using whatever means necessary in order to blend in—we find that when we show up in a world like that and inevitably break the rules (because we did not know the rules), somehow *we* are the ones who end up with the scars to prove it.

If you are not familiar with this iconic Tim Burton film starring Johnny Depp and Winona Ryder, the storyline is basically this: Edward (Johnny Depp) is being assembled high up on the hill in a creepy, gothic-style castle, by a well-meaning father figure in the form of Vincent Price, aka "The Inventor." What started with holding up a heart-shaped cookie to a robot on his conveyor line quickly turns into The Inventor replacing this robot piece by piece with human parts until all he is missing is his hands. (Which still currently consist, as you might have astutely surmised from the title, by . . . *scissors . . . for hands*. Thus . . . *Scissorhands*.)

Sadly, The Inventor dies suddenly before he can finish giving Edward everything he needs to go out into the world as a wholly complete human. And with one *ding-dong* from the Avon Lady calling (played to perfection by Dianne Wiest), who promises she can help him cover up all the self-inflicted nicks and cuts on his face with her cosmetic powers of blending in . . . *everything* changes. Edward is suddenly pulled from the dark, hidden places that had always kept him safe, and dropped right into the middle of the midday sun in cutthroat suburbia, his delicate eyes blinking back at the sudden glare now burning down on all his most visible scars.

The poster for this movie when it first released in December 1990 showed an image of Edward embracing his love interest in the film, Kim (played by Ryder), while his sharp blades for fingers are perilously positioned all around her. The tagline reads, "The story of an uncommonly gentle man." And the juxtaposition of those words against the backdrop of all his sharpest edges threatening to ruin everything he loves makes the comparison all the more jarring.

I can't help thinking how this is us, the ones with the missing handbook.

We go out into the world with all these missing parts. Our well-meaning father (and mother) figures equipped us as best they knew how with what they had available at the time. But somehow it still wasn't enough. Because of this, we would prefer to stay hidden, to keep to ourselves in the safety of the dark corners we have always called home. But when we are thrust out into the open, when we bump into all these other people with all their unspoken rules . . . it turns out we are somehow the ones who bleed little by little, this death by a thousand cuts.

All the pretty-pastel smiling ladies, who promised they could help us hide away our ugly scars so we would never again make anyone uncomfortable, looked at us and immediately decided that *we* were the dangerous ones. But in their grass-is-always-greener world, with all its hard red lines and blinking yellow-light "should I stay or should I go" social cues, the reality is we were always the ones in danger of being run right out of town.

You could have the gentlest heart in the world.

You could have nothing but good intentions.

But all it takes is one slip and everyone will instantly turn on you.

So, is it any wonder we spend our whole lives being terrified of ever getting it wrong again?

We Believe There Is Actually a Right or Wrong Answer

In a world of unspoken rules, certainty feels like safety.

Psychologists agree, telling us "people second-guess themselves because they think there are 'right' and 'wrong' answers or ways of doing things," and since they are under the illusion that there is a "perfect" answer, they continually spin out and get caught up in questioning and relitigating every decision they make.[2]

Dr. Sanam Hafeez, a neuropsychologist with a faculty appointment at Columbia University, adds that "second-guessing oneself is a form of insecurity, anxiety and lack of self-confidence about whether you have made the right decision or not." She continues that it can become "pervasive," saying, "People who tend to second-guess themselves usually don't do so in an isolated manner. It tends to permeate much of their life."[3] A 2003 study in the journal *Personality and Individual Differences* confirms this, adding that it found "those who constantly doubt their own judgment are especially prone to a wide range of psychological problems such as mood swings, lower self-esteem, anxiety and depression."[4]

But it was Rizza Bermio-Gonzalez, in an article titled "When Anxiety Makes You Second-Guess Every Decision," who said this in a way that made me want to stand up and slow clap, Nick Jonas GIF style: "There are *often expectations of yourself that you feel you just can't reach*. . . . When it comes to making decisions, you envision that every choice you make is somehow still below these standards. . . . You then end up beating yourself up for not doing the right thing, *no matter the choice you make*."[5]

There is a saying I think about often: "I would never want to be a part of any club who would ever have *me* as a member."

That's how I approach second-guessing.

On the one hand, there is no one harder on me than . . . *me*. I hold myself to the highest expectations. I am driven. And ambitious. I have goals and a vision for where I'm headed, and I will never stop pushing myself until I get there.

But on the other hand, there is this other, very real part of me that also secretly thinks it will never happen. *Because* it's me.

How can we be so driven and so doubtful at the very same time?

In a dilemma of causality (think chicken or the egg) that would make even a metaphysicist's head spin, we find ourselves asking: Does my deep insecurity give rise to my determination for something more . . . or does my deep desire and determination for things that so often feel out of reach, in fact, give rise to my insecurity?

As my coaching client Kristen put it, "The missing handbook makes you feel like you're constantly making it up as you go along. But I will say, it has also built in me an ability and a determination to keep taking the next step. It's like there's already a fog so I just keep moving forward in fortitude.... It's built in me a tolerance for the uncertain."

In their book *The Triple Package*, about how three unlikely traits explain success, Yale Law professors Amy Chua and Jed Rubenfeld* offer us an answer by identifying one of those unlikely traits as... *insecurity*. They explain, "The paradoxical premise of this book is that successful people tend to feel simultaneously inadequate and superior.... This unlikely combination of qualities is part of a potent cultural package that generates drive: a need to prove oneself that makes people systematically sacrifice present gratification in pursuit of future attainment."⁶

> I both forever want more and also forever doubt I'll get there.

Oh, do I get that. I both forever want more and also forever doubt I'll get there.

Because I always seem to choose the long way around. Because I seem to repeat the lesson until it is learned (only I never seem to learn it). Because everyone else seems to instinctively know things I don't. Because it's *me*.

And all that doubt does... is make me work harder.

What We're Really Experiencing Here Is "Hard-Story Fatigue"

I played a lot of Nintendo as a kid, and there was always this rumor that you could enter some code to skip to the end or start with ninety-nine extra lives: A, A, B, B, up, down, up, down... or some such nonsense like that.† With it, everyone else kept skipping right to the end to face down their dragons. Meanwhile, I just kept leaping off the same brick ledge, falling to my death over and over again.

Forever repeating Level 1.

---

*In a fun full-circle moment, they were actually professors at Yale Law School while I was there.

†I don't *know* the actual code. I guess I've *never* been someone who knows all the best shortcuts in life.

This is how it feels to never trust that your instincts or decision-making will ever be as good as someone else's.

Other people never seem to make a single misstep. And if they ever do, they know all the right buttons to push that will have them pick right back up where they stumbled. They never have to go all the way back to the beginning just to once again fight their way forward to their previous personal best like the rest of us do.

They just keep scaling up and up, walking the outer brick precipices of their wildest dreams without ever once a fear of falling. Each level unlocks a new level. They know all the cheat codes we never will. They apparently got a complete user's manual that someone forgot to include with our game.

Like I said, if second-guessing ourselves had an origin story, this missing handbook would be it.

But really what we're talking about here is that we're just bone-tired of it always being so much harder than it has to be.

We're exhausted.

We've spent all this time stumbling our way through without the playbook, making mistakes that would cost us for years, wondering how everyone else knew to zig at the exact moment we had already committed to the zag. Even the things that were going well for a while have now fallen into disarray and disrepair because we just didn't know how to manage them well. We are a cautionary tale in the form of a cartoon cat in a very confusing semiserious relationship with Paula Abdul. *Two steps forward, two steps back.*

And we're just at that point in our lives where if we *never* see another bootstrap again, it will be more than fine with us. We're tired of picking ourselves back up. We're tired of being the strong ones. We're tired of having to be the first in our family tree to figure out . . . [gestures wildly at everything] . . . just *all* of this.

> **We're just bone-tired of it always being so much harder than it has to be.**

We're tired of having to muster up some endless supply of grit, all the while pretending that this sandpaper existence doesn't rub us the wrong way. That it hasn't, in fact, been ripping us wide open for years. I'm going to call all of this "Hard-Story Fatigue."

My client Heather put it this way: "I just don't want it to keep feeling so HARD all the time. For those of us who had to parent ourselves, I really don't like it when people say 'you're the parent you needed.' I wish I didn't HAVE to be. I find that I avoid even *putting* myself in a situation to go after something big because it's easier that way. Mostly, I dread starting anything new because I don't want to feel so ALONE out there on the mountain. I just don't want it to be that hard again."

Alone out there on the mountain.

That line in particular hit me like a punch to the gut.

It's the feeling that everyone else is going on without you. They are not waiting on you to catch up each time you fall behind. They have no desire to let you look over their shoulder at the handbook you weren't smart enough to pack from home like they did before setting out on such an important climb. They're just afraid that if they told everyone where the shortcut was, the path would become far too crowded. Meanwhile, you have been sent out here to this mountain with a blindfold and some limiting beliefs turned lead weights tied up around your ankles, your only partially self-inflicted scars now on full display.

Can we just have an honesty hour here?

We're *tired* of having to become the grown-up in the room who can be trusted, even if we do believe it will be the thing that changes everything. I think we just need to pause here for a minute to say the quiet part out loud before we can move on to any of the rest of the work we came out here to do. We have been holding on to the weight of the world for far too long, bearing up the entire future of our family tree on our already breaking backs. *We're exhausted.* And that's why *alone out there on the mountain* becomes one of the moments when we MOST want to give up.

It's quiet out there in the middle of the mountain.

It's just you and your thoughts and the miles now separating you from everyone else. Far enough apart that no one would hear you scream if you wanted to. But instead, you just lie down and quietly press your face into the well-worn rocky path, this hill you once again came out here to die on. Overhead, a vulture circles. With each concentric pass it closes in on your most recent downward spiral, diligently scavenging for any new signs of decomp now rising in the once rarefied air. The death of yet another dream lost out here to the perils of the climb.

How quickly these missing pieces of ours can turn into a fatal flaw.

the shift

Second-guessing has told you there is a right and a wrong answer, and you don't have the handbook to know how to choose well. Therefore, you always take the long (wrong) way around. *Instead, trust that character and curiosity are forged in the not knowing.* None of this will be wasted. And with each slow trek up the mountain, you are becoming the kind of person who will one day turn around and point the way for others.

5

"not enough" is a blank space

I ONCE PULLED an all-nighter to pack for a two-day trip.

True to form as the epic procrasti-packer I've always been, I had put it off until the last minute. And then a snowstorm came through and knocked all the power out. I'm not sure if you've ever tried to pack by flashlight before, but I *don't* recommend it.

What followed next was a meltdown of epic proportions.

Every "But I'm not _____ enough" and "Why am I the way I am?" insecurity I'd shoved down for twenty years came rushing back all at once. I just knew that everybody else going on the trip would have somehow gotten the memo for *exactly* what to bring that I once again missed out on.

Whatever I did, I already knew ... I was going to be the one to show up *wrong*.

This called for some drastic measures. So, I decided to employ a very scientific process of elimination by first going through *every stitch of clothing* that I owned, holding it in my hands, closing my eyes, and trying to imagine ANY possible scenario for why I might get there and beat myself up for not packing it.

It was a deductive reasoning of delirium-induced proportions, an absolute fevered pitch of paring down that would have left Marie Kondo herself dry heaving in the corner.

"But I'm not _____ enough."

It turns out, for most of us that handbook isn't the only thing we think we're missing.

We're One _____ Away from Belonging

If there's one thing the rise of the Influencers* has taught us, it's that we are all just one purchase away from belonging.

I don't know if for you it's been the perfect pastel pink shade of Stanley mug† that you see everyone else carrying, the celebrity-endorsed vitamin C serum that promises the best glow, a dress made especially for napping (What *felicity*! Jane Austen would be so proud!), or the "it girl" designer cross-body bag that costs at least a thousand dollars for every letter in its logo.

Whatever it is, we always feel like we're one good purchase away from finally feeling like enough of something that, up until now, has always been missing.

Believe me, I get it.

In *Dirt*, I wrote an entire chapter called "Belonging Is a J.Crew Sweater":

> It was only two weeks into classes when I swiped my card and bought that gray sweater, without another thought of how long that money actually needed to stretch. It was the most I had ever paid for a single article of clothing, and I took special pride in the fact that I had paid full price. . . . When the word *Approved* flashed across the

---

*Here I can't help but picture the rise of the machines, and a brand-new breed of Terminator that tries to bring about the downfall of humanity by using . . . TikTok "Get Ready with Me" videos. Hey, I wonder if Arnold would be in for *that* sequel?
†Yeti is better.

screen, the lady at the register tucked my receipt in a tiny square envelope... and sealed it with their logo sticker—the J.Crew stamp of approval....

I wish I could say that gray cardigan was the first and only time I tried to fill a deep, ugly hole in my heart by buying pretty things.

It wasn't.

But when I think of that sweater in particular—its stiff, sewn-in tag scratching at the back of my neck, clawing at my backbone with all its crisp newness—what I remember most is how it didn't make me feel different, like I thought it would. The cashmere-wool blend itching on my arms only served to remind me that I hadn't also, somewhere in the process, been able to zip myself out of my own skin and step into somebody new.

I was still me. Just me in a gray sweater.[1]

For most of us, we have spent a lifetime feeling like we don't look the part.

Or, we will go to extreme measures to make sure that we do.

In my second book, *Slow Growth Equals Strong Roots*, I called this second option "The Most Put-Together Woman in the Room." It's not because she ever sees herself that way and not because she would ever do it to make anyone else feel small,

BELONGING IS A J.CREW SWEATER

the cashmere-wool blend itching on my arms to remind me I was still me. Just me in a gray sweater.

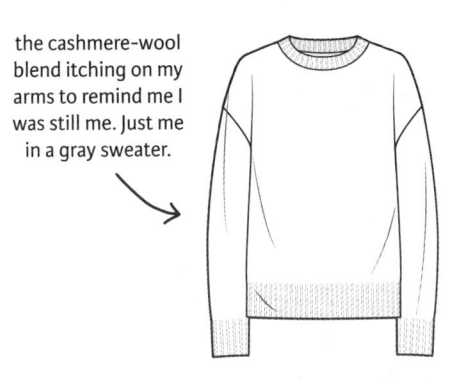

we're all just one _____ away from belonging

but because "she has convinced herself that [being the most put together] is actually the *bare minimum standard* she has to hit just to be welcome in most rooms. Just to be invited to have a seat at most tables."[2]

So, it's not surprising that people who didn't grow up with a lot can wind up becoming major spenders as an adult. To be clear, people who didn't grow up with a lot can also turn into major *savers*, as well. In either extreme, they are just trying to outrun the circumstances they grew up in. But studies show that as a whole, people who were brought up in lower socioeconomic conditions were "more impulsive [with spending], took more risks, and approached temptations more quickly."[3] As one article put it, "People ... who have grown up with scarcity, often feel a sense of urgency to spend when money comes our way. ... [We] feel the need to spend money to feel like we belong, to validate our own financial good fortune."[4]

Or, as my client Heather put it in one of our calls, "We got really good at hiding when we were teenagers, making sure our friends never knew how we were living."

It turns out, we're still doing it.

Somewhere along the line, we got the message that the "good jeans" would somehow equal a "good life." We started to treat these outer labels like camouflage, making sure we always blend right in. Like I said in *Slow Growth*, "Eventually, my only antidote to scarcity becomes this experiment in excess. My overstuffed closets rain down on me in stacks of clothes there could never be enough versions of me to wear."[5]

That all-nighter packing stint left me with some very real scars.

(Or maybe more to the point, my very real scars led me to an all-nighter packing stint.)

Either way, I spent the next twenty years or so convinced that someone was always going to show up better than me.

And then, like a currency of confirmation bias, I would look for the proof until I found it.

We Overidealize Other People

I think we both know it's not really just about the clothes. When I say that someone was always going to show up better than me, I mean it in every sense of the word. That's what we're really talking about when we examine this currency of confirmation bias. Everywhere we look, we're searching for the proof that someone would do this better than we would.

Someone else would know how to grow this faster.
Someone else would already be so much further along.
If they were facing this problem, they would know exactly what to do.
They never would have gotten themselves into this situation in the first place.
If they walked into this same room, everyone would instantly like them more.
I find it hard to imagine a world where they would ever feel this left out.

They have the "It" factor. The influence. It all comes so easy to them. Whatever that particular cocktail of personality traits is that turns a person from mere mortal to megastar, they apparently got a double shot.

And we got skipped right over.

In Enneagram speak (especially for all of us Type Fours out there), they call this feeling a *fatal flaw* or missing piece. "Fours often report that they feel they are missing something in themselves, although they may have difficulty identifying exactly what that 'something' is. Is it will power? Social ease? Self-confidence? Emotional tranquility?—*all of which they see in others, seemingly in abundance*."[6]

What I know from nearly two decades of coaching entrepreneurs is that this is hardly limited to just one Enneagram type. *Most* of the people I've worked with, in fact, have a tendency to overexaggerate other people's successes and minimize their own. It's like they have these rose-colored glasses on, a perfecting filter that makes everything

> Most people have a tendency to overexaggerate other people's successes and minimize their own.

someone else does seem so much bigger, so much more important, and so much more successful than it actually is.

Heather put it this way, "It always feels like someone else out there would be better for this than me. Because of that, I never feel like I can operate at that next level."

But Heather is certainly not the only one who reports a feeling of not being enough of something to step into the very kind of success she is simultaneously working so hard to achieve.

For my client Jessica, it's more about questioning how she shows up in the world. "I always find myself getting really intimidated by very educated or distinguished people," she says. "I'm always afraid I'll end up saying something stupid in front of them. I guess it's just a leftover feeling of always being less-than because of how I grew up."

Meanwhile, Liz can't even picture herself stepping into that position in the first place. "It honestly scares me to see myself as a 'winner,' someone who is successful like that. I would like to think I would know what to do with it, but if that kind of success ever were to happen, I think I would freeze. It all feels so foreign."

This all reminds me of a conversation I had with author and licensed therapist Jason VanRuler when he was on my podcast to talk about his book *Get Past Your Past*. He said, "I would bet on the person with trauma in their story a hundred times out of a hundred . . . but the thing is, that person would never bet on themselves."[7]

I felt that in my wisdom teeth when he said it.

Or rather, in the raw, exposed nerve endings that were once left in their wake . . . these metaphorical wide-open, gaping wounds yet again recoiling at the rush of cool air.

In that episode, Jason and I also talked about how some of us with hard stories fell in love with self-help and self-improvement when we were little. And now we don't know how to stop. In his book, Jason writes, "Growing up, I loved, and still love to this day, self-help books on personal development and growth. I love reading about how to dress, how to be, how to succeed. But unfortunately, that created in me the idea that *I always need to be different*."[8]

I call this feeling "The Illusionist in the Distance." There is always some illusioned, illuminated, perfect version of me way off in the distance, glowing in radiant, gilded light on all the mountaintop moments I have still yet to climb. She turns if only for a minute—white robes billowing in the pristine air surrounding her, her long hair floating but never seeming to land. She stares me directly in the eyes, these dimly lit mirror reflections of her own. She smiles a sweet, superior smile . . . and then goes on without me. She never once waits for me to catch up. This is the me I am always trying to become. And I don't feel like I can get started on any of these dreams until I finally reach her.[9]

It turns out we overidealize other people . . . even when it's just our future selves.

Replace "But I'm Not _____ Enough" with "I'm Becoming _____"

For me, overidealizing other people is this constant nagging feeling—a droning low hum of pre-disappointment, if you will—that someone out there is doing everything better than I would, at the exact moment I most want to be doing it.

Before I even begin, they have already bested me. They have already arrived at the summit before I even take the first step. These broken scripts of "But I'm not _____ enough" and "Sure, but it's easy for them" become my constant anthem on repeat, the gauzy-synth soundtrack to all my best efforts at playing small.

When that happens now, here is what I am quick to remind myself.

"It's all been done" is not a permission slip for bowing out of your entire life.

I'm not sure if any of fear's lies have killed more dreams than "It's all been done." Therefore, this is no longer an acceptable permission slip for you bowing out of showing up. "Please excuse (your name here) from the rest of their entire life, it turns out someone else got there first" will no longer count toward your perfect attendance at playing small. Yes, it's going to require you doing the *hard* work to figure out what you add to the conversation, to zero in on what you bring to the table that no one else can. To see how you can turn these things you only thought were all your missing pieces into the source of some of your greatest strengths. Remember that quote from Kim? "Our greatest points of impact will come from our deepest places of empathy." Make no mistake, it's going to take work. And it's going to be hard. But in the wise words of Tom Hanks in *A League of Their Own*, "It's supposed to be hard. If it wasn't hard, everyone would do it. The hard is what makes it great."[10]

NO ONE knows how to do this when they first get started.

We assume everyone else is doing it perfectly and unless we can do it just like them, we shouldn't show up at all. But no one, I mean absolutely NO ONE, who has done the thing you're most dreaming of right now knew all of the steps in the perfect order before they took the very first one. They just had the courage to start anyway. They got really comfortable figuring it out as they went. They fail, they stumble, they have hard days where they feel like they're getting it all wrong. Just like you do. And if they are continuing to push themselves, I can *promise* you that they feel the fear with them on *most* days. Stop assuming that other people don't have the same side steps, fears, frustrations, doubts, questions, long ways around, starts, stops, stumbles, and start-overs that you do. The biggest difference separating them from where you are right now is that they never allowed fear to make them quit.

Fear will monopolize any perceived misstep as a chance to say "told you so."

Fear is going to pick up on any insignificant imperfection or perceived misstep you make and use it as a chance to say, "Someone else would have done that right," or "SEE? Just further proof you don't have what it takes." Cool. *Cool, cool, cool.* Add yet another boring script to fear's very limited repertoire. I mean, it's great to see fear branching out and all, adding some new material to the lineup. But just like all the others, as soon as you can spot this one once, you'll be able to see it coming from a mile away. And as we've already established, when fear shows up in all its boring ways . . . it means we're about to do work that matters.

The tricky sleight of hand fear uses next is "But I'm not a _____."

You have to look closely for this one or you'll miss it. Just when fear is hitting you the hardest with all the "But I'm not _____ enough" lies (not young enough, not attractive enough, not loud enough, not outgoing enough, not ambitious enough), that's when it's going to hit you with this tricky sleight of hand. It will change "But I'm not ____ enough" to "But I'm not a _____" where that new blank is the thing you most dream of doing.

In other words, it shifts from attacking you at the surface level and moves to attacking your very identity itself.

Can I just tell you how many people come to me for writing coaching who will sit there and read me the most beautiful, prolific words, and then five minutes later in the conversation turn right around and say, "But I'm not a writer."

From here on out, I want you to catch that suffocating lie midsyllable. Every time you hear yourself saying "But I'm not a _____," I want you to take a deep breath and exhale the following words instead: "I'm BECOMING a (insert your dream here)." You are allowed to shed old skins. You are allowed to be a work in progress.

You are *allowed* to become a new thing.

When fear can't get you to go under . . . it will give you a case of "The Overs."

When fear can't get you to *under*estimate and disqualify yourself by pointing out all your missing pieces, all the many ways you are "still not _____ enough," it will instead try to send your brain into overdrive by giving you a case of the "The Overs": overthinking, overwhelm, overapologizing, and, of course, as we've already established . . . overidealizing others. We'll talk about those other three Overs in upcoming chapters. But before we go, one more note about overidealizing other people.

We Get to See Other People as a Curse or a Guide

One of my favorite things I always tell people who are feeling stuck is, "Look for the guides. At the right time, a guide will be provided. So, if a guide has just appeared, *maybe now is the time.*"

Sure, it suffers from a bit of circular logic. But pesky categorical fallacies aside, it gets the point across.

Here's the other thing I tell people when I really want to make them mad (that, if I'm being honest, might make you just a little bit mad at me right now too).

When there's someone in our life we can't stop overidealizing, someone who is doing the exact thing we most want to do at the exact moment we most want to do it and seemingly doing it better, we either get to see them as a curse . . . or a guide.

We can either think that they have been brought into our life purely to punish us, to make us miserable, to wake us up at three in the morning spiraling out over how much better their life is than ours . . . believing that they alone are responsible for all our acid reflux, premature wrinkles, and latest outbreaks of adult acne.

Or . . . we can think to ourselves, "Great! Here is a guide! *Maybe it's time.*"

The bottom line is, **we get to choose.** And *whatever* we choose, that is what they will become to us from this point forward.

A burden or a blessing. A hindrance or a hope. A punishment or a path forward.
A curse... or a guide.
You choose.

the shift

"Not Enough" wants you to overidealize other people and tells you that someone else will always show up better than you would. Instead, shift "But I'm not ____ enough" to "I'm becoming _____" and choose to see other people as the guides who have been sent to help you get there.

scenic overlook #1
resilience is a long road ahead

Here at our first wide, spacious overlook in the climb, pause to soak in these words: *We're going to be okay.*
    We're tired.
    We're scared.
    We're weary.
    We're numb.
    We woke up at a place in our life where we never thought we'd be.
    The setbacks and disappointments crash over us in wave after wave and fill our lungs with a wild animal roar turned wail we don't even recognize.
    We're wounded. We want to run and hide. We grieve. We feel like giving up. We wonder if anyone would even notice.
    And yet somehow . . . we rise.
    We take these stones meant to break us and we build bridges. Foundations. The very groundwork that will raise the rafters and change generations.
    We take everything that could harden our hearts and we become a soft place to land. We learn from our mistakes. We forgive others for theirs. We decide to try again. *This time not out of proving, but out of curiosity.*

We chase these wild threads running like ribbons through our story and let them show us who we were created to be.

We trade our numb for raw nerve endings because at the end of them at least we feel alive. We'll sleep when we need to. And when we rise, we'll finally open our eyes and wake up to every dream already coming true standing right in front of us in wild, vivid, blinking color.

Exhale.

You have no idea how far you have ALREADY come. How PROUD little you is of this life you are building. And the family tree that will never be the same because of the roots you are putting down right now.

We're going to be okay.
We're going to be okay.
We're . . . okay.

6

impostor syndrome is a sheet of thin ice

Don't double dare yourself to walk on thin ice just because you have something to prove.

The year I turned twelve, I invited a small group of girls over to our single-wide trailer for a time-honored tradition of staying up all night, watching copious amounts of teen slasher movies, eating our body weight in ice cream cake turned little bowls of crunchy melted chocolate soup . . . and generally getting up to no good.

In other words, a slumber party in the 1990s.

When we got off the bus that afternoon, we knew we would be totally unsupervised for at least three hours until Dad got home from work. If you didn't live through them yourself, let me be the first to tell you: The '80s and '90s were basically a Quarter Quell cornucopia of Hunger Games–style free-range parenting (before that was even a thing). *May the odds be ever in your favor.*

To fill the intervening hours, we decided to walk down to a nearby frozen pond where I . . . [checks notes] . . . *double dared MYSELF to* walk out to the center of the ice to make sure it was solid enough for everyone else. Everything was going great until I got a few steps from dead center. And that's when I heard it. The ominous *crack, crack, crack* in the already shaky foundation beneath me. Just before the bottom dropped out. And I found myself instantly in over my head.

I came up sputtering and gasping at the sudden shock of my unintended ice bath. (Wait, did I invent cold plunging?) My desperate friends screamed in horror as they watched all of this happen in slow motion from the safety of the shore. They would never be able to get to me in time. So, the only choice I had left was to pull myself up onto the ice over and over, only for it to break apart again each time, as I slowly clawed my way out of this mess of my own making.

By the time my friends got me back to the trailer, I was without a doubt in one of the early stages of hypothermia. *Toes are supposed to be a deep plum shade of necrosis, right?* They put me in the bathtub and turned on the water as hot as I could stand it.

Pro tip: Never do that. Turns out, it can result in shock, or even worse, *death* by sudden arrhythmia.

But none of us were concerned about any of that.

All we knew was that *no one* could ever find out.

The Fear of Being Found Out

It turns out, the "fear of being found out" can make you think some pretty stupid stuff.

Like that it's somehow more important to not get into any trouble than to, say, lose a few toes here and there. (Don't worry, all ten digits are still accounted for.)

More than that, it is one of the most shame-filled, isolating tactics fear uses. It makes you think you're the only one. It makes you think you must stay hidden or risk being discovered. It makes you think there are cracks already appearing in your fragile façade and the entire bottom is about to fall out at any second. That at any moment, someone is going to be able to see right through you, to give you a quick once-over and instantly identify you as the fraud you really are.

Ironically, for such an isolating "I'm the only one" tactic, it's actually one of the *most common* fears people struggle with.

Don't believe me? Still think you're the only one?

That's because you might not know it as the "fear of being found out."

You most likely know it by its far more popular name: *Impostor Syndrome*.

I like to think of it this way.

If "Not Enough" is the fear that tells you all your missing pieces turned fatal flaws disqualify you before you even begin . . .

. . . then Impostor Syndrome is the fear that soon everyone else will realize it too.

Leadership expert Dr. Margie Warrell tells us living with the "nagging fear of being 'found out' as not being as *smart or talented or deserving or experienced or (fill-in-the-blank)* as people think is a common phenomenon. So common, in fact, that . . . researchers believe that up to 70% of people have suffered from it."[1]

But Dr. Warrell explains that falling into this group might, in one very specific way, actually be a *good* thing.

"Impostor Syndrome is the domain of the high achiever. Those who set the bar low are rarely its victim. . . . It's a sure sign that you aren't ready to settle into the ranks of mediocrity."[2]

In fact, Pauline Clance and Suzanne Imes, the two psychologists who first coined the phrase in 1978, described it as "an internal experience of intellectual phoniness which appears to be particularly prevalent and intense among a select sample of high achieving women."[3]

And there are certainly many exceptional high achievers who have admitted to feeling this way.

Nobel laureate Maya Angelou often felt like a fraud, saying, "I have written eleven books, but each time I think, 'Uh-oh, they're going to find out now. I've run a game on everybody, and they're going to find me out.'"[4]

Two-time consecutive Academy Award winner (and six-time nominee) Tom Hanks put it this way: "No matter what we've done, there comes a point where you think, 'How did I get here? When are they going to discover that I am, in fact, a fraud and take everything away from me?'"[5]

And Hermione Granger herself, actor Emma Watson, has said, "It's almost like the better I do, the more my feeling of inadequacy actually increases, because I'm just going, 'Any moment, someone's going to find out I'm a total fraud, and that I don't deserve any of what I've achieved.'"[6]

Dr. Warrell goes on to explain that people who share this fear of being found out tend to credit their achievements to "external factors—like luck or a helping hand," and that even though we now know both men and women can experience Impostor Syndrome, "unsurprisingly, women tend to do this more often than men, who are more likely to attribute their successes to a combination of internal factors, such as grit, talent, brains, and sheer hard work."[7]

Those of us with Impostor Syndrome simply don't believe we've done anything special to get here.

So, we also believe *it can all be taken away in an instant.*

Impostor Syndrome vs. Reality Is a Venn Diagram

Cartoonist and financial expert Carl Richards, known as the creator of the Sketch Guy weekly column in *The New York Times*, once drew a Venn diagram on a cocktail napkin. In the left circle, he wrote the words "Making Something Look Easy," while in the right he wrote, "Discounting Its Value." And in the middle, with an ink arrow pointing to the shaded-in overlap, he wrote the words "The Impostor Syndrome." He went on to say in his column, "When we have a skill or talent that has come naturally we tend to discount its value. Why is that? Well, we often hesitate to believe that what's natural, maybe even easy for us, can offer any value to the world."[8]

The more impressive we are at something, the more prone we are to believe that it must be no big deal. We think if it's this easy for us, it must come this easy for everyone. If we know something valuable and important, everyone else must already know it too.

A second sketch I came across demonstrated Impostor Syndrome vs. Reality this way: For Impostor Syndrome, it had one small circle entirely contained in a much larger one. The small circle was labeled "What I Know" and the larger circle that contained it read "What I Think Everyone Else Knows." Meaning, we believe everyone else already knows everything we know . . . *and then some*. Whereas, the Reality diagram showed the two circles, this time of equal size, this time with only a very small overlap.[9]

But, ironically, high achievers just can't believe we have that much to offer the world. We also think we're the only ones who've ever felt this way.

When Clance and Imes first published their findings, thus coining this Impostor phrase, they actually referred to it as "The Impostor *Phenomenon* in High Achieving Women."[10] I have to be honest, I like that better. The word *syndrome* makes me feel like I've contracted some sort of rare strain of self-doubt virus, an all but eradicated disease not seen around these parts since the turn of the 1900s. And now I must quarantine in isolation—the lone, sole patient zero—as I wait for these self-sabotaging symptoms, general malaise, and an absolutely raging case of female hysteria* to pass.

> Ironically, high achievers just can't believe we have that much to offer the world.

Phenomenon makes me feel far less alone. It makes it feel like something we are all experiencing. This destructive force of nature to be reckoned with. Something we know we can't avoid entirely—it's already been let loose on the world—but we're collectively learning how to adapt to and navigate together . . . things like earthquakes, locusts, and TikTok dance videos.

Describing this phenomenon, Clance and Imes say, "Despite outstanding academic and professional accomplishments, women who

---

*Side note: Female "hysteria" was once succinctly defined as any sort of behavior at all that has "a tendency to cause trouble for others." Time to get hysterical, ladies.

experience the impostor phenomenon persist in believing that they are really not bright and have fooled anyone who thinks otherwise. *Numerous achievements, which one might expect to provide ample objective evidence of superior intellectual functioning, do not appear to affect the impostor belief.*"[11]

Yeah. I get that.

In *Dirt*, when I wrote about the day I found out I got into Yale, I summed up my Impostor Syndrome this way:

> What if success was where the real trouble began?
>
> What if we got everything we ever wanted, only to find out it doesn't change a thing about not liking this skin we have to do life in, this dirt still caked under our fingernails. That once we go home and tuck ourselves between the cool cotton sheets, where it's just us and the darkness settled in, it hasn't changed a thing about how easily we can lay our heads down and fall asleep at night. We feel like a fraud, a walking, waking impostor. And we hate ourselves for still feeling this way. If anything, it just makes us hate every raw, exposed nerve ending all the more.
>
> "You should be better than this," we whisper to our thin epidermis. "What on earth could you possibly still be screaming for? You have *everything* you ever wanted."[12]

I don't think Clance and Imes would be surprised at all to read these words about a woman getting into the number one law school in the country . . . only to still not have it change a thing about how she sees herself.

In fact, they might even argue that it only served to reinforce her Impostor Syndrome all the more, through what they call "magical ritual" thinking.

In their study, Clance and Imes refer to a self-perpetuating cycle in which all this fear of being found out actually fuels more diligence and hard work, which in turn only leads to more achievements and approval from authority figures. They write, "The woman feels elated temporarily and such feelings of success make the cycle very hard to give up. *She develops an unstated but vaguely aware belief that if she were to think she could succeed she would actually fail.* Her belief takes on the quality of a *magical ritual* which will guarantee at least an overt success. However, the success is an empty one, and the good feelings are short-lived because the underlying sense of phoniness remains untouched."[13]

Can I tell you something? I actually sat with my mouth gaping wide open when I read that paragraph.

And, true to form when it comes to Impostor Syndrome, *I thought I was the only one.* I had no idea that thinking you actually have to *expect* to fail in order to succeed—like some sort of superstitious baseball player refusing to wash his dirty socks—was common enough for someone to write about, let alone give it an official name.

Magical ritual, indeed.

In *Slow Growth Equals Strong Roots*, I describe a parallel experience when it comes to achieving for our worth:

> We *used* that adrenaline. We became addicted to it. We feared we would forget how to move forward altogether if we didn't have something constantly clawing at our heels. The greatest fear for those of us who are trying to break free from all this achieving for our worth is this right here: What if I do the work to get healed and in doing so, I lose all my drive?
>
> What if I lose my edge? What if I suddenly have to be content just being ordinary ... average? What if ... I just disappear altogether?[14]

If "Achieving for Our Worth" and "Expecting to Fail" were ever put into a Venn diagram of their own, the shaded-in overlap part would definitely read "The (Very Unhealthy) Fuel on the Fire That Drives Us."

Oh sure, it'll get the job done. But you'll burn yourself down in the process.

It turns out there are a lot of us out there who think if we start believing in ourselves for even a second, if we dare to put ourselves out there on that kind of thin ice ... that's when the entire bottom will drop out.

MAGICAL RITUAL THINKING

(if we were to ever think we could actually succeed,
that is when we would fail)

[Venn diagram: "Achieving for Our Worth" overlapping with "Expecting to Fail", with overlap labeled "The (Very Unhealthy) Fuel on the Fire That Drives Us"]

And when it does, not only will we be found out as the fraud we always knew we were, it will also confirm this much deeper fear that was lurking there beneath it all along.

That all of this will have been a waste of time.

Waste of Time Is a Self-Fulfilling Prophecy

In a lot of ways, Impostor Syndrome is one of those phrases that has been used so much in casual conversation that it's started to lose all its meaning.

Which is exactly why anytime I heard someone use it, I started pressing them and asking, "Well, how would you actually define that?"

Their answers were very telling.

> Self-defeatism. It's quitting before even starting, assuming I don't have what it takes anyway.
>
> Being disappointed has become a habit . . . I go into every new situation expecting to be let down.

I don't trust myself to follow through. I tell myself, "You've been saying you'll do this for years. This is who you are, a person who doesn't follow through on things."

It's feeling like if I get there, I'm not going to be able to maintain it. I always end up letting things fall off.

And what they are *telling* me is that Impostor Syndrome is another one of those places where fear divides us into two camps:

For some of us, expecting to fail is actually the fuel that drives us. It keeps us succeeding with our magical ritual if only to go one more day without being found out.

But for others of us, expecting to fail makes us believe we already know the fatalistic outcome—*we've already seen this movie, and we know how it plays out*—that ALL of this will have been a waste of time. And that's exactly what keeps us from getting started in the first place.

In this comedy of errors turned absolute exercise in futility, we put off the dream, not wanting to waste our time . . . never realizing that the clock goes on ticking anyway. And the surest way to waste this time you've been given is a life spent wondering *what if*.

Dr. Warrell warns us that this fear of being found out can cause us to play small, count ourselves out, and refuse to raise our hand for opportunities because we don't want to do anything that might put us at risk of being exposed as a fraud.[15]

That can play out in a lot of different ways. Here are just a *few*.

> We put off the dream, not wanting to waste our time, but the clock goes on ticking.

High achievers have their first major failure and it sends them reeling.

In a lot of ways, success can become a prison of our own making: It feels like the only direction we have to go from here is *down*. High achievers build up this track record for always coming through, and even though they feel like a fraud on the inside, they still never want to disappoint anyone else.

They develop a "Praise Dependency," as my coaching client Jessica called it, where they continue to seek out that approval from others, even as they feel they don't deserve it. So, they go on trying to rack up successes, garnering all the gold stars. But when they get their first major failure or setback, or the results are disappointing, it sends them reeling.

Now they don't know who they are. They feel this intense sense of shame for coming up short. They want to withdraw and isolate. They feel the urge to hide in order to self-protect. All they know is that they *never* want to repeat that feeling. So, they decide to just stay stuck rather than ever risk failing again.

On the flip side, they feel unworthy of praise, so they avoid it.

Even those who are praise-dependent have a limit to how much praise they can tolerate before their Impostor Syndrome takes over. The second they start seeing the possibility that a *lot* of eyes might suddenly be on what they're doing, they freeze up. It's that feeling of being SEEN. Only rather than making them feel important and loved, they feel *exposed*. This is true not only because they feel unworthy of anyone else's adoration, but also because they don't feel like they have the *capacity* to handle it.

Some of my coaching clients have reported having a social media post go semi-viral, and it feeling like an immediate drain suddenly having all those eyes on something they created. They feel like they can't keep up with it, they can't get back to everyone fast enough, they don't even know what to say to such kindness they ultimately don't even believe they deserve.

These people report that by the time they finish overthinking every response and get back to everyone, they have gotten nothing else done. It doesn't feel productive. It doesn't feel sustainable. In Enneagram speak, we would call that a *critical depletion of resources*, this feeling that something is going to drain you so much you'll never be able to come back from it. They don't feel worthy of the praise, and they don't think they have the capacity for what that level of success would require of them. So, they go ahead and quit before they waste any more time.

They make data the enemy.

I'm going to be honest with you, for years I made data my enemy. Data told me that no matter what I was doing, I was already failing. The numbers were always disappointing. I was never where I wanted to be. I wasn't growing nearly fast enough. Someone else was always growing faster. Data was just a numerical confirmation that everything I was doing still wasn't working, and that I'd already wasted years of my life trying to move the needle with no success. It told me that, for all this effort, it had all been such a waste of time.

That until the numbers moved, *I* was such a waste of time.

> *How many podcast downloads?*
> *How many followers?*
> *How many likes did that post get?*
> *How many email subscribers?*
> *How many copies did it sell?*

But something that changed all that for me was this quote from Jon Acuff in *Finish*:

> That's the funny thing about failure. It's loud ... You know when you've blown it. Progress, on the other hand, is quiet. Perfectionism screams failure and hides progress. That's the reason a little data can make a big difference. It helps you see through perfectionism's claims that you're not getting anywhere and helps you celebrate your achievements. Without data, progress virtually disappears.[16]

We have to learn how to make friends with the data. We have to be willing to deal with it head-on and allow it to point us to the problem areas so we can fix what needs fixing. Maybe it will tell us we're not where we want to be yet . . . but it can also remind us just how far we've come.

Something happens to make them think, "I guess I'm not as good as I thought I was."

Data is not the only thing that can be disappointing. The truth is, even the smallest setback, perceived slight, missed opportunity, lukewarm response, email that ended in a period rather than an exclamation point, or simply seeing someone else be really good at the thing we most want to do (*that we still haven't started yet*) can send the best of us tail-spinning into a cobra maneuver that would make even Maverick and Rooster proud.

And when that "I guess I'm not as good as I thought I was" moment arrives, we sit right down and determine not to try again. We wax poetic and philosophize in fatalism, a modern-day Aristotle with higher thread-count sheets, knowing that the outcome has already been decided. As my coaching client Tracy put it, "It's this nagging pessimism that it won't work out. So, I go ahead and throw in the towel, because what's the point in doing all this work if it won't work out anyway?"

They feel disqualified because of a gap in their knowledge, skills, and abilities.

They will say things like, "I would love to write a book, but I don't have really great grammar." Or they will want to start speaking on a topic, but they'll say, "Who am I to teach on this? I didn't go to school for it. I don't have a degree."

When that doesn't work, they then turn to, "I just didn't know what I *didn't* know. There's so much that goes into this, and my total lack of knowledge feels like it's confirming I'm just not meant to do this."

And when, finally, none of that convinces me they should just go ahead and quit, they have one last resort: "What if I've missed my window to get good at this? What if it's *already* too late?"

Guess what? You'll never know until you try.

They overidentify with all the worst parts of their track record.
They point to that one time they started something and didn't finish it, and they believe they are forever destined to be a quitter. They remember that other time when they weren't consistent with something, and they now believe they are missing the gift of follow-through right down to the cellular level. The echo rings in their ears of all the times before when they said they would start, how they've been saying they would get started for years. Now, even *they* don't believe it when they say it.

They start to overidentify with all the worst parts of their track record.

Like my coaching client Stacey told me, "For me, Impostor Syndrome is actually me playing down to what the worst version of me would do. I expect that I'm not going to be able to see it all the way through, so that's exactly how I show up."

They feel like a hypocrite because they are not "there" yet.
Finally, one of the biggest ways I hear about Impostor Syndrome keeping someone from trying again is by pointing out what a "hypocrite" they would feel like for trying to help someone else when they are still a work in progress themselves. They'll point out how they're not where they thought they would be by this point in their life, they haven't always done it all perfectly. And they still haven't dealt with some of the not-so-pretty parts of their *own* lives.

What I always tell people at this point is no one wants their leaders to be perfect. They want their empathy instead.

Think about it. Would you want to learn how to get out of debt from someone who has never once struggled with money and has been living off their family's trust fund since they turned eighteen? *Me either.*

So, this tells me there's actually something deeper beneath this fear: It's not just the fear of being a hypocrite that keeps us stuck . . . it's the fear that if you put it out there, you might actually have to *change* something you don't like about yourself.

My coaching client Liz put it way: "I am fearful of both what it takes to get to that level and what the world would expect from me once I was there, even though I know I am meant to do great things and rise above my circumstances. In the process of that transformation, *I self-sabotage out of fear of change and losing the parts of me that helped get me here... even when those parts no longer serve.*"

We can now see how that "this will all be a waste of time" fear quickly becomes a self-sabotaging, self-fulfilling prophecy.

> No one wants their leaders to be perfect. They want their empathy instead.

We expect we're not going to follow through, so we don't.

We expect to be disappointed, so we wind up disappointing ourselves.

We look at the worst parts of our track record and believe that's all we'll ever be.

If we want to change that, we're going to have to *look for evidence to the contrary*.

Look for Evidence to the Contrary

I went to college on a full debate scholarship.

Which I know sounds very fancy.

But I can assure you, it looked less like the navy blue blazers with gold crests emblazoned on the pockets you might be imagining—the "Rory Gilmore Goes to Chilton chic" aesthetic, if you will—and much more like a bunch of bleary-eyed college students wheeling around moving dollies stacked four bins high full of all our most crucial arguments.

All with one goal in mind: to overwhelm our opponents with *evidence to the contrary*.

Each blue bin, or "tub," as we called them, contained thousands and thousands of sheets of loose-leaf white paper filled with photocopied articles, all underlined and highlighted and pointing directly to one unfortunate and unavoidable outcome: Whatever it was our opponent was proposing, it would *surely* lead us all directly into the imminent threat of nuclear war.

"Oh, you want subsidies to grow more corn in Iowa, Brad? Congratulations, buddy, you just sent us into DEFCON 1." In the upside-down world of college rapid-fire debate, if you could prove we're all about to be incinerated . . . you WIN!

I spent all four years of my time in college on the debate team, including coaching the novices my senior year about how to structure an argument and really take down your opponents, to drown them in their own evidence. Which now means two things: (1) You should never pick a fight with me, casually over truffle fries in some chain restaurant, unless you have a few extra hours to spare, and (2) I spent years perfecting the craft of anticipating any and all objections before they ever come.

This makes me a great debater.

And . . . it also gives me *chronic* Impostor Syndrome.

If there's a scenario for how it can all go wrong, you best believe I have the receipts to back it up. Thousands and thousands of loose-leaf arguments, all filed away in row upon row of neatly stacked blue bins in the fluorescent-lit corridors of my mind . . . all just waiting to tell me how this latest dream is going to detonate in my face.

Generally speaking, I know what the criticism is going to be before it ever comes. This allows me to hem and haw and hedge my way into safer arguments, a skating-on-thin-ice, watered-down version of what I really believe. It's like a tap dance on the *Titanic*. Sure, the water is freezing and there aren't enough boats. And the entire ship is going down with me still on it. But even then, I don't know how to stop performing for your approval.

One thing I've been doing lately when Impostor Syndrome gets loud is something that I learned from those early debate days: *I look for the evidence to the contrary.*

I look for all the little ways I am already showing up and becoming a person who stewards what I'm trusted with. My friend Hannah Brencher calls that "small things on repeat."[17]

When the lie says, "I always mess things up," I will literally list off ten recent examples where I actually came through.

When the lie says, "I never prepare for anything in advance," I think of ten times recently when I took care of things way before I had to.

When the lie says, "I didn't do anything special to deserve this," I remember ten times when I sat down diligently to practice my craft.

You've heard of two truths and a lie? Well, for me, that ratio is more like *ten* truths and a lie. Hey, you do whatever it takes to change your own mind.

Evidence to the contrary.
Drown your opponent in their own arguments.
Go nuclear on fear.

It turns out, Clance and Imes would agree with this plan of attack, only with one very important caveat: It needs to be a *specific* kind of evidence.

Citing their findings, they said, "We have been amazed at the self-perpetuating nature of the impostor phenomenon. . . .We have *not* found repeated successes alone sufficient to break the cycle."[18]

In other words, we can't just achieve and gold star our way out of this.

This is why I could get into Yale Law School and still feel like a fraud. This is why the women in Clance and Imes's study could get into prestigious programs and believe their admission was a mistake. Or why another woman in the study could have multiple advanced degrees, including a PhD, and still feel "unqualified to teach remedial college classes."[19]

There is not enough external success in the world to loosen Impostor Syndrome's grip on us.

Instead, this needs to be evidence about who we are *becoming*.

Clance and Imes suggest that those suffering from Impostor Syndrome should take "small, incremental steps" to prove to themselves that they no longer need to rely on self-doubt as a way of fueling their success. "For example, she is encouraged to study for an exam with the expectation, 'I will do well on this exam' rather than, 'I may fail.' When she is able to succeed without the self-doubting beforehand, she has made a major breakthrough in undoing her ritual of predicting failure."[20]

However, they warn that this must be a slow, steady process: "Trying to give [this] up too quickly, before other attitudes and habits have been experienced as personally more satisfying," can lead to being pulled right back into the Impostor Syndrome cycle.[21]

As with most things that matter in life, this process can't be rushed. And it starts with the power of small things on repeat.

the shift

Impostor Syndrome wants to tell you that you are a fraud who will be found out at any moment. Or that this will all be a waste of time. It will shout that you didn't do anything special to get any of this success, so it can all be taken away in an instant. Instead, look for the evidence to the contrary . . . not of your achievements, but of how you are showing up with small things on repeat to become the person who stewards this success with excellence.

7

overthinking is an orange safety cone

I ONCE HEARD A SPEAKER at a conference say, "You leaped the first time. But will you leap again the next time the ledge comes back around?"

For the life of me, I don't remember a single other thing he said in his talk. I don't remember what he was wearing. Or what the room looked like. I don't know if he was using notes or winging it, had a handheld mic or a lavalier. I couldn't tell you what kind of chair I was sitting in, what my own outfit looked like, or what day of the week it was. I honestly couldn't even tell you if it was a quick thirty-minute talk or a full two hours.

But for the last fifteen years or so since I first heard him say it, I haven't been able to get that one line out of my head.

Will you leap again the next time the ledge comes back around?

Sitting in that room (whatever it looked like), shifting uncomfortably (in whatever kind of chair it was), I also remember exactly how I felt.

I remember the red creeping up my neck, jumping the hard perimeter of my jawbone, and consuming the flesh of my cheeks in an instant. I remember how it was somehow both hot and icy-stinging chill at the same time, like a controlled burn setting wildfire to a hornet's nest. Where you're not really sure if it's the flames or the venom that will kill you first.

I remember how I could taste the adrenaline on my tongue, bitter like battery acid, acrid like two-day-old underarm sweat. It rushed in from the wild-eyed animal parts of my brain, a fight-or-flight flood of survival chemicals that saturated every fiber of my being, made every muscle twitch and ready itself to run.

I *know* what it feels like to know that you were brave once... but that you haven't been brave again in a really long time.

For some of us, that last big leap we can remember taking had to have been somewhere around the time we took those first few tentative, wobbly steps when we were little. But a hard face-plant early in life quickly taught us that it was safer to just sit still where you are than to continue trying to gain any important ground at all. This group becomes the people who believe it is better to hide in plain sight than to risk falling flat on your face in front of everyone ever again.

For others of us, though, we leaped again later in life.

And we somehow stuck the landing.

Sitting in that blur of a vacant room, I knew that I had been incredibly brave once. I had leaped, believing the net would appear (which is just terrible aeronautics advice, by the way—it's the Schrödinger's Cat* of goal-chasing). And *that* time I had been caught gloriously on the way down. Cirque du Soleil style. Fate had grabbed me by the hands in a tight wristlock and flung me in a triple somersault all the way back up to this highwire act of every dream I had been chasing.

And I guess I just thought from that moment on... *life would always feel this way.*

---

*In the Schrödinger's Cat experiment, a cat is placed inside a box with a radioactive atom and some poison that *may* kill it, but we are not sure. So long as we don't look in the box, the cat's fate can be both dead and alive to us at the same time. It's the same thing with the net. It might appear, it might not. And the only way to find out for sure is on the way down. Except in that scenario, *we* run the risk of becoming the dead cat.

There is this thing that happens in the movies when the hero finally gets everything they ever wanted.

The score swells, the screen fades to black, the credits roll. What we DON'T talk about enough is how the very next day, *the day after everything*, the hero has to wake up and go on living. We act as if all our life stories will fit neatly within the confines of the average 120 minutes of a cinematic reimagining. As if once our main character makes it over that first big hurdle, they will never again stumble. They will have ARRIVED.

And in the silver screen economy, arrival is everything.

But then the next day comes. And real life settles in.

Plot idea: We as the hero of our own story get everything we ever wanted in the first five minutes of our film. And then the audience spends the next two hours watching us wake up, pay bills, go to the grocery store, get cut off in traffic, answer angry emails, have trouble sleeping, and walk around with this constant low hum of low-grade anxiety about whether or not our best days are already behind us. It's not exactly *main character energy*, is it?

Pretty soon, these long stretches of even more setbacks, disappointments, and failures than we ever could have imagined play out in real time. There is no three-minute movie montage to help us skip to the good part. At times, it even feels like they are playing out in slow motion. Possibly even stuck skipping on repeat.

You now know what it is to stumble.

You now know what it is to land with a thud.

You now know what it is to face-plant as a full-grown adult.

And suddenly you become a person who flinches at the ledge.

Overthinking Begins with the Missing Blueprint

If second-guessing is a missing handbook, overthinking is a missing blueprint.

At least that's how it starts.

What's the difference? The missing handbook is internal. It's every perceived gap in your own inherited wisdom, your lack of basic understanding of the universal laws for how the world works, these missing shortcuts that mean you always take the long way around.

The missing blueprint, on the other hand, that's something *external*.

You could have been given the best handbook ever written growing up, set up for success from the very beginning. Your entire future could have been laid out in front of you like one bright, bedazzling horizon full of boundless possibilities. The deep blue ether of the stratosphere might represent your only upper limit.

But that still doesn't mean you could walk into NASA tomorrow and know how to build a rocket ship.

The handbook is everything you believe is missing in you generally.

The blueprint is the missing step-by-step instruction manual for how to build *this* dream in particular.

In other words... you second-guess yourself.

You overthink the dream.

Overthinking, at its core, is a fear of the unknown. It's believing that until you know all the perfect steps in just the perfect order, you shouldn't even start. It's staring out into the murky, thick, gray fog of the abyss—this great gapped divide now separating you from the dream—and believing that one misstep, one slip of your unsure footing, will undoubtedly send you plummeting directly to your death.

It is *catastrophizing* at its finest. A survival-games exercise in "worst case scenario."

You start to buy into the lie that there is a specific order of steps, a precision-level number of cords to cut in just the right sequence— *red wire, blue wire... red wire, blue wire*—and if you get those wires crossed even the slightest, the whole thing will blow up in your face.

Pop quiz, hotshot. What do you do? *

If you're anything like me, you freeze. Your mind goes blank.

---

*Yes, this begins an amalgamation of *Speed* references, starring one Keanu Reeves. A movie I saw in the theater when I was just fourteen years old, and loved it so much I went back the very next day. We still watch it several times a year. "There's a curve up ahead. We're gonna speed it up!" *Speed*, directed by Jan de Bont (20th Century Fox, 1994).

Overthinking, at its core, is a fear of the unknown.

Here it is, your hero moment. You are seconds away from taking the next big leap (city bus off a bridge that's only finished on the map style). The wide expanse stretches out in front of you.

And at the last minute... you flinch.

You determine to sit right down where you are—deer in the headlights look—and not move forward again until you know all the answers. You hope to run out the clock just long enough that you never have to make a decision again.

3 . . . 2 . . . 1 . . . BOOM.

"Let's be honest," you console yourself amongst the rubble as yet another dream detonates and scatters around you like ashes, "it was probably always going to blow up anyway." (Especially with such a cheap gold watch as a timer.)

There was no point in even trying.

One possibility for why we might react this way is called *predictive brain theory*.

This approach goes more formally by the name Bayesian Brain Theory, which assumes that the brain uses existing beliefs and probabilities to "generate predictions about sensory input, then uses prediction errors to update its beliefs."[1]

In other words, and put way more simply, "The brain is a prediction machine: It knows how well we [will do] something before we even try."[2] Therefore, in an effort to keep us safe, its default mode will always be to try to predict and control everything, to get us to only stick with what we already know we're good at rather than brave the unknown.

A 2021 study from Oxford University suggests this prediction machine determines the goals we are most likely to go after as it "guides us towards tasks and problems we are likely to solve, and away from those that might be too hard."[3]

So, when we set out to start a new goal—and we think we're missing the all-too-important, step-by-step instructions for how to do it—our brain quickly predicts that it will be too hard and we won't succeed. And it once again backs us away from that ledge.

It turns out, the prefrontal cortex plays an important role in our excessive overthinking and catastrophizing.[4] This is especially true when a new goal doesn't come prepackaged with a paint-by-numbers instruction manual and would require us to do some actual problem-solving to figure things out on our own.

In fact, an area of the brain called the dorsolateral prefrontal cortex (DLPFC) is responsible for "cerebral thinking and higher executive function" as it serves a "pivotal role in automating cognitive processes to solve problems by applying previously learned rules." However, the research goes on to say that despite being an efficient form of problem-solving, "the DLPFC's powers of automaticity can backfire if previously learned 'rules' create roadblocks when someone needs to solve an unfamiliar problem that requires fresh ideas and thinking outside the box."[5]

Roadblocks. That's a nice way of putting it.

Anyone who has ever been stuck in overthinking, you know that it feels far less like being held up in a little bit of traffic, and more like banging your head against a brick wall over and over again to see if it will somehow give you any of the answers. All the existential angst in the world gets pent up right behind your forehead. You get so stuck in the problem. And the harder you push to solve it, the more blocked up you get.

At this, I picture the prefrontal cortex nearing full temper-tantrum meltdown stage. In my head, for some reason, it's wearing little white gloves and matching boots and vaguely resembles Jon Lovitz as the red M&M. It stomps its little feet and squeezes its little hands into balled-up fists as it makes an "eeeehhhhhh" sound. Poor thing just gets so frustrated. *Bless its heart.*

And the more stressed it gets, the worse it feels.

If you've ever wished that you could just turn off the overthinking part of your brain, (a) you are not alone, and (b) you just might be onto something.

In fact, researchers report that "using a targeted electric current to temporarily suppress a particular region of the frontal lobes called the left dorsolateral prefrontal cortex (DLPFC) helps to break the mental constraints linked to 'rut-like thinking.'"[6] These results led researchers to conclude "certain cognitive functions, especially those required in creative problem solving, could benefit from inhibition rather than excitation of the prefrontal cortex."[7]

Now, no one is saying you should run out and hook electrodes up to your forehead the next time you find yourself overthinking. But what this study is pointing out is that when the problem-solving center of your brain (the prefrontal cortex) can just relax a little, the more creative parts of your brain like the limbic system can take over to come up with some truly innovative solutions.

My friend Ally Fallon, author of *The Power of Writing It Down*, describes the limbic brain versus the prefrontal cortex this way:

> I like to think of the limbic brain as that old filing cabinet you keep out in the garage. It's where we store old memories that we don't need to regularly access and traumatic experiences we'd prefer not to revisit.... You can see why we don't visit the old, rusty filing cabinet very often. It seems pretty inconvenient and out of the way. Plus, we're not sure what we'll find if we go digging through it. Everything seems much more organized and orderly inside the house. So instead of venturing out to the garage, we stay inside.
>
> The *prefrontal cortex* is sometimes called the "higher-level thinking" part of the brain, and while this is true, it's also a tad misleading. Most of our modern lives make use of the prefrontal cortex—the part of our brain that's used for carefully evaluating, planning, organizing details, time management, productivity, and efficiency. Things are organized and orderly in there. The "house" of our brains is the prefrontal cortex. It's the garage (or the basement or attic), the limbic brain, where everything is out of control....
>
> While the prefrontal cortex is indeed the "higher-level thinking" part of our brain (and we need it), what this doesn't accurately represent is that the limbic brain is much better at creativity, emotion, imagination, and play. This is the "muscle" in your brain you're exercising

when you spend time in your limbic system.... You've [now] stumbled across your most powerful resource for positive change.[8]

The limbic brain is where your imagination and innovation really come alive.

This is the part of your brain "responsible for novelty seeking and for providing creative drive."[9] This is also the part of the brain that can take random memories, experiences, data, new information (and if you're anything like me, pop culture references), and connect the dots in brand-new ways, thus giving rise to our most creative ideas. This is referred to in the literature as "conceptual blending."[10]

As one article put it, "Innovation demands new ways of thinking and doing, or novel ways of stitching existing ideas together to come up with a better solution. As we know from Einstein, 'we cannot solve our problems with the same thinking that created them.' But there's a technical hitch: your brain will always try to solve a problem based on what's worked in the past."[11]

Author Estanislao Bachrach, who wrote *The Agile Mind*, uses the metaphor of thoughts or ideas being like liquids, free to combine, until they become frozen. "At school we are taught to define, divide, segregate and label things into different categories. For the rest of our lives these categories remain separate, they never combine. It's as if the fluid thinking of children becomes frozen, like ice cubes in a tray ... our thoughts become frozen."[12]

Thoughts and ideas as ice cubes ... talk about some innovative conceptual blending to explain something in a brand-new way!

But this is exactly what our organizing, productivity-minded prefrontal cortex does. It compartmentalizes our free-flowing thoughts into the ice cube tray. It takes spaghetti and makes waffles.* It makes a rainbow color–coded bookshelf out of all our best ideas instead of actually noticing what's on the page.

To begin this act of noticing, we have to be willing to let our mind wander.

---

*Why yes, that is a reference to the book *Men Are Like Waffles, Women Are Like Spaghetti*.

Bachrach compares this to another powerful metaphor, saying, "Stars are invisible during the day because the light from the sun eclipses them. Similarly, many ideas remain undiscovered because, like tiny lights, they are eclipsed by the brain's activity."[13]

The reason for this has to do with our default mode.

> Your brain only has a chance to make connections (and even notice your ideas) if you create some space.... During these times our Default Mode Network engages. Think of the DMN like a light switch ... it can only turn on when you turn your brain off from tasks.... It moves things around, bringing different pieces of information to the top, connecting things together in new ways.... Mind wandering (and rest!) are really important for your brain to forge [new] connections and tell you about them![14]

Mind wandering and rest.

If you've ever had your best ideas in the shower, now you know why. Rest, therefore, becomes an *active* part of this work of foregoing other people's step-by-step blueprint instructions for our lives, and instead innovating a brand-new set of our own best-laid plans.

The next time you find yourself stuck in overthinking, trying to think right through your forehead, instead try allowing yourself to get bored. Meditate, gaze out a window, color in a coloring book, hop back in the shower.

Even better, do something that gets you moving. Like Ally Fallon said to me on our podcast episode, "When you think limbic, think *limbs.*"[15] Stretch, go on a walk, have a dance party in the kitchen. Anything that shifts you out of the problem long enough for the answers to find you.

So yes, overthinking begins with what we believe is a missing blueprint.

But it turns out, the actual perfect design for creative problem-solving was in us all along, *if only we'll just learn to relax a little.*

That, however, gets infinitely more complicated when perfectionism shows up to lend overthinking a hand.

In my experience, that can play out in three extreme ways.

1. The Colossus of Clout (THE COLOSSUS OF CLOUT!)

There is a defining scene in the 1990s summertime cult classic *The Sandlot*.

The main character, Smalls, has just let on that he doesn't know who The Great Bambino, Babe Ruth, is. And the rest of the boys on his backyard baseball team can't believe what they've just heard.

> Ham: What did he say?
> Bertram: What? Were you born in a barn, man?
> Yeah-Yeah: Yeah yeah, what *planet* are you from?
> Smalls: [*narrating*] But there was no *way* I could let them know.
> Squints: You've never heard of the sultan of swat?
> Kenny: The titan of terror.
> Timmy: The colossus of clout.
> Tommy: THE COLOSSUS OF CLOUT!
> Benny: The king of crash, man.[16]

That movie is quotable for many great lines ("For-Ev-Errr" being one of the most well-known). But in our house, we also can't stop quoting that repetitive one-two punch from the brothers, Timmy and Tommy: "The colossus of clout. THE COLOSSUS OF CLOUT!"

We use it anytime we know one of us is letting our perfectionism make mountains out of milestones.

One of fear's favorite tactics it uses on repeat when it comes to overthinking is to give us just enough of a glimpse of what the thing *could* be that we build it up into this mythical colossus in our own minds.

It's no coincidence, then, that the boys in *The Sandlot* spend the whole movie being terrified of "The Beast" living next door, a specter of fear they've only caught glimpses of through the fence. They've let their imaginations run wild, only to find out in the end (spoiler alert) he's just a regular, sweet dog... named *Hercules*.

A *mythical colossus* ... but only in their own minds.

Sounds familiar, right? Overthinking tells us everything the goal *could* be, every permutation and possibility playing out on repeat. Then perfectionism swoops in for the one-two punch to tell us it therefore *should* be all of the above.

My coaching client Tracy put it this way: "I just build it up into this colossal, insurmountable thing. I think it has to be perfect and include ALL these ideas I have in my head. And then, before I know it, it feels too BIG to even start."

Before we know it, we're frustrated ×2.

First, we're frustrated thinking it has to be "the BEST (fill in the blank thing) that's ever existed." And then we're frustrated by the imperfect nature of our progress.

Ultimately, though, what we're most afraid of is that we won't be happy with the results no matter *what* we do.

So, our predictive brain tells us . . . *we may as well not even try.*

2. "The Princess and the Pea" Problem

When fear can't get you to quit by making that big-picture, highest version of your dream look too colossal, it will swing to the other extreme by trying to turn even the tiniest problem into an insurmountable obstacle.

I like to call this "The Princess and the Pea" Problem.

When I was growing up, I once heard a (*wildly* condescending) fairy tale about a prince who was looking to take a wife. The problem was that this particular kingdom was apparently chock-full of counterfeit princesses who kept trying to pass themselves off as the real deal.

The prince, taking way too long to admit he needed help, finally decided to turn to the wise old "crone" of a queen for advice. (Who, let's be honest, in this scenario was probably only forty-two, had already been thinking about chucking it all, including the patriarchy, to *Eat, Pray, Love* her way across some neighboring kingdoms, and wished for nothing more than to be excluded from this narrative.) In my mind, she side-eyed the ageism, and then came up with what

I can only presume was a joke of a plan she never thought anyone would ever take seriously.

The next night, a terrible storm came through, and a soaked-to-the-bone supposed princess stood knocking at the castle gate.

The queen said nothing, but went into a guest bedroom, pulled off all the bedding, and laid a single pea on the box spring. She then proceeded to stack *twenty* mattresses and (I'm guessing) *twenty* IKEA down comforters on top.

I have just SO many questions.

Where did she get all these mattresses? Do castles just have twenty extra sets of bedding laying around? Were they memory foam or Sleep Number? Because that's going to change things. How *tall* were these ceilings? I'm just saying, your girl sounds like she's about to be pressed right up against the rafters. Did the thread count of the sheets come into play at all? Were they Egyptian cotton or Belgian flax? (Because I've got to tell you, I know some real *princesses* in real life who have some *opinions* about that.) And just how hard was this pea that it didn't immediately smush under the weight of, y'know, twenty Posturepedics? I mean, I'm assuming this was some sort of freeze-dried situation. But did they even have that kind of technology back then?

It's safe to say there are some real plot holes in the storyline.

Nevertheless... *this* was the plan.

The supposed princess had to lie on a pile of this absolute nonsense the entire night long. And in the morning, she was asked how she slept.

(This is the part where the original fairy tale version clearly kicks back in.)

Oh, very badly! said she. I have scarcely closed my eyes all night long. Heaven only knows what was in the bed, but I was lying on something so uncomfortable, so that I am now black and blue all over my body. It's horrible!*

And that was when the prince knew she was the real deal, and they could all live happily ever after.

*Thanks for that, Hans Christian Andersen.

Because nobody but a real princess could be as delicate as that.
Yeah. Like I said. *Wildly* condescending.

But it does give us a good metaphor for those times when we let our Overthinking make us lose sleep over the tiniest of details.

I had a coaching client of mine, Jennifer, say to me once at one of our retreats, "I haven't started building my email list yet because I haven't decided what I want my email to be."

"Oh, you mean you don't know what you want your message to stand for yet? You're not sure exactly how you want to show up and serve your people?"

No. She meant she didn't know what *email address* she should settle on to *send* the emails from.

I'm pretty sure you could hear my eyelids audibly clicking. *Blink, blink . . . blink, blink.*

I told her she had until lunch to decide, or I was going to decide for her.

PrincessAndThePea84@aol.com

With her permission, I'm picking on Jennifer here just a little bit all in good fun. But the truth is, we *all* do this. We get so hung up on the tiniest stumbling blocks that we make a boulder out of what should have only ever been an annoying pebble in our bed. And we don't feel like we can move forward an inch until we think through every possible outcome—a veritable butterfly effect turned tsunami of worst-case scenarios—all stemming from that one tiny decision.

In 2007, a parody of the Johnny Cash biopic *Walk the Line* called *Walk Hard* was released about a fictional singer named Dewey Cox. The movie begins in Folsom Prison with an all-in-black-clad John C. Reilly staring down at the wall. A crew member with a clipboard emerges to try to get him to finally, *finally* take the stage. His longtime friend and drummer, played by Tim Meadows, says, "Give him a minute, son. Dewey Cox likes to think about his whole life before he goes on stage."[17]

This is why I will also sometimes refer to this "Princess and the Pea" Problem by another name.

The Dewey Cox Problem.

We have to think about our *whole life* before we move on to the next stage.

This can lead us into what I call The Research Riptide.

3. The Research Riptide

When I was working on my thesis papers in both my Master of Philosophy in England and again in law school, there were two important overarching rules we had to follow.

1. You had to **survey the landscape** enough to know what else had been written—in other words, to see what had *already* been said.
2. You then had to **move the conversation forward** in a meaningful way by contributing your own *original* work (new thoughts, arguments, ideas, paradigm shifts). It couldn't just be a book report on what everyone else had said.

It's no surprise, then, that when I begin work on a big new project now, my first instinct is always to research what else is out there.

At its best, surveying the landscape like this allows me to observe, study, learn, pivot, and contribute something truly original. It allows me to learn from what has worked before, but also to find out how I want to do it differently. A "know the rules to break the rules"* approach to creating, if you will, that has always served me well.

If ever I find myself asking, "What am I *supposed* to do? What is everyone else doing?" and turning that into a step-by-step blueprint I must now follow, I know I am *already* on the wrong path. Certainly the most crowded one.

At its *worst*, though, it pulls us into what I have coined The Research Riptide.

In the beginning, it feels *amazing*. You're out there floating along in a sea of new people you now look up to, people who are already doing exactly the thing you most want to do. You let their work and

---

*As opposed to in the movie *The Skulls* where they would say, "We live by the rules, we die by the rules."

their words, their wisdom, their style, and all of their best practices wash over you in waves. This is the golden hour of beginning to work on the dream. You are positively buoyant. You have no idea how deep you've gone. How far from the shore you've already drifted.

And then, like a rip current instantly sweeping you out to sea, suddenly you are in way over your head.

Reality comes crashing down on you, as you swallow up an ocean's worth of other people's opinions and their very specific ways of doing things.

You panic and paddle desperately back toward the safety of the shore—a perfect storm of "it's all been done, it's all been done better" churns the water even more—but the harder you try to fight it, the more you feel yourself being pulled under.

In a real-life riptide situation, they tell you your only bet is to stop expending so much energy trying to swim back toward what is now only the *illusion* of safety. The harder you try to reach that shore, the farther the riptide will drag you away. Instead, you must *make a hard 90-degree turn from where all the trending currents are headed.*

It's not so different with building the dream.

The Research Riptide could also easily be called "Overpreparation as a Delaying Tactic." We overprepare and overplan as a way to create the illusion of certainty and control. As long as we are still "researching," we get to stay in the covert phase and stay hidden. We don't actually have to do anything about building this dream ourselves. And we'll happily float along that way for years.

But sooner or later, we find ourselves thrashing in three distinct undertows: (1) It's all been done; (2) I have to do it exactly like them in order to be successful, even if it means watering myself down in the process; or (3) I'll never be as good as them anyway . . . *so what's the point?*

This Research (It to Death) Phase, therefore, takes on a very predictable cycle:

Research → Comparison → Oversaturation → Feel Defeated → Quit

THE RESEARCH RIPTIDE

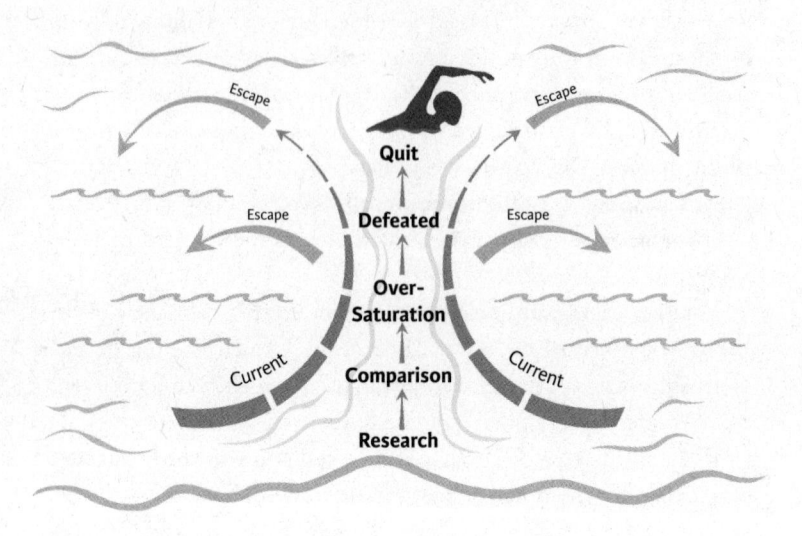

Diagram: A swimmer caught in a riptide cycle labeled (from bottom to top): Research → Comparison → Over-Saturation → Defeated → Quit, with "Escape" arrows on either side and "Current" labels flanking the cycle.

We research to see what else is out there, only to quickly compare and determine everyone is already doing it better. This leads us to realize just how many people are already doing this dream of ours and how saturated the market actually is. We instantly feel defeated, determine there is no need or place for us here . . . so we quit.

We lean right into the riptide and let it carry us away. Because the truth is, we felt ourselves getting a little too close to actually having to DO something about this dream. So, anything that puts a little space between where we are and taking action is just fine with us.

Even if we're drowning in the process.

Enter: The Bandwidth Shifts

Overthinking is exhausting.

No, really.

There's a reason you feel entirely drained and depleted of all energy after a good bout of ruminating. It's *science*.

And researchers now have new evidence to explain why. A 2022 study reports that when "intense cognitive work is prolonged for several hours, it causes potentially toxic byproducts [called glutamate] to build up in . . . the prefrontal cortex" and also notes actual evidence of fatigue "including reduced pupil dilation." They added that this toxic buildup "alters your control over decisions, so you shift toward low-cost actions requiring no effort or waiting as cognitive fatigue sets in."[18]

> Overthinking is exhausting. No, really. It's science.

While the researchers note that some widely accepted theories have proposed the fatigue is nothing more than an "illusion cooked up by the brain" to make us pursue more instant gratification, they argue that their research actually shows this shift to low-cost activities serves a much more crucial purpose: "to preserve the integrity of brain functioning."[19]

When asked if there was a way to avoid this thinking fatigue, researcher Mathias Pessiglione suggested rest and sleep, adding that there is solid evidence that glutamate is actually broken down in the prefrontal cortex during sleep.[20] It seems resting our mind is even more important than we thought.

Overthinking makes us shift toward low-cost actions that require no effort for reward. With my coaching clients, I call these *Bandwidth Shifts*. And in my experience, they typically take one of two forms.

Bandwidth Shift #1: I don't have the time/energy/resources/focus right now.

We already saw this one come into play with our all-or-nothing thinking back in chapter 1. Fear wants to tell us that if we tried to start right now, we wouldn't be able to start well (let alone finish in one sitting). We look at how colossal it all feels . . . and we immediately go into scarcity thinking. We don't have the time. We don't have the focus. We don't have the energy. We don't have the money. It's this foreboding feeling that tells us we can't create anything of value if ANY of our resources feel crunched at all. So, we wait for the day when we don't feel so spread thin.* And in

---
*Spoiler alert—that day never comes.

the meantime, we shift our efforts to something that *can* be completed today, unintentionally forever delaying the dream in the process.

Bandwidth Shift #2: GUILT tells me that everyone else has to be taken care of first.

This second shift is like the trickier evil twin of Bandwidth Shift #1. That's because it plays on all of our guilt, telling us that EVERYTHING and EVERYONE else have to be taken care of first before we can ever get started on the dream. It whispers how everyone is counting on us (and how we can't count on *anyone*). It keeps us spinning out—checking off an endless list of "more pressing to-dos"—and telling us how very irresponsible it would be to let anyone down... unless, of course, it's *ourselves*.

When I talk to my coaching clients, these are some common versions that I hear:

> I just feel all of this GUILT when I try to work on one of my big dreams. I can't shake the feeling I'm just WASTING time.
>
> Every time I try to sit down and work, a flood of all my other to-dos comes rushing into my head and pulls my focus from what I'm working on.
>
> It's the "tyranny of other people's urgent"... I put people-pleasing above protecting my own boundaries for deep work.
>
> What's keeping me stuck? Never wanting to disappoint anyone, overwhelm to the point of shutting down.

Overwhelm to the point of shutting down.
And now we see what Overthinking was really up to all along.

Overthinking to Overwhelm Is an Orange Safety Cone

There is a flip side to feeling like you never got the missing step-by-step blueprint instructions for how to build this dream.

It is the moment you find out *exactly* what will be asked of you. You know that meme that goes . . .

13-year-old me: Don't tell me what to do!
Me now: Could someone please tell me, in chronological order and with great detail, *exactly* what I have to do?

This is us.

We walk around telling everyone who will listen that if someone would just sit us down and tell us exactly how to do this dream, list it all out from start to finish for us just once, we would never get stuck again. We're not "playing small" people, we're DOERS. If we knew *how* to do it . . . trust us, we would go DO it! We just need someone to show us the way.

But then someone calls us on our bluff.

They sit us down and tell us exactly what will be required of us. They lay it all out in proper Roman numerical outline form—a 57-point, four-phase plan with at least six "if-then" variable iterations—where the subpoints all have subpoints going all the way down to the little lowercase ii's.

Suddenly, a Jodie Foster–worthy *Panic Room* door slams shut. And "I can't do this because I don't know every step in the staircase" turns into "I can't do this because it all sounds like too much right now."

This is the moment when we don our favorite neon reflective vest and most conscientious hard hat. And one by one we start putting out our best orange safety cones of excuses. But we don't place them around the perimeter of the ledge, mind you, just to remind us where it is. *Danger: Steep Drop Ahead.* Instead, we place them in more of a straight-line buffer, straight back in reverse. *BEEP, BEEP, BEEP.* Forever backing ourselves up further and further from taking the next leap.

Now is just not a great time.
There's too much going on at the moment.
Everybody's schedule is so busy right now with school letting out.

We've got a few trips coming up, and I've got so much going on at work. This month is just not a good month; it will be better in the spring/summer/fall.

With each orange safety cone we place, we feel a little more breathing room. The tight grip of our fear of (all these new) heights subsides with every tentative step away from the brink. We've avoided the embarrassment of another full-grown face-plant. We've walked away from the threat of once again landing with a sickening thud. We now congratulate ourselves for being the *very* responsible people that we are.

We probably even go ahead and log a few quick wins just to remind everyone of how truly capable we are (even if we did just balk when the ledge came back around).

We cross a quick win off our to-do list. *Instant gratification.*

We people-please and put out a fire for someone else. *Automatic approval.*

We clean out that junk drawer instead of starting our new chapter. *Dopamine hit.*

OVERTHINKING IS AN ORANGE SAFETY CONE

the ledge coming back around

you leaped the first time...

As my coaching client Ashlee put it, "This is going to sound so silly, but when I spend the day writing, I have nothing to show for the work I'm doing right now, no finished product I can point to and say, 'Here's what I did today.' It doesn't feel PRODUCTIVE. And that also means there is no 'thank you' waiting for me at the end of the day. No gold stars. No checkmarks. I can't show my work and instantly be appreciated for it the way I can when I do something for someone else."

There it is.

The ledge is long, lonely, dangerous work.

Going after the big dream means being okay with going through these long stretches of thankless days. It's putting in day after day of steadfast, relentless "butt in the chair" work . . . and still not having anything to show for it. It's trading the high of easy daily dopamine hits for the unsexy long-haul work of *true* discipline.

It's hard to put value on something only you can see right now.

It's far easier, in those moments peering over the ledge, to want to run back to the safety net of the low-cost effort instead. It's understandable to prefer the gold stars, daily double taps, occasional thank-yous, and falsely inflated feelings of productivity that a life full of checking off boxes only to appease other people will promise you.

That's especially true when your exhausted, predictive brain keeps telling you to just stick with what you're good at, kid. Stick with the quick win.

Back away slowly from the ledge.

Wait until you know all the answers.

Put as many orange safety cones as you can between you and the next leap.

Even if it means you cease moving forward altogether.

the shift

Overthinking wants you to exhaust yourself to the point of Overwhelm, with the main goal of getting you to shut down and back yourself away from taking the next leap. Instead, when you feel yourself spiraling out, learn to rest your mind rather than pushing harder. Get quiet enough to let the answers find you. This is when you'll realize you never needed someone else's step-by-step instructions. You had the blueprint to truly innovate inside you all along.

8

procrastination is a double-edged sword

It takes 14 minutes and 37 seconds to get from the Papa John's parking lot in Morgantown, West Virginia, to the first floor of Woodburn Hall.

I know this because I walked that path daily in my last few years as an undergrad at West Virginia University. I lived on the other side of town from the campus, so I'd drive downtown to park my little Dodge Neon at a friend's apartment—which, as it turned out, was right above the Papa John's and came with free parking and the occasional free pizza. Then from there, I'd hike the remaining approximately forty-seven thousand* steps straight up the side of the hill to get to Woodburn Hall sitting proudly at the top.

This was where Dr. John C. Kilwein's Constitutional Law class was waiting.

Dr. Kilwein was one of those professors whose classes filled up instantly each time registration went live. He taught Constitutional

---

*Give or take.

Law in the fall semester and its fraternal twin sister First Amendment in the spring. And every year there were seniors who graduated without ever making it into either one of his classes.

So, I considered it lucky when I found myself sitting in his classroom in one of those cramped, grade-school-looking chairs, the kind with a desk attached to it, in the fall of my junior year.

Kilwein was one of those professors who really changed the way you looked at everything. He was notoriously *tough*, but fair. And he didn't want anyone taking up one of those elusive desk-chairs who didn't really want to be there. So, he had a very . . . *challenging* . . . approach to his grading.

Everyone in the room started with 100 points. And those 100 points corresponded directly to the grading scale. Which meant that if you lost more than seven points combined on any of the multiple exams and one final term paper throughout the semester, you were instantly dropped below an A.

I lost five and a half points on our very first exam.

Which, if you weren't a math major, meant I could only lose 1.5 more points total on *every other assignment* from there on out if I wanted to keep my straight-A streak* alive. This first exam was administered right before the drop period ended, and the rumor was Kilwein used it to weed out anybody who wasn't serious about being there.

I had a decision to make.

Every A+, gold star, "anything less than perfect is a failure" synapse in my overachiever brain begged me to run.

Instead, I decided to stay. To see what would happen when I didn't instantly bail on something the second it got hard.

Kilwein was big on attendance and class participation. You could even earn back some of the lost points by asking good questions. And he had one major rule about our upcoming final paper of the semester: It had to be turned in on time, IN class the day it was due.

---

*Well, straight A's except for one B+ my freshman year, which made me so mad I swore it would never happen again. In true overachiever fashion, I also somewhere along the line decided that A-minuses didn't count either.

I put off writing that paper for weeks.

I agonized over it. Catastrophized it. Played out every scenario for how I was destined to fail. And then, when the deadline finally got close enough and what I call "The Terror" at last kicked in, I wrote that paper like Bruce Almighty sending email, my fingers flying across the keyboard. I stayed up all night to finish it ... and still I kept typing.

The morning the paper was due came and went, and still I kept typing.

A lunchtime meal of occasionally free pizza came and went, and still I kept typing.

The time that the class *began* came and went ... and STILL I KEPT TYPING.

Finally, at fifteen minutes before the end of class, I printed out the pages at my friend's apartment and went sprinting up the hill.

It takes 14 minutes and 37 seconds to get from the Papa John's parking lot to the first floor of Woodburn Hall.

Panting, breathless, red-faced for more than one reason, I took one final "*why am I the way I am*" wallow in my own impending embarrassment. Then I turned the squeaky brass handle as fifty shocked faces looked up at me at once.

Kilwein paused a long, hard second, staring me straight in the face, deciding if he would let me in.

And then he kept talking.

I silently and sheepishly placed my paper on top of the stack with all the others that had been sitting there for nearly ninety minutes at that point and squeezed myself awkwardly into the tiny desk-chair, trying to make it look as casual as possible. I no sooner sat down than ...

Class dismissed.

I literally turned that paper in twenty-three seconds before the end of class. But I turned it in, IN class. Kilwein made some joke about how the rule of law is always open for interpretation. He laughed. I laughed. The whole room laughed.

I got a 100 on that paper and an A in the class.

And I have been chasing that high every day of my life since.

I Always Feel *Horrible* When I Procrastinate

I learned long ago to make friends with what I call "The Terror."
 There are a lot of other names you could call it. Pressure. Panic. A good old-fashioned procrastination-induced hysteria. It is a fisticuffs fight for survival when I finally sit down to write, battling back all these destructive, dead-on-the-inside, *de-composing* monsters of my own making. A *World War Z*–level outbreak of absolute pandemonium in the streets. Only all of it is happening in my own head. While on the outside it just looks like I'm sipping this delightful hazelnut latte.
 Me, I prefer the simplicity of The Terror.
 But call it what you will, *it is that moment when you are finally more afraid of losing the opportunity . . . than of what will happen if you try and it isn't any good.*
 James Clear calls that moment the "Action Line." It is the exact threshold when these *future*, far-off consequences you've been putting off finally transform into *present-day* consequences, and the "pain of procrastinating [has at last] escalated" enough that it propels you into action.[1]
 Clear goes on to say, "There is something important to note here. As soon as you cross the Action Line, the pain begins to subside. In fact, being in the middle of procrastination is often *more painful* than being in the middle of doing the work. . . . The guilt, shame, and anxiety that you feel while procrastinating are usually worse than the effort and energy you have to put in while you're working. The problem is not *doing* the work, it's *starting* the work."[2]
 Oh, do I get that.
 I always feel *horrible* when I procrastinate.
 By that, I don't mean that I feel *bad* for procrastinating (although that part's true too).
 I mean that I *feel* HORRIBLE. It either feels like I'm getting sick, having an existential crisis . . . or both.
 When I'm in full-blown procrastination phase, it will literally feel like I have the flu. My joints ache, my muscles feel weak, I'll have full-body head-to-toe chills like I have a fever, my head hurts, I crave

ginger ale and crackers, and I'll be so wiped-out exhausted to the point that all I want to do is sleep for hours on end.

It turns out, it's not just in my head.

In fact, "When stressed, a person's brain may think their body is in danger and trigger the sympathetic nervous system (SNS). The SNS is a network of nerves that activates the fight or flight response. The SNS also activates the adrenal gland hormones adrenaline and noradrenaline. A rush of adrenaline surging through the body can cause flu-like symptoms, such as weakness, nausea, and headaches."[3] And a 2015 article in the National Library of Medicine also made the connection from stress to inflammation, which would explain the achy joints and fever.[4]

When I'm not feeling *physically* sick, I'll feel like I'm on an emotional downward spiral, like I need to get my whole life together before I can even *think* about moving forward. There's that Dewey Cox Problem come back to bite me. *I have to think about my whole life before I move on to the next stage.*

But worse than either of those horrible feelings—and this is the one I find the *most* frustrating—is that I don't know how to get my BEST work to show up until I am almost out of time.

Something I have come to realize is that the way I'm wired, my brain always has to start off writing the stuff I will *never* use. I'm not talking crappy first draft here, where you just get it down Anne Lamott style and then go back to fix it later and it ends up being good.[5] No, I'm talking more like Oscar going over the budget with Michael Scott right before he declares "BANKRUPTCY!"

"See this scary black bar here, this is the stuff that no one ever, EVER needs."[6]

Apparently, *these* are the words I always like to get out of the way first.

Every time I sit down to start a big new project, my lizard brain (the part that is screaming the entire time, saying "WE CAN'T DO THIS!!!" in the voice of Bill Hader) likes to flood the rest of my brain with so many fear chemicals that my IQ drops at least one standard deviation. (That's science, look it up. Don't worry, it comes back.)

The words I write during this time don't even feel like me. It's not my cadence, my voice, my wordplay. My brain literally feels different, like someone else is at the keyboard. Normally, when I'm writing, my brain feels like it's vibrating on a different frequency, almost like it's making a *"wohm wohm"* sound when I hit that state of flow. Like it's inhaling and exhaling while a white-hot light is pouring in through the top. *Weird, right?*

THIS feels more like I'm trying to sneeze through my forehead.

As you can imagine, this part of the process feels horrible. It involves a lot of pacing, curling up in the fetal position, staring up at the ceiling, existential crises (plural), questioning man's search for meaning... and whether this string cheese in the back of the refrigerator is still any good.

This is where The Terror comes in.

Ironically, in a sort of "you have to fight fire with fire" meets "I'm rubber, you're glue" brand of logic, the only thing that can ever snap me out of this fear-induced mediocrity is... yet ever MORE fear.

Stay with me here.

See, it's one thing for me to feel stuck in an endless loop of hours upon hours of soul-crushing procrastination because every sentence I write feels like it is being pulled from the depths of my back molars with some sewing thread and a well-timed door slam.

It is quite another when the threshold—that Action Line—is finally crossed, where the clock is ticking on the deadline, I'm almost

I'M ADDICTED TO "THE TERROR"

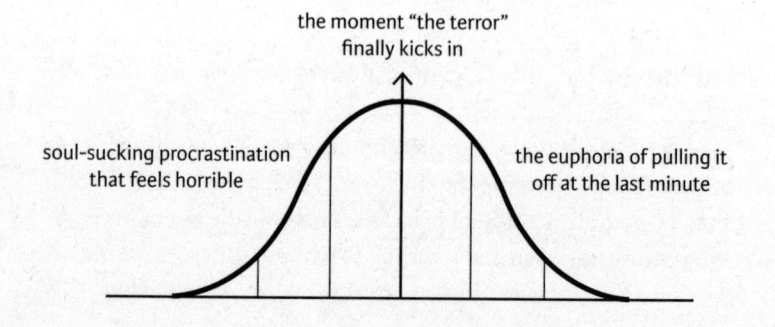

the moment "the terror" finally kicks in

soul-sucking procrastination that feels horrible

the euphoria of pulling it off at the last minute

out of time, and this chill goes through my entire body telling me that this, THIS might be the time when I'm not able to pull out another A+ win at the very last minute like I always do. That *this* might be the time when I finally fail and show everyone what a fraud I actually was all along.

This is the moment when The Terror finally takes over.

Suddenly, a sort of crystallizing clarity shoots through my veins—like vampire venom in a wildly popular YA novel—as every word on the page instantly snaps into focus. Time both slows down and starts moving in fast-forward. Entire hours can go by, the sun can completely set outside, day giving way to dark, and I don't even look up to realize it's happening. In my younger years, I could stay up all night if I had to and still show up on time to class at eight o'clock the next morning looking as fresh as a Noxzema commercial.* However sick or emotionally fragile I feel, the second The Terror takes over I magically feel better. Most importantly, now every sentence I put down on the page flows as freely and effortlessly as if I'm just taking transcription from someone much smarter than I am who was actually the one doing the writing all along.

I am . . . *addicted* to The Terror. I am dependent on The Terror. I don't know how to be any good at something if I'm not pulling it off at the last minute against all odds. And every time I do it I develop a little more tolerance, so that my brain has to raise the stakes the next time just to get the same amount of high.

Psychologists like to tell us, "Some procrastinators contend that they perform better under pressure, but while they may be able to convince themselves of that, research shows it is generally not the case; instead, they may make a habit of last-minute work to experience the *rush of euphoria* at seemingly having overcome the odds."[7]

Rush of euphoria, indeed.

> I am . . .
> *addicted* to
> The Terror.

---

*Why yes, that IS a *Gilmore Girls* reference. Thank you for noticing!

And with its double-shot cocktail of dopamine[8] while I'm putting things off and adrenaline when I pull off another last-minute win, it's no wonder procrastination keeps me coming back for more.

By the time I was a senior in college, I had signed up for an independent study in philosophy where I was supposed to turn in *five* 5,000-word essays on five different philosophers of my choosing at any time throughout the semester. I opened up a blank Word document the day before the semester ended, pulled an all-nighter, and turned in all five essays—all 25,000 words—the next day at the last possible minute, catching my advisor as she was walking out of the building, keys in hand.

I got an A+ on all of them.

And my tolerance cranked up a little higher.

I wrote the bulk of a 50,000-word thesis for my master's degree in England over a long three-day holiday weekend. I graduated with high honors.

Ratchet the dial up even more.

I turned in my final law school paper at the literal last minute, 11:59 p.m. EST, from the hotel room of a photography conference in Las Vegas and again received high honors. Two years later, at that same Vegas conference, I ditched and rewrote an entire talk for the biggest stage I had ever spoken on with an all-nighter the night before.

I got a standing ovation.

Yes, I feel horrible when I procrastinate.

But it is absolute *Euphoria* when I pull it off just in time.

It's Time to Do "Future You" a Favor

There is a phrase in the literature around procrastination, something economists refer to as *hyperbolic discounting*.[9]

It essentially means that "people [will] choose smaller, immediate rewards, rather than larger, later rewards" against their own better future interests, which is why this phenomenon is also sometimes called "present bias."[10]

The classic example often used to illustrate hyperbolic discounting is that, given the choice, many people would choose $100 now over $110 a week from now ("a bird in the hand" and all that). But given the choice between $100 a year from now and $110 a year and a week from now, most people will choose the latter, thinking, "I will have already made it that far, I may as well see it through."

Put another way, it is the reason why "Future You" is so much more well-behaved than "Right-Now You." Future You has lofty, noble goals to study Latin, eat that bag of kale in the back of your refrigerator, run a marathon, get rid of half your possessions, backpack across Europe, and memorize the unabridged complete works of William Shakespeare . . . in the proper Queen's English.

Right-Now You would rather have a donut.

Right-Now You is *great* at putting things off until tomorrow. No matter how horrible it feels.

"Cognitive dissonance" is the psychological term given to "the discomfort a person feels when their behavior does not align with their values or beliefs."[11] It is the pit-in-the-stomach feeling we experience when we think to ourselves *why do I not do the thing I say I most want to do?* And, if we're not careful, it means procrastination can easily become a habit. Here's why.

HYPERBOLIC DISCOUNTING

(why future you is so much more well-behaved)

FUTURE YOU
wants to study Latin, eat that bag of kale, run a marathon, backpack across Europe, memorize the complete works of Shakespeare . . . in the proper Queen's English

RIGHT-NOW YOU
really wants a donut

As Dr. Alison Cook said in her follow-up book, *I Shouldn't Feel This Way*, "If you don't consciously face the discomfort of dissonance, you open the door for your mind to start playing tricks on you. A meaning-making part of you will jump in to reduce the inner tension. You might start to rationalize, defend, or justify the incongruence."[12]

And, in fact, this is exactly what we see with most procrastinators. We repeat the lesson until it is learned. Only we *never* seem to learn it.

One of my favorite TV shows is *Mom*, mostly because I love all things Allison Janney.*

> If we're not careful, procrastination can easily become a habit.

There is an episode where Bonnie (played by Janney) has taken on the job as an apartment building superintendent in exchange for free rent. Only she's pretty terrible at the job, the tenants are now all complaining, and her annual review is coming up fast. In a last-ditch effort to save her job, not to mention her home, she starts checking off as many of the backlogged requests as she can.

In one particularly telling moment she says, "Case in point, Mrs. Slivkin in 2E now has a working light fixture in her bathroom. Ignoring her took six months, fixing it took six minutes. There's a lesson in there somewhere."[13]

Only you get the distinct impression that Bonnie still hasn't learned *a thing*.

The reason most procrastinators don't learn their lesson is because of something psychologists call a "downward counterfactual."[14]

An article in the Association for Psychological Science's journal *Observer* explains the idea this way:

> In general, people learn from their mistakes and reassess their approach to certain problems. For chronic procrastinators, that feedback loop seems continually out of service. The damage suffered

---

*Excuse me, I mean Oscar, Golden Globe, SAG, BAFTA, and seven-time Emmy AWARD–WINNING Allison Brooks Janney. *That's Ms. Janney, if you're nasty.*

as a result of delay doesn't teach them to start earlier the next time around. An explanation for this behavioral paradox seems to lie in the emotional component of procrastination. Ironically, the very quest to relieve stress in the moment might prevent procrastinators from figuring out how to relieve it in the long run.[15]

Procrastinators, in an effort to avoid any and all negative feelings (which is what led them to procrastinate in the first place), will then double down by trying to find any shred of good in how it all turned out. The downward counterfactual is both a *silver linings playbook* and an exercise in "at least."

In our *Mom* example above, Bonnie would likely say something along the lines of "*At least* I got her light fixed before the tenant reviews were due" (downward counterfactual), as opposed to something like "If only I had done it when she first asked, I would have saved all this time, stress, and hassle, and she would probably be writing me a glowing review right now."

That second type of response, known as an "upward counterfactual," seeks to learn something from the situation and use it for the future. But that process often proves too painful for procrastinators to admit what they've brought on themselves. "The mood regulation piece is a huge part of procrastination," says professor of psychology Fuschia Sirois. "If you're focused just on trying to get yourself to feel good now, there's a lot you can miss out on in terms of learning how to correct behavior and avoiding similar problems in the future."[16]

And here is where hyperbole really comes back into play.

If procrastinators have a tendency to overvalue immediate rewards over later ones, they also have a propensity to overestimate how much "future them" will have grown. They tend to "comfort themselves in the present with the false belief that they'll be more emotionally equipped to handle a task in the future," believing that they will have somehow been able to "develop these miraculous coping skills" by then and "be better able to handle feelings of insecurity or frustration with the task."[17]

Do you *really* want to do Future You a favor?

Start breaking your habit with procrastination right now. And that means dealing with what we're *actually* afraid of.

The Fears We're Really Avoiding

Can I be honest with you?

What procrastination really is for me is a "break in case of emergency" rescue apparatus that I carry with me at all times in my purse. It's kind of like one of those "as seen on TV" all-purpose tools that both break your car window and slice your seatbelt in half if you ever run your car right off the road and into a lake.

Mine is always with me, always at the ready, in case I'm about to drown in my own expectations.

If hyperbolic discounting is what makes us choose short-term instant gratification over long-term rewards, I think the second phase of procrastination for me—the one I spend the *majority* of my time in—is something more akin to hyperbolic excuse-making. I use procrastination to make excuses for myself, running it to the extremes on either end.

Future Me always gets to say, "Just imagine how good *it would have been* if I'd had more time."

And Right-Now Me always has a built-in excuse, a last-ditch failsafe . . . on the off chance that this is the time I actually *fail*.

This is a double-edged cop-out. On the one hand, it means I never have to journey to the edge and outer limits of my own abilities. Here I picture a little weathered sign hammered into the desert sand that reads "the end of what you are capable of," as a lone tumbleweed rolls by and bumps up against the dry, desiccated bones of every dream I ever quit too soon because I was not instantly good at it. Procrastinating

> Right-Now Me always has a built-in excuse on the off chance that this time I actually fail.

means I never once have to come face-to-face with the realities of my own limitations. I never have to deal with the possibility that maybe I'm not as smart as I think I am. Or as talented as I one day hope to be.

This is why psychologists tells us, "Procrastinators are often perfectionists, for whom it may be psychologically more acceptable to never tackle a job than to face the possibility of not doing it well."[18] We would rather numb out and avoid the work than to give our best effort only to find out that it will never be as good as we want it to be. And each time we avoid it, our brain gives us little hits of dopamine like a PEZ dispenser doling out sugary-sweet rewards. That's because when our brain is left to its own devices, it will choose numb over pain any day.

By numbing out and procrastinating, we never have to say to ourselves, "This was as good as it was ever going to be. This is the full measure of how much talent you actually have. You had all the time in the world, you could have written down anything you wanted, and now you will be graded accurately on your fullest, best effort."

Nobody wants that.

So, we build in all these last-minute, down-to-the-wire deadlines, like a ticking doomsday clock, which allows us to still be oh-so-proud of ourselves for the very best effort we put in under such dire circumstances. This elusive promise of what it *could* have been with just a little more time tucks us in at night as the sirens go off over our heads. And we can sleep safe and sound, warm in our beds, knowing the vast expanse of all our most hidden potential has not yet been captured.

Meanwhile, on the off chance that all our worst self-sabotaging, self-fulfilling prophecy fears finally come true, and this is the one time in our life when we actually do fail, we never have to internalize that into our identity. *We're not people who FAIL at things. We're just people who were up against impossible circumstances this one time.*

Ironically, we seek to maintain an internal locus of control about who we really are and what we think we're capable of in the broader expanse of our lives by saying *this* time it was out of our hands.

So, what are some of these underlying fears we think procrastination will protect us from?

We've already been introduced to many of the names fear goes by. Here are a few more we can now add to the list.

The Fear of Not Being Good Enough. This is the fear behind all the other blank spaces in "But I'm not _____ enough," the fear that whispers we might not have what it takes after all. And if we put ourselves out there even a little bit, we're about to find that out for sure. So, it's best not to start at all. Or at the very least, procrastination whispers, we should just put it off so long that no one could ever blame us for coming up short. In this weird way, procrastination actually helps set us free from our perfectionism. But only *temporarily*.

The Fear of Being Judged. This is that "What if they say, 'Who does she think she is?'" fear. And it's one of the most common fears among all the people I've ever coached. If I had to guess, I would say that movie *Mean Girls* really did a number on all of us. Raise your hand if you've ever been personally victimized by the imaginary Regina George in your own head. We can already imagine all the snarky things people will say about us if we dare to put ourselves out there. How they'll talk about us behind our backs. How they'll pick apart whatever we create. How *cringe* they already think we are. And we would just rather wait our whole lives to get started on the dream than to have to endure even one day of being judged by them. *Yeah. That seems like a fair trade-off.*

The Fear of Negative Evaluation. Very similar to the fear of being judged, but specific enough that it needed its own category, the fear of negative evaluation is the belief that going after the goal will make others misunderstand or judge us *down to the very core of our character*. "People who have experienced some negative outcome in the past after doing well— such as being derided for being a 'show off' or enduring hardship because of this success—may also fear doing well again in the future."[19] As my coaching client Ashlee put it, "I've bought into the lie that I'm selfish if I chase my dream. I've been labeled in the past as 'a control freak, you like to be in charge, you're so selfish.' I guess it goes back to not wanting to prove that they were right about me all along."

The Fear of Disappointment. The fear of disappointment is not that we're afraid WE will be let down in pursuit of these dreams . . . but rather, that our going after these dreams will be a disappointment to everyone else around us. Going after these dreams might require parting ways with someone else's plan for our lives. It might mean saying no to them for a while, holding a boundary, or "inconveniencing" other people. Then add in the possibility that we just might try and fail and fall flat on our faces, letting everyone down in the process. The result is that this "good kid" urge in us to never be a disappointment to anyone can keep us procrastinating on the dream forever . . . even when it means *disappointing ourselves.*

So, What Type of Procrastinator ARE You?

Are you a thrill-seeker? That is one of the five types of procrastinators experts often identify (in addition to the perfectionist, avoidant, indecisive, and overbooked types).[20] But while the other four procrastinate to avoid some type of pain, the thrill-seeker (sometimes called the "crisis-maker"[21]) is the only one who seems to bring this upon themselves *on purpose* because they "enjoy the rush of racing to meet deadlines, so they hold off on working to feel that rush."[22]

Thrill-seeker. Crisis-maker. *I feel personally attacked.*

But it turns out, this difference in motivation actually makes a big difference in the outcome. To prove this point, researchers narrowed the field down to two broad types of procrastinators: passive and active.[23]

Passive procrastinators are considered to be a *nonadaptive* type, who "delay the task because they have trouble making decisions and acting on them." While active procrastinators are considered to be an *adaptive* type, who "delay the task purposefully because working under pressure allows them to 'feel challenged and motivated.'"[24]

Studying a group of adults who were asked to first identify three personal goals and an action plan to achieve them in a two-week period, researchers found that meaningful progress on their personal goals "correlated positively with active procrastination and negatively with passive procrastination." Even more than that, they discovered that "active procrastinators had an advantage in temperament" in that they were "associated with dependable temperament, well-developed character, and high emotional intelligence and [that this adaptive style] predicts meeting personal goals," and also that they "correlated positively with personality traits that confer resilience, conscientiousness, and emotional stability."[25]

They went on, "While passive procrastination is a self-destructive process in which self-doubt, anxiety, and distress accompany the non-accomplishment of tasks, and the failure to meet deadlines, active procrastination is a self-regulating time-management strategy" that allows for a preference for working under a tight deadline, an intentional decision to procrastinate, and the ability to still successfully turn in work on time.[26]

See, I knew it. The Terror CAN be our friend.

What I like about what this research adds to the conversation is that it makes space for the fact that some of us just *are* wired differently.

Lately, I've been talking to some of my fellow authors and favorite creatives—people who are truly at the top of their game and recognized as the ones who set the industry bar *very* high for everyone else around them. And two things we all realized we have in common are (1) how much our work changes from the first draft to the final draft, sometimes to the point that it's unrecognizable, and (2) how our BEST work often doesn't show up until there's some sort of *real* looming deadline.

A lot of people can have some real shame around that.

They think if people knew their brains worked this way, everyone would just assume they were lazy. Or that they don't take their work very seriously. They can start to think they *should* be able to just sit down and outline the entire project, start to finish, the very first day they begin the work and never once deviate from the plan. That if they were truly *good* at what they do, the creating would always be a very tidy process, indeed. And therefore the work would always be accomplished *way* ahead of time. They see their messy minds as the proof they are, in fact, a *fraud*.

Me? I've started to see it as the hallmark of originality.

Book reports get outlined quickly.

Original thought is born out of the mud.

And that's just going to take us a little longer.

I said to a friend recently that for me writing is like carving a statue. The thing reveals itself to me in stages, where each pass somehow uncovers more detail. It's like I can simultaneously know somewhere in my "knower" what I ultimately want it to be. And yet I could never tell you exactly what that is or how it's going to get there.

The work itself guides the way.

Something we will have to make peace with, find *relief* in even, is that creating is messy. You never fully know what it's going to be until it's done.

And yet, what we can't do is allow that to keep us from starting.

> Creating is messy. The work itself guides the way.

Those of us who are wired to have our best work show up at the end can still fall prey to procrastinating for all those passive, pain-avoidant reasons listed above. We get stuck and don't want to start because it won't be perfect from the very beginning. We get indecisive because we aren't sure of the best way forward. We overbook ourselves and avoid the work because we don't believe we're going to be able to get it "there," across the finish line of what we want it to be this time.

But as the old adage says . . . write messy, edit ruthlessly.

Even if your best work never shows up until the end, know this: It would have never been unearthed without all the messy, hard work that came before. All those scraps left on the cutting room floor?

They were guiding your hand all along, revealing new depth and detail with each attempt.

If you wait for it to be perfect, pristine, and tidy, the true work will never begin.

Allow yourself to go bravely and curiously in the direction of things that don't make any sense just yet. Go against the grain. Let the thing reveal itself to you in stages.

The work itself guides the way.

Procrastination Is Not Laziness, It's Physiological

Charlotte Lieberman explains in a piece for *The New York Times* that the word *procrastination* literally breaks down to mean "to put off until tomorrow against our better judgment." (Aristotle also called that a "weakness of the will."[27])

> Etymologically, "procrastination" is derived from the Latin verb *procrastinare*—to put off until tomorrow. But it's more than just voluntarily delaying. Procrastination is also derived from the ancient Greek word *akrasia*—doing something against our better judgment. . . . That self-awareness is a key part of why procrastinating makes us feel so rotten. When we procrastinate, we're not only aware that we're avoiding the task in question, but also that doing so is probably a bad idea. And yet, we do it anyway.[28]

To figure out why that is, we first have to understand that procrastinating is not necessarily a laziness problem, a character problem, or an apathy problem. It is "first and foremost a *physiological process*" and it's "what happens when your brain perceives a real or imagined threat."[29]

Going back to our limbic system versus the prefrontal cortex, what we have is quite literally a battle of the wills. The limbic system has also been referred to as the "paleomammalian brain" because it is "one of the oldest and most dominant portions of the brain" whose "processes are mostly automatic."[30] And one of its main jobs is to stop you from doing undesirable things like putting your hand on a hot stove, but also things you don't *want to do* like starting the next big project.[31]

The prefrontal cortex, on the other hand, is a "newer, less developed, and as a result somewhat weaker portion of the brain," and "because the limbic system is much stronger it very often wins the battle, leading to procrastination. We give our brain what feels good *now*."[32]

This comes back to the automatic nature of the limbic system and something called *immediate mood repair*. The prefrontal cortex operates best when we "consciously engage" it. The limbic system, on the other hand, is "always waiting, ready to take over as soon as you disengage from the (unpleasant) task at hand." As soon as it does, the limbic system begins the work of immediate mood repair, which essentially means "doing a more pleasant task provides the brain with a small amount of dopamine." So, when it comes to procrastination, "you're being rewarded for not doing the task that you're supposed to because it feels better for your brain."[33]

So, while the default mode nature of the limbic brain is great for imagination and creative problem-solving, it is also at least partly to blame for our procrastination.

Remember that procrastination is what happens when your brain perceives a real or imagined threat, which can include the stress of an impending project. When that happens, "your autonomic nervous system will deploy a fight/flight/freeze response."[34]

As Lieberman says, "Even if we intellectually recognize that putting off the task will create more stress for ourselves in the future, our brains are still wired to be more concerned with removing the threat in the present. Researchers call this the '*amygdala hijack*.'"[35]

When this happens, it again divides us into two types of procrastination. Only this time it's not passive and active. It's much more *physiological* than that.

Britt Frank, author of *The Science of Stuck*, explains it this way. She first draws the distinction between two types of responses when someone is stuck in the "intention-action gap" of procrastination. There is parasympathetic nervous system procrastination (PNSP), which Frank calls the "brake pedal" of the body. And there is sympathetic nervous system procrastination (SNSP), which she refers to as the "gas pedal" of the body. And depending on which type of procrastination you are stuck in, you will need a different approach to shift yourself back into action.

Frank goes on to explain that the parasympathetic nervous system is meant to relax you, but when it perceives danger it can cause you to experience such symptoms as "exhaustion, muscle fatigue, [being] glued to your screen." A person may also feel "sluggish and forgetful" with a "sense of heaviness or dread" and "struggle to make decisions." This is often referred to as a *freeze* response. She explains that the solution to this functional freeze response is to "up-regulate" using such techniques as stretching and allowing your eyes to slowly wander around the room in front of you as you take in your surroundings.

The sympathetic nervous system, on the other hand, is meant to energize you, but when it perceives a threat it may result in what Frank calls "productive procrastination," which can include things like racing thoughts and doing everything on the to-do list except the one project you keep putting off. It can also include symptoms such as "restlessness, irritability, and elevated heart rate." This is referred to as a *fight-or-flight* response, and the solution is to "down-regulate" using techniques such as "jumping... laying on the ground, making extended eye contact with someone you trust."

Fortunately, for those of us stuck in procrastination, Frank tells us that we don't have to feel *motivated* before these techniques can work. We regulate and the motivation follows.

And, as always, the way forward is to start with small steps. As Britt Frank tells us, "A micro-yes that moves you forward is preferable to a macro step untaken."[36]

The Antidote to Procrastination Is Noticing

Have you ever read "The Habit Poem"?

Its second line refers to habit as "your greatest helper... or your heaviest burden."[37]

At this I can't help but picture us stalled out somewhere midway up the mountain—boulder raised up high over our heads in some

Rocky Balboa pose, biceps trembling, sweat beading up on our furrowed brow as it glistens in the midday sun.

The longer we make procrastination a habit, the heavier this burden becomes.

The paradox of all this is that we *think* procrastinating makes us feel better.

Does it, though? Does it really?

Oh sure, in the moment it feels better to binge re-watch an entire season of *The Marvelous Mrs. Maisel* than, say, open up a blank Word document and stare at a blinking cursor. It feels so indulgent to numb out on your couch with—*purely hypothetically speaking*—an entire bag of SkinnyPop popcorn and a family-size package of peanut M&Ms.

But it never lasts.

Like I said before . . . when I procrastinate, I feel *horrible*.

And actually *noticing* that fact just might be how we stop.

Dr. Judson Brewer is the director of research at Brown University's Mindfulness Center and the author of *The Craving Mind*. In explaining what he calls a *habit loop*, he says, "The standard habit loop is: trigger, behavior, reward. It's set up for survival . . . and also procrastination."[38]

In the scenario above, the trigger is the blinking cursor, the behavior is to avoid it and procrastinate by binge-watching Midge and Susie's witty banter, and the reward is the "relief you feel from not doing [the work]—which obviously doesn't last."[39] The nature of this brief relief only furthers the procrastination habit loop as we seek the next reward.[40]

But according to Brewer, curiosity and noticing are the ways we can break that habit loop. He suggests we try, just one time, tackling the work ahead of time so that it's not hanging over our heads. Notice how great it feels to have it done. He explains that we can use that mindfulness to get that new information to our brain and break the cycle of the procrastination reward.[41]

Need some help getting started? Try these the next time you want to put off your work.

Get Yourself a Deadline

Notice I said GET, not GIVE. If just giving ourselves a deadline worked, we would never struggle with procrastination and all of our best work would show up right away. I want you to get someone to hold you accountable in a major, public way where you don't get to miss that deadline without consequences.

A few years ago, I had the honor of having fellow Yale Law alum and *New York Times* bestselling author Gretchen Rubin on *The Mary Marantz Show* to talk about her book *The Four Tendencies*.[42] In our conversation, she identified four archetype personalities that are sorted based on how well a person (a) keeps commitments to themselves and (b) keeps commitments to others. The "Obliger" type—the *largest* of the tendencies according to Rubin's research—has no problem breaking a promise to themselves but easily comes through when there is someone they are accountable to, because they never want to let anyone else down. If that just resonated with you, GET yourself a deadline, let it motivate you . . . while you work on building that muscle of keeping promises to *yourself*.

Double-Dutch the Work

A common phrase in the literature around procrastination is to "on-ramp" the work, meaning to get a running start at it. I like to call that "double-Dutching" the work.

A key way I do this with my writing is that I will begin each day by reading the last *good* thing I wrote the day before. It warms my brain up, it gets the words flowing, it gives me the confidence and cadence that I *do* actually know how to do this, and it gets me in a good rhythm. Nine times out of ten, as soon as I do that, the next words jump right in, like a good game of double-Dutch. They just had to get the timing down and get a good running start at it first.

Chunking

Another common phrase around procrastination is "chunking," meaning to break down these Colossus of Clout projects into the next bite-sized piece. "By breaking a larger task into smaller, more digestible components, individuals can progress incrementally, reducing the overwhelming nature of the entire endeavor. Chunking helps dismantle this mental barrier by transforming an intimidating task into a series of smaller, achievable steps."[43]

Self Esteem vs. Social Esteem

Finally, studies have shown that "non-procrastinators focus on the task that needs to be done" and "have a stronger personal identity." They are concerned more with their own self-esteem versus what psychologists call "social esteem" (how much others like us).[44] They don't spend time worrying about whether other people will judge them, be disappointed in them, or reject them, so they are able to get started on new goals much faster.

In other words, they waste no time trying to please other people. And we'll talk about *that* next.

the shift

Procrastination wants to convince you that forever delaying the dream somehow feels better than doing the actual work, because at least then you don't have to deal with the pain of disappointment of "what if it's not as good as I want it to be." Instead, spend some time *noticing* how you actually feel when you put off doing the work. And how the pain dissipates the second you cross the Action Line. The more you notice how you actually feel, the less your brain will reward you for "avoiding pain."

9

people-pleasing is a lonely intersection

THERE IS NO *THERE* THERE.

Playing Small loves nothing more than to sing a siren song to you about this mythical "there" (as in "I'm not there yet") that exists somewhere at the lonely intersection of "paid their dues" and "waited their turn."

When I picture this intersection, for some reason in my head it always looks like Tom Hanks at the end of *Cast Away* on some dusty, beat-up road stretching out for miles in every direction from the four-way-stop, asphalt epicenter of a sparse Texas landscape. It's the kind of *plain* that runs on forever.

We met a woman once at a workshop we did in Texas. She said the place where she was from was so flat that you could sit out on the front porch and watch your dog run away for three days straight.

1. I've never laughed at something so hard in my life.
2. This is the kind of expansive, dusty no-man's-land we're dealing with when we go looking for "there."

When I google that scene from *Cast Away*, the top result tells me, "In the movie's final scenes, Chuck finds himself at a literal crossroads in the middle of nowhere. The crossroads symbolize Chuck's life at that moment—he can go in any direction. His life on the island taught him to survive, but now he has to learn how to live again."[1]

That's the problem with Playing Small. It leaves most of us sitting in neutral.

We stall out somewhere on the way to arriving, and we decide to just stay right there on the side of the road.

Like that call you put in to some off-brand AAA and then have no idea if anyone is ever showing up, we spend all our time waiting for someone else to save us . . . someone who will give us the all clear and tell us that it's now safe to move forward. We have this idea in our head that there will actually come a point in time when someone will finally pull up alongside us, motion for us to roll down the

PEOPLE-PLEASING IS A LONELY INTERSECTION

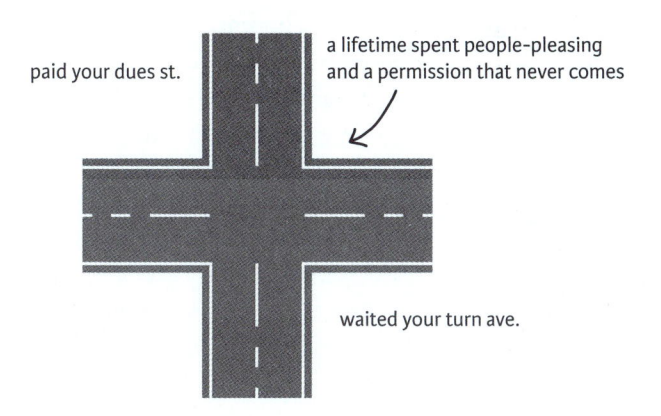

paid your dues st.

a lifetime spent people-pleasing and a permission that never comes

waited your turn ave.

window, and say to us from the other side of the road less traveled, "Now. NOW you're good enough to start."

Like I said, this place called "there"—also known as *Arriving*—exists at this lonely intersection of "paid their dues" and "waited their turn." Which really is to say, it's composed of two parts.

There's the "waited their turn" part, which stands for all our people-pleasing ways.

And then there's the "paid their dues" part, which represents a permission that never comes.

We've been stalled out here on the side of the road for a while now.

We're not going anywhere, anyway.

So, we may as well spend some time talking about *both*.

Don't Block the Box

There is a saying in Connecticut: "Don't block the box."

I'm sure this is a saying that exists in other parts of the country too. For all I know, it's part of the official student driver's manual in all fifty states.

The point is, we *especially* need it here in the land of *The Gilmore Girls*.

Don't let Amy Sherman-Palladino fool you. This state is not everything Stars Hollow would have you believe. Oh sure, there are plenty of picturesque, charming towns with white steeples spiraling out of the kind of perfect fall foliage that would make you expect to see Luke and Lorelai come strolling around the corner at any minute. While a troubadour serenades them from the sidewalk.

But running right through the middle of all *that* . . . is the I-95 corridor.

And believe me when I say, the drivers would just as soon mow you down as they would wave at you delightfully from the other side of the street.

There is a dark side to all this charm.

> In the people-pleaser's world . . .
> everyone else gets to go before they do.

Mostly, though, what it means is that everyone is in a hurry to get somewhere, and every single one of them thinks that they should be the one who gets to go first.

If entitlement was a driving lesson it would be . . . *don't block the box.*

Blocking the box, if you didn't happen to study that when you turned sixteen, is when a driver is so impatient to get through a red light, they end up stuck there blocking the intersection for all the other drivers who just got the green. And it's something our people have to be reminded not to do. *Often.*

Connecticut drivers are most decidedly *not* people-pleasers.

This is why the "waited their turn" portion of the lonely intersection is the perfect illustration for the people who ARE.

Can't you just see them sitting there in their car at that dusty, four-way stop? Hands placed dutifully at the ten and two position, only ever lifting them off the wheel for barely even a second . . . just long enough to motion the next person through. And then the next person, and the next person, and the person after that.

In the people-pleaser's world . . . *everyone else gets to go before they do.*

I imagine our people-pleasers would sit there all day if we let them, baking in the hot Texas sun. Getting burned on both sides through the glass. Looking left and looking right, *looking left and looking right* . . . just about to pull out when they see someone else coming from a mile away. "Oh, not just yet," they think to themselves. "Better let this one go first too, and *then* it'll be my turn."

Where you lead, I will follow.

Arrival, then, becomes both a moving target and a stalled-out intersection: It keeps us sitting still as we watch everyone else blur by. It's disappointing. It's discouraging. It's defeating. It makes us doubt that it will ever be our turn, as we shrink ourselves up a little smaller to get out of everyone else's way.

And it turns out intersections are not the only box we get stuck in.

The Masquerader and The Contortionist

Chances are, ever since you were little the world has told you how to contort yourself into the one-inch by one-inch square box of the "good kid," the likable one, the one who never causes trouble or asks for too much. These cubed containers of *just enough* and *never too much* that stack so nicely and keep us tidy in our place on the shelf.

In some ways, this has even turned you into a really good champion of other people.

Kind. Humble. Servant-hearted. You are always the first one pushing others to take center stage and finally feel the spotlight on their face. You love watching other people step into their gifts and you are always the one cheering the loudest when every dream they have comes true.

But your cheering for other people has now drowned out the roaring silence in the room, all these places in your life where you have gotten really comfortable playing small. You're not sure you could handle it if it didn't work out. So, you find clever ways to hide in plain sight. You would rather not even go after something, not even break ground on building the dream, than risk disappointing yourself or anyone else in the process.

In *Slow Growth*, I called these two flip sides of the same coin The Masquerader and The Contortionist.

Every day you are out there walking this tightrope into a trapeze act, a contortionist twisting yourself up into tiny tethered knots, doing backbends until your back breaks, trying to squeeze yourself into a corner that takes up even one inch less space in this world.

Because to contort is easier than to be criticized. . . .

So you have become a master of disguise, masquerading in these qualifiers. Wearing all the different masks and all the different hats.

Spinning plates and spinning fates and spinning out, but never once letting anything drop, including the act.
You find clever ways to hide right there in plain sight.[2]

I say flip sides to the same coin because the result is always the same: The world winds up worse for your absence.

The Contortionist can spend their whole life trying to be enough of something for other people. The people-pleasing side of them turns them into the proverbial "yes person." They become addicted to taking on more than any one human should simply because they equate saying yes to earning both approval and love. Capable. Competent. They are the epitome of "The One Who Always Comes Through."

But all of this twisting themselves up in knots just to please other people has at last left them exhausted. If you resonate with The Contortionist, you are most likely finally reaching that point where you are *starting* to see all the places in your life where you are shrinking into "supposed to be" simply because it makes other people more comfortable. But bending until you break does not serve the world.

The Masquerader can spend their whole life hiding in an effort to keep other people from disapproving of them. Whether it is with the clothes they wear, the masks they put on, or just staying quiet, this person thrives on blending into the background. They excel in helping people believe in themselves and being their biggest cheerleader.

But if you resonate with The Masquerader, what you need to hear right now is this: You do not have to reserve that kind of belief only for other people. If the tables you are trying to sit at require your silence in order to belong, those *aren't* the right tables for you. And there is no amount of hiding that will make people love you.

Whether it's contorting or hiding, people-pleasers are known for their ability to be a "chameleon," shape-shifting into whatever people need them to be. "They're adept at taking the temperature of the room, tuning in, intuiting their assumptions of what other people think and feel and need. And because they've been doing it their whole lives, they can be shockingly accurate in their assessments."[3]

All of this shape-shifting to make other people comfortable can lead the chronic people-pleaser to believe:

(a) No one wants to hear what I have to say anyway; my voice doesn't really matter (also known as the "Who is ever going to care about this?" fear).
(b) It would be better if I could just disappear altogether because then it might not feel so bad never truly feeling seen.

This, of course, comes from a deep-seated sense you have always had.

You think you must disappear in order to be safe.

The Root Causes of People-Pleasing

People-pleasing is often referred to as self-neglect and is rooted in "sociotropy," which is characterized as "feeling overly concerned with pleasing others and earning their approval as a way to maintain relationships."[4]

This strong need for social acceptance is commonly associated with low self-esteem or poor self-image, insecurity, social conditioning, trauma, codependency, seeking acceptance, and anxiously avoiding rejection or abandonment. But it can also be associated with perfectionism and a tendency to overachieve, as these people "want everything to be 'just so,' including how other people think and feel" about them.[5]

At its core, people-pleasing is rooted in a "deep mammalian need" to self-protect by appeasing others since "our brains link that external validation and approval with our own survival."[6] Dr. Britt Andreatta, author of *Wired to Connect*, tells us, "This is largely thanks to the ancient part of our brains—where evolution taught us that if we were outcast from the tribe, we were more likely to perish."[7] She continues, "When our brains perceive that we are being forced to the fringe, it reacts just as it does when faced with a physical threat. In fact, one of the most shocking discoveries I made . . . exclusion lights up the same regions of the brain as physical pain—creating the same neurological reaction as if you've been hit. *Exclusion then, is just as threatening to our survival and as painful as a physical injury*."[8]

It is not surprising then that so many of our people-pleasing tendencies took their earliest roots during childhood, when we were most dependent on others for our survival.

In fact, codependency coach Victoria Albina believes "people-pleasing can have its deepest root in a lack of parental attunement." She writes,

> If your caregivers [were] not tuned into you, which can look like busy parents, distracted parents, emotionally vacant or checked out parents . . . parents dealing with trauma, stress, crisis or substance use issues, or pushy parents who demand that you excel in a certain way, then you may have taken that in as a child. And as an adult, you may feel like you're going to get rejected or abandoned, [so] your focus is on what other people think or feel as a way to keep them happy with you.[9]

Psychologists tell us that *fawning* or excessive people-pleasing is the fourth way our brains might respond to a perceived threat (in addition to fight, flight, and freeze), and it is characterized by "trying to gain the affection and admiration of those they fear as a means of survival."[10] As one article explains, fawning is a type of "trauma response in which a person immediately moves to try to please a person to avoid any conflict and re-establish a sense of safety. . . . We are biologically driven to form an attachment to a parent or caregiver even when they are also a source of critical, shaming, neglectful, or abusive behaviours. . . . For children, this can be defined as a need to be a 'good kid' in order to escape mistreatment by an abusive or neglectful parent."[11]

And if we're not careful, that "good kid" complex can follow us the rest of our lives.

We Shrink So Much We Forget Who We Are

If you spend your whole life chasing approval, you will inevitably have to carve off everything about yourself that made you interesting in the first place—all those smart, sharp edges at the extremes now surgically removed with precision as you whittle yourself down to the middle. Or, as the great philosopher Niles Crane from *Frasier* once said, "Mediocrity is the hallmark of popularity."

This at its core is what it is to have a "Good Girl Complex": After years of people-pleasing and playing small, it's gotten to the point where we don't even recognize ourselves anymore.

It makes us question everything, mostly ourselves.

We lose our voice and start to sound like everyone else around us.

It's been so long since someone asked, we don't even *know* what we like anymore.

And all this shrinking can lead us into three distinct conforming behaviors.

Over-Apologizing and Taking the Blame

Out of a desire to avoid conflict, which people-pleasers believe will lead to them being rejected or abandoned again, they will often find themselves over-apologizing for things that did not require an apology at all, or worse, taking the blame for things they did not do in the first place.[12] People-pleasers are willing to take the blame so long as they can maintain that closeness. They would rather be wrong than be alone.

The "Oliver Twist" Problem

The Charles Dickens classic *Oliver Twist* is a story about an orphan in nineteenth-century London, most notably known by the one-liner phrase "Please Sir, can I have some more?"* as the young boy asks for

---

*The line is actually "Please Sir, I *want* some more." But enough people remember hearing it the other way that it has become a Mandela Effect. Most likely it is because this second wording more accurately reflects the implied meaning of the scene: having to beg someone else for scraps. *Oliver!*, directed by Carol Reed (Columbia Pictures, 1968).

a second helping of gruel. Little bowl raised high, eyes pleading, a giant gulp in between words... this is how we approach people when we don't believe we are worthy of their approval.

I see the "Oliver Twist Problem" play out in so many of my coaching clients. And I see it play out in myself. Most commonly what this looks like is being terrified to ask anyone for help. We believe people don't really want us around or that we're being a bother to them just by existing. Or, on the flip side, we wind up saying yes when we should say no, because we are just so *honored* to be asked, or we accept the first offer that comes along because we are afraid there won't be any more. Whether that's a romantic relationship, a client that you know isn't a good fit, or signing a contract with the first person you meet with... they all boil down to asking for scraps when you were meant for so much MORE.

Performing to Prove You Are Not a Waste of Time

While The Masquerader and The Contortionist seek to please people by disappearing to nothing, there is an alternate approach in the form of The Performer who loves nothing more than to show people how far they have come. But it's not always for the selfish reasons you might think. In this case, they want people to know about their successes not so they can brag... but so they can show these other people that spending time together *won't be a waste of their time*. In *Dirt*, I wrote about it like this:

> When I walked into any room, it was my latest accomplishment that walked in first.... [It] goes before me into any room and announces why I am a person worth talking to. Not because of my inherent worth as a human. Not because I have a good story to tell. Not even because of my witty sense of humor, old soul, or kind heart. It's because I've done something, achieved something, that would make me a good person for them to know.... Therefore, *and for this reason only*, I'm worth paying attention to.[13]

I want them to know I won't be a waste of their time.

Pick Me, Choose Me, Love Me, Let Me Make You Happy

And that, of course, brings us to the other axis in our lonely intersection: the "paid their dues" kind of permission that never comes.

We grow up and we're taught to follow the rules of the road. If the sign says to yield, we yield. If the sign says to slow down, we ask, "How slow?" We stay in our lane, we follow the flow of traffic, we wait our turn and zipper merge with the best of them.

We are good at going where they tell us to go.

It's an entirely different thing to chart our own course.

I have coached entrepreneurs and creatives for years, and if there was a word cloud chart for words people have uttered to me during those sessions, "Wait . . . can you DO that?" would be the biggest bubble.*

The Permission Gap is referred to as "the distance between the things we do and the things we *actually want* to do."[14]

At its core, permission is really about us seeking validation from others that we have arrived, we are "there," and it's safe now for us to proceed. Or, sometimes more to the point, we're hoping that they will tell us that we're NOT there yet and in doing so give us the *permission* we're looking for to once again back ourselves away from that ledge.

Either way, it comes down to not trusting ourselves.

Permission-seeking, it must be said, is also an exercise in avoidance. It's about *talking* instead of *doing*. It's hashing and rehashing all the pros and cons, trying to get as many people as possible to cosign your plan. But when we ask ten different people, we get ten different opinions, which only leaves us spinning all the more. Talking *feels* productive, and of course it's always good to get some outside input, but the problem is it

> Permission-seeking, it must be said, is also an exercise in avoidance.

---

*I don't think that's actually how word bubbles work, but you get the idea.

comes with major diminishing returns. The more we talk, the more confused we are.

So why do we do it, then?

It's because "seeking approval and validation from others is a hallmark trait of a people-pleaser. This person wants assurance that he matters to the people around him. He doesn't look for validation from within, he seeks it everywhere else."[15] More than that,

> When you do something and someone else validates you, you get a hit of oxytocin [and] dopamine. The problem is that people pleasing is buffering. It keeps you from feeling your real feelings.... When you do things to get that dopamine hit, it is so fleeting.... So you have to please another person and another and another if you want to get that dopamine that makes you feel good. It's an endless and exhausting cycle.[16]

Or, as my coaching client Brittany put it, "We're all the GOOD GIRLS, so that need for permission is still so ingrained in our bones. We keep waiting on someone to say 'Yes, you may.'"

Like I said, I spent years teaching marketing to photographers and other creative entrepreneurs, and one of the concepts we always went over was this idea of *positioning*.

Positioning says, "I am _____ because I am not _____," where the catch is that both blanks have to represent *arguably good* things.

Right? It would be cheating for someone to try to create a positioning statement that said "I am good because I am not bad" or "I am talented because I'm not a hack" because that's never going to create a visceral reaction among potential customers. No one is ever going to come along and say, "Oh my gosh, I'm good too! What are the odds!"

Instead, a good example would be something more like, "I am someone who believes classic never goes out of style, because I am not trendy." Reasonable people can now agree to disagree—classic and trendy can both be arguably good things—and now *your* people who agree with what you believe feel like they just found someone who really gets them.

We taught our students it had to be two arguably good things because that started to tell your people something with substance about *who you are* and *what you stand for*. And it allowed them to either connect with you in a meaningful way... or not.

And here's the secret... either one is a win.

When you share something of substance about who you are, the people who love you will love you all the more.

And the people who don't? They were *never* going to get it anyway. Simon Sinek in *Start with Why* put it this way,

> This is largely the pattern for almost every [company] on the market. ... They focus on WHAT they do and HOW they do it... they act like commodities. The more we treat them like commodities, the more they focus on WHAT and HOW they do it. It's a vicious cycle. But only companies that act like commodities... wake up every day with the challenge of how to differentiate. Companies... with a clear sense of WHY never worry about it. They don't think of themselves as being like anyone else, and they don't have to "convince" anyone of their value.... They *are* different, and everyone knows it.[17]

The same is true of people.

Positioning starts by you (a) knowing exactly who you are, and (b) being unafraid to OWN it.

When a person knows *exactly* who they are and they aren't afraid to put it out there *without apology*—when they don't wait for a permission that never comes, when they just *instinctively* know the world needs more of them—then it becomes very easy for them to find their people.

Unsurprisingly, this was one of the hardest things people struggled with in the course.

THE POWER OF POSITIONING

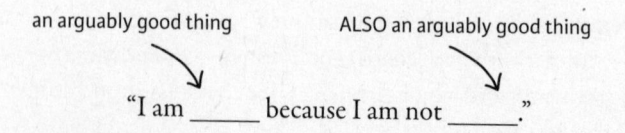

an arguably good thing   ALSO an arguably good thing

"I am _____ because I am not _____."

It's hard enough to know exactly who you are. It's even harder to *own* it.

I told every person in our course that what the world *needed most* was for them to choose to be a Popeye in a Julia Roberts world.

In the movie *My Best Friend's Wedding,* Julia Roberts runs up to Dermot Mulroney (behind poor Cameron Diaz's back) at the end and says something along the lines of . . .

"*Pick me. Choose me. Love me. Let me make you happy.*"

If there was ever a slogan for our recovering people-pleasers sitting around waiting on a permission that never comes . . . this would be it.

This is what Playing Small does.

It tells you to run around in the world, asking other people to let *you* make *them* happy, begging them for seconds on their scraps. It tells you to run to the middle. To play it safe there by looking just like everyone else. To do everything you can to avoid showing up as an outlier in a copy-and-paste world.

But in doing that, you become just another commodity.

And you lose yourself in a million little ways carving yourself up like that.

Meanwhile, in a Julia Roberts world, Popeye simply shows up and says . . .

"*I am what I am.*"

And we don't need *anyone's* permission to do that.

Warning: People-Pleasing Is a Self-Perpetuating Cycle

We have spent far too long stalled out in neutral.

So, it's going to be disorienting when we first pull out the map and decide once and for all to chart our own course. What's more, the people who have been so very *pleased* by our waiting on their approval for every single thing we do . . . they aren't going to like it one bit.

They are going to have opinions. And they are going to make them known.

This is our crossroads moment.

That's because people-pleasing is a self-perpetuating cycle. And the longer we stay in it, the harder it is to break. "Constantly believing you must ask for permission whittles away your sense of Self, and invites self-doubt, feelings of inadequacy, and fear of failure. Other people loom large and more knowledgeable. You override your own internal wisdom and make decisions based on what you think others want you to do."[18]

And the more you do it, the more you erode any remaining trust you have in yourself.

Just like small shifts forward can *expand* our capacity, it turns out these "small things on repeat" in the *wrong* direction only serve to expand our fear.

The heartbreaking part for most of us is that this work should have been started so much sooner when we were little.

> Childhood plays a major role in whether we seek approval as an adult.... Successfully going through childhood development typically imparts a solidified sense of self-worth and value.... When a child is repeatedly given approval, they build up their sense of value. They eventually become confident in their internal sense of validation: they don't need outside approval because they can often validate and approve themselves.... Repeated approval reinforces and builds validation. Criticism undermines [it].[19]

If we didn't get that growing up, once again we have to *become* the grown-up in the room who can be trusted. We have to be that permission for ourselves.

We have to be the ones to look ourselves in the mirror and put a gentle but urgent hand on each of our cheeks as we lean in real close to say, "What are you WAITING for?"

We have to GO.

We have to try.

We have to be willing to say . . . we can't stay here.

People-pleasing and permission, that was always about us surviving. But now it's time for us to *live*.

the shift

People-pleasing and permission-seeking have convinced you that you can't be trusted and everyone else's opinion should be valued more than your own. In an effort not to be rejected, you have now forgotten who you are. Instead, realize that this cycle is self-perpetuating and must be broken to release its grip. Begin to practice owning who you are through a simple exercise like positioning.

10

perfectionism is hiding with better PR

A SELF-PRESERVING ENNEAGRAM FOUR with a *strong* Three wing, a child of the 80s, and a proud Appalachian walk into a room.

No, this isn't the start of some hilarious joke I'm telling. And no, those are not three separate people I'm talking about.*

The truth is, I am all three of these people. All three of these people are me.

And together, they form a lot of opinions about how I walk around in the world.

From the first moment I ever heard about the Enneagram on some podcast somewhere, I was convinced without ever taking the test that I was a clear Enneagram type Three. If you're new to the nine

---

*Side note: If that line didn't immediately make you think, "Why yes, that IS French they're speaking. And no, these kids aren't French, they're *American*!" then I can tell you right now that you are probably *not* at least one of those three things. (And if you're stumped, it's from the classic 1980s Muzzy language learning commercial. Trust me, just google it. *Je suis la jeune fille!*)

perfectionism is hiding with better PR 159

types,† Threes are The Achievers. The gold star accumulators. The A++ students. The Most Likely to Succeed (at Having a Nervous Breakdown). Or as the popular meme so aptly puts it, "Shout out to all the 'gifted' kids from grade school who are now the grown-ups walking around with high-functioning anxiety."

I grew up in a single-wide trailer and ended up at Yale for law school. I got all straight A's in undergrad, except for one B+ that I'm still mad about twenty years later. I was in the gifted program, every AP program, I was class president, on student council, head cheerleader, prom committee chairperson, and was voted Most Likely to Succeed... *twice*.‡ I have anxiety. My anxiety has anxiety. That anxiety in turn has a little pet miniature OCD anxiety that it buys tiny argyle sweaters for and carries around in an oversized purse. Type Three seemed like a pretty safe bet.

That all changed when I had Ian Morgan Cron, coauthor of *The Road Back to You: An Enneagram Journey to Self-Discovery*, on my podcast a few years back. In his book, Ian walks through all the different Enneagram types and the things that might have happened to them in childhood when they first learned to put on the "mask" of that specific type... in other words, when they first got the message "*this* is who you have to be in order to be loved." And he talks about who they become as adults.

In discussing unhealthy type Threes, he talks about how they can become these "shape shifters who can switch personas to match the environment."[1] He calls them "social chameleons" who are willing to "cut corners"[2] if they have to, in order to get to the goal faster.

Given that some of my most absolute nonnegotiable core values in life are Authenticity, Excellence, and Originality... I knew that something was off with me being a total type Three. So I asked Ian about it during our episode.

There is a golden rule in the Enneagram where you are not supposed to "type" other people; it's meant to be *self*-discovery, after all. So instead, Ian just told me to make sure I looked up a Self-Preservation

---

†*Ennea* means "nine," by the way, and there's your Greek lesson for the day.
‡True story. Once in junior high, once senior year.

type Four.[3] Type Fours are known as The Individualist (excellence in authenticity and originality, check, check, check), but he said a Self-Preservation Four will often look like a type Three as they try to *achieve their way into safety.*

And there it was.

Achieving = Safety.

A flash of scarlet letters on the page ribboned from somewhere in the deep, dark corners of my mind as The Girl in the Red Cape and the Big Bad Wolf ripping at her heels came back all at once to bite me.

I included that imagery in *Dirt* to show how for some of us, this self-preservationist switch gets flipped in us where we feel like if we stop escaping for even a second . . . it just might kill us. We run and don't stop running. We run so hard from our story that we stumble into success. An "after" so pretty and perfect on the outside that you would never guess the hard things we've gone through before.

I included that story because I wanted people to understand how *primal . . . visceral . . . survival* this constant drive to be better can become. Some people think the only side effect to all this running is wild, unbridled success . . . so how bad could that be? The truth is, the side effect—the whole dang disease really—is never knowing how to stop.

Achieving is our oxygen. If we go too long without it, we don't know how to breathe.

Achieving = Safety.

I had never felt so understood in my life.

A Self-Preservation Four is known for being "stoic" and "long-suffering." Often called the "Dauntless" or "Tenacity" type, they believe they earn love by being strong, resilient, and never asking for too much.[4] They also forever feel like they have a fatal flaw in the form of a missing piece. And that they are always just barely out of reach of this version of themselves they were always meant to be.

> I want people to understand how *primal . . . visceral . . . survival* this constant drive to be better can become.

As Beatrice Chestnut points out in her book *The Complete Enneagram*, "This Four works hard to get what others have that he or she lacks. Instead of hanging out in their longing in a way that prevents them from taking action, they strive to get 'those distant things' that give them the feeling of being able to obtain that which was lost. Whatever they get, however, *never feels like enough*."[5] She goes on to say,

> These Fours may also *masochistically enact a need to prove themselves by working against themselves*: they make efforts to get what they need and want, but unconsciously work against themselves at the same time.... They spend a lot of energy on being afraid of what's happening instead of dealing with problems and making improvements, so they habitually postpone actions necessary to achieving what they want and then blame themselves for doing so. They wear themselves out seeking and striving in ways and places where they know they'll fail, which ensures the perpetuation of a cycle of effort and devaluation. They may be ambitious, but they deny and work against their own ambitions.... These Fours will often work at cross-purposes, *unintentionally thwarting their own efforts*.[6]

And the boulder rolls all the way back down the mountain.

Add in that I'm a #ChildOfThe80s, where we were all basically feral cats left to fend for ourselves growing up. And that I am also the hyperindependent by-product of this strong, proud, truly Appalachian tradition in my family of never, EVER wanting to ask anyone else for help.* What you are left with is this perfect storm trifecta—this three-in-one, three-strikes-you're-out character combination—that means I am now a person who never, *ever* wants you to see her struggle.

This makes me walk into the world in some very specific (self-sufficient turned self-sabotaging) ways.

First, I don't want your pity. I don't want you averting your eyes from me in some sort of sympathy shame on my behalf. I don't need you feeling sorry for me.

---

*In the eternal words of my Grandma Goldie, "I'll DO it myself!"

While we're at it, unless I specifically ask for it, I don't need your advice, guidance, input, best practices, suggestions, or generally good ideas either. They burn in my ears, run down my throat, and taste like condescension.

I also don't need you asking me a bunch of inane questions about what I'm going to do next. Trust me, I've already thought of all of them. I spend my whole life questioning myself, I don't need you doing it too.

I never, ever want you to know that something isn't working, not even just for pride's sake but because I don't need you worrying about me. Then I'll just have to *worry* about you worrying about me.

And finally, don't even *think* about telling me that it's "good enough," better than what most people would do, or that I should just be proud of myself for trying. *Trying?* I don't even know what that means.

Maybe you know this particular brand of hypervigilant self-sufficiency too.

Regardless of what your Enneagram type is (or if you'd ever even heard of it before today), what decade you were born in (the BEST one or any decade other than the 1980s), the socioeconomic background you experienced, or where you call home... we all know what it is to walk into the world and not want to show any kind of weakness whatsoever.

> Priding yourself on not needing people is a great way not to have any.

We put on this bespoke stoic armor of shiny achievements. We wear these accomplishments like a bright, blinking, neon camouflage, seamlessly blending into the background by, *paradoxically*, forever standing out. If all they can see is our latest win, then we'll never have to worry about them getting close enough to see our many flaws.

As you can imagine, this leads to a very *lonely* existence, indeed.

It turns out priding yourself on not needing people... is a great way not to have any.

These Walls Keep Tumbling Down

When I was little, this wild thing, untamed growing up on Fenwick Mountain, I used to sit out in the yard with a blue spiral-bound notebook drawing and redrawing plans for how we could turn our single-wide tin can of a trailer into a *real* house overnight.

I spent hours dreaming up how we could build walls around it. Put a roof over it. Layer on more and more until no one would ever know what it once was . . . even though I already knew the flimsy aluminum would never be able to bear the weight. Hour after hour, I would sit out there and reimagine everything it *could* be.

But do you want to know what I never once drew?

In all of my best-laid plans, I never once drew what would happen if we bulldozed that trailer all the way to the ground and started with a firm foundation.

I only realized that recently.

It hit me out of nowhere midsentence while I was doing a podcast interview for one of my books. "Build walls around it. Put a roof over it." It was *always* about putting up facades. These pretty, white-picket dream house exteriors where no one would ever guess I was still just The Girl in the Trailer on the inside.

I don't know why it never occurred to me to tear down that trailer first. I sure *hated* it enough to back then. I would have given anything to get away from that trailer growing up. And yet, there it always was . . . right at the center of all my future plans.

I don't know why it didn't dawn on me that sometimes we first have to rip out the wreckage and the rubble of what no longer serves—all these hollow tin-can versions of what we thought we'd always have to be—before we can dig in and build something new.

I don't know why we build these lives that look better on the outside than they *feel* on the inside. Or why we'll go right on breaking the backs of our littlest selves, piling on these burdens of all our heaviest expectations their tiny shoulders were never built to carry.

But I do know that we keep hiding everything that's crumbling at the very center of us.

We keep holding the world at arm's length, far enough away where they can't see any of these fatal flaws in the facade, the places where the prop scenery turns two-dimensional and painted-on when you look at it from the side, and these blue-sky, happy-days-are-here-again backdrops fall right over with the slightest push.

We keep putting up a pretend front to the world.

We keep wishing for a different start to the story.

We keep turning the blank page and starting over from scratch.

But no matter how much we draw and redraw these temporary hard lines in permanent ink, believing the next draft of us will surely be the one to finally make us feel real, to finally make us feel safe—no matter how pretty and perfect we look on the page . . .

These walls keep tumbling down.

Perfect Does Her Very Best to Keep Me Safe

Every now and then, I think it's good to remind myself that Perfect is not ALL bad the way I like to make her out to be.

Mostly she's just looking out for me in her own messed-up, meddling sort of way. Perfect is sort of like that well-intentioned but seriously misguided relative at Thanksgiving who cares a lot but gives the absolute *worst* advice.

You know the one.

You would think with a name like Perfect she would show up acting like Margot Robbie, pretty in pink, sweet as can be, and always on her toes. But it turns out, up close and personal, when the mask falls off, Perfect is a lot more like Shirl from *The Marvelous Mrs. Maisel*.

Brash. Pushy. Overbearing. Absolutely stuffed full of unsolicited opinions, which she always shares freely. (But make no mistake, they *will* cost you.) She arrives dressed to the nines in these loud floral-print dresses, tied up in a pretty bow with the delicate apron strings she still refuses to cut. She sounds like gravel and she smells like Aquanet-scented cigarette smoke, this combustible cloud of criticism following her everywhere she goes. She's convinced I'm not doing *anything* right, and she never misses an opportunity to tell me.

But mostly, she's just looking out for me.

In all honesty, Perfect does her very best to keep me safe.

Perfect knows how hard it is to have the critics come for you. These projectile-hurling armchair quarterbacks throwing their opinions around from the safety of the cheap seats. Perfect knows how when the words hit just right, it knocks the wind out of me every time, leaves me curled up and bleeding on the field. So, Perfect likes to whisper about how maybe I just shouldn't put anything else out into the world until I know it's so good that no one could ever criticize us again.

What Perfect *doesn't* whisper is how that moment will never come.

Perfect tells me people won't love me if I'm weak, so I better always be strong.

Perfect tells me people only love me for my results, so I better always come through.

Perfect tells me to work harder than anyone else in the room, even when it's killing me.

Perfect tells me to nod sweetly and say yes even when I mean no.

Perfect tells me nobody cares about gentle spirits, kind hearts, or old souls anymore, so I better always have something shiny and brand-new ready to impress them.

Then she takes a long drag on her cigarette, brushes the hair out of my eyes, and tells me I would be so much prettier if I smiled more.

Yes, Perfect does everything she can to keep me safe.

Even if it means I disappear entirely in the process.

What If Perfectionism Is Just HIDING with Better PR?

Being a perfectionist is one of those noble vices we love to claim. Like being too diligent with our flossing, too conscientious in our refusal to ever take eleven items or more through the "ten items or less" checkout lane, or self-deprecating our way into "works too hard" as one of our supposed weaknesses in a job interview. *Nailed it.*

We say it without actually thinking it's a bad thing.

You know that meme with the Volturi from *Twilight*, standing on a balcony in their silk jackets and ruffled Beethoven shirts, looking down on everything and everyone in their path with unrestrained vampire disdain?

That's what my perfectionism looks like when I even *think* about putting something out into the world that is just "good enough."

"Oh, done is better than perfect, you say?"
"Imperfect progress is still progress?"
"At least you tried your best?" (Your *best*? Losers always whine about their best!*)

Pfft. Peasant.

If we're being honest, that's the kind of soul-sucking superiority we put on when we treat our perfectionism like a virtue.

We're happy to say things like:

"Of course I haven't put this thing out into the world . . . it's just not 'there' yet."

"Of course I'm really nitpicky about all the details and have to think about my whole life before I hit publish . . . that's just the perfectionist in me."

"Of course someone else might think this is good enough . . . I guess I just have higher standards I hold myself to."

But here's what we're *not* willing to say:

"I'm afraid of being seen."
"I'm afraid of being criticized."
"I'm afraid it's not any good."
"I'm afraid I don't have what it takes."

---

*Thanks to Sean Connery in *The Rock* for this gem on repeat in my head. *The Rock*, directed by Michael Bay (Buena Vista Pictures, 1996).

And the one underlying all the others:

"I'm afraid of raising my hand and finally saying out loud for maybe the first time ever that THIS is what I want to do with my wild, untamed life... because then I'll actually have to go DO something about it."

The judgy, overly confident, overly ruffled shirt no longer seems to fit now, does it?

No, we don't like to tell the truth.

That we've gotten so comfortable in our hiding, we've actually convinced ourselves it's this whole other thing. A noble thing. An excellence thing. An overachiever thing. An attention-to-detail thing. A thing that only the A+ people of the world will understand. This incessant desire to not give up until it's perfect? This is just our cross to bear. Oh to be one of the common people who are perfectly content to phone in a C- performance. They will never know the self-loathing and existential dread that comes from being one of the truly set apart.

Or.

Or, it just feels safer to blame perfectionism rather than admit we're afraid.

What if "perfectionism" is just HIDING with better PR?

Not since the "Got Milk?" people has there been an ad campaign that has made something so plain-Jane vanilla seem so sexy and sought-after.

I wonder how *that* staff meeting went down.

I wonder what kind of storyboards the *Mad Men* stiffs in power suits had to put up that day to convince all their focus groups that indefinitely delaying their entire future and every single dream they can't go a day without thinking about would all be worth it so long as no one ever had anything bad to say about them *ever* again.

I wonder if there was a catchy jingle. *Dial 877 PLAYSMALL, 877-PLAYSMALL.*

I wonder if there was a tiny mascot. The Perfect Parrot, perhaps, a jewel-toned, tone-deaf squawking macaw with a jaunty little British accent. Or an Australian accent. Or one of those news anchor

PERFECTIONISM IS HIDING WITH BETTER PR

not since the "Got Milk?" people has there been an ad campaign that made something so plain-Jane vanilla seem so sexy and sought after

NO-accents, for all they care. So long as you never sound like your real self again and get really good at mimicking all these lines they keep feeding you about how "now" is not the best time.

They went digging into all of our collective hidey-holes—these dark corners we can disappear into where no one will ever find us, these enigma-ridden white-rabbit trails that lead us to an upside-down world where creating nothing is somehow safer than creating failure—and then they slapped a milk mustache on them.

"Drink me" the tiny tag(line) beckons to us.

Drink me. And I'll shrink every one of these doubts down to bite-size, transform them into something far more palatable, an adorable little game of chess that will keep you here, a pawn forever trapped in a world of make-believe. You're not hiding, forever suspended in the upside down. You're just waiting on perfect. (And if we have our way, you'll be waiting here a very long time.)

Because, Really, What's the Alternative?

Let's be honest here. Deep down, we WANT to believe Perfect can keep us safe. We want to believe that if we're perfect enough, we can somehow transform ourselves into someone new ... an exercise in pretty pink eraser, rubbed all the way down to the metal end like nails on a chalkboard until there is nothing left of us but shreds. These pieces of us that are left behind and scattered with shallow breath when we blank-space entire parts of our story, all in the name of fitting in.

We NEED to believe Perfect can keep us safe.

Because, really, what's the alternative?

The alternative is we'll have to admit we're going to get our hearts broken.

We'll have to admit we're going to get our as-yet unscarred palms ripped wide open in pursuit of getting our hands dirty building this dream.

People are going to be cruel. Crueler than we ever thought possible. And when they're not being cruel, they'll just ignore us altogether.

We're going to be disappointed. The most disappointed we've ever been. We are going to kick and scream and flop on the ground, temper-tantrum our way into saying "fine, maybe I should just QUIT!" more times than any grown person ever should.

We will have to shed a thousand old skins, be torn down to nothing and built back into something new so many times that it will be hard to recognize us anymore. We'll evolve so hard that we'll have to reintroduce ourselves to the people who only *thought* they once knew us.

So, it is no wonder we go running back to Perfect every chance we get. And for her part, Perfect is happy to take us back every time.

> We think if we're perfect enough... no one will ever leave us again.

We WANT to believe that if we can just be perfect, we will finally be chosen, accepted, included, safe... *loved*.

Let's just call it what it is.

We think if we're perfect enough... no one will ever leave us again.

In *Dirt*, I talked about the aftermath of my mom leaving when I was nine years old and how it turned "perfect" into a weapon for me.

> Over time, I've realized this thing I do when I think someone is about to leave me. Right then and there, I determine to become something

so much *more*. I decide to go out and become so successful at something in life, to achieve something so great, that it will make them regret missing out on any of it. It makes me want to go out and do something so beautiful, so extraordinary . . . if for no other reason than it will make them sad that they weren't there to see it firsthand.

"That'll show them," I think to myself. "I bet then they'll wish they had stuck around."

The obvious problem with this plan, of course, is that it implicitly gives away my most deeply held fear and belief: *maybe they were right.*

Maybe without all this *more*, I was never someone worth staying for to begin with. . . . And maybe I will have to spend my entire life being more of something if I ever want the people I love to stay.[7]

Beatrice Chestnut's words about the Self-Preservation Fours come back again to haunt me: "They strive to get 'those distant things' that give them the feeling of being able to obtain *that which was lost*. Whatever they get, however, *never feels like enough*."

And just like that, we are once again The Illusionist in the Distance.

There is this version of us always up ahead, glowing in radiant gilded light from our mountaintop moments. We call out to her to wait, to let us catch up. We fall down again and again, trying to reach her. She turns if only for a minute. She stares us directly in the eyes, these dimly lit mirror reflections of her own. Smiles a sweet, superior smile.

And then goes on without us.

In *Slow Growth* I wrote:

You know that feeling of being left behind. Whether in a dream or a waking nightmare, you know the feeling of running after someone who would not stay. That pit pounding in your chest, the sputter of sobs rising up that steal your breath away, the familiar arms that once held you now always arm's length beyond your grasp. You know what it is to lose someone.

"Don't go. Don't go. Don't go."

But perhaps the greatest heartbreak of all is the day you lose yourself.

It's the day you realize there are a thousand supposed-to-be versions of you standing on a thousand illusioned, illuminated mountaintop moments in the distance. And not a single one of them cares enough about you to let you catch up.[8]

The trap with all of this, of course, is that we think if we're perfect enough, no one will ever leave us again . . . but we end up *abandoning ourselves* in a thousand different ways in the process.

the shift

Perfectionism has convinced you for years that perfect can somehow keep you safe. Meaning that until that elusive "someday" when you are finally perfect, the only alternative is to stay hidden a little while longer. It wants you to believe that these fragile facades are all that matter, and it's better to walk around in the world not needing anyone. But deep down, that's just because we never want anyone to ever hurt us again. Instead, each time perfectionism tries to convince you to play it safe, smile sweetly and remind it that "safe" was never a fair trade for indefinitely delaying the dream.

scenic overlook #2

grief is a story not yet lived

Can I tell you something?

It is okay to grieve the story you thought you would be living by now.

It is okay to mourn the best-laid plans that were drafted by your own hands now scattered like ashes all around you.

It is okay to say, "This is not the plotline I would have chosen . . . but it is the story I have been given. So right here, even in the pain, I will believe that the character and endurance this is building in me will carry me further than I've ever been before. And who I am becoming will one day all be worth it."

Listen, I know that you feel like quitting.

I know that every day you are walking around, this internal dialogue is on repeat like an intercom tied tight around your neck. Barking out the morning announcements of how you *still* haven't gotten it right yet. And how much further ahead you would be right now if you hadn't had to pause along the long, slow climb to do all this healing first.

You see everyone around you doing exactly what you want to do and doing it with ease. Meanwhile, you can't stop thinking about every mistake you've ever made that you still haven't found a way to forgive yourself for. All the ways you've messed up and keep messing it up, somehow still repeating the unlearned lesson all these years later.

But if I could show you what I see . . . I would want you to know how BRAVE it is to me that you keep going.

Sure there have been missteps, sure there have been times when you've stumbled. I know that because I have had missteps and stumbles too.

But I want you to know that every time you rise, there is a whole stadium of future yous—drafts upon drafts upon drafts of the "you" you are becoming—who jump to their feet and cheer you on.

They are who *they* are because today you chose to pick yourself up, dust yourself off, and begin again. It's time to forgive yourself for all the time that you've wasted playing small. It's time to forgive yourself for waking up once again back at the starting line.

It is okay, radically BRAVE even, to be a draft in progress.

And for what it's worth . . . I'm *already* so proud of the "you" that is standing here today.

11

failure is a bankrupt identity

You are here.
 You are... here.
 You are... HERE?!
There is an urban legend among writers that goes a little something like this: A group of author friends got together and made a bet that none of them could tell an entire story in just six words. Supposedly Hemingway* scribbled down something quick on a piece of paper and submitted the following: *For sale: baby shoes, never used.*† At which point the rest of the group immediately paid up without saying a word.

---

*It has been often attributed to Hemingway but never proven. Some argue the link is unlikely, but like all great stories, the point is not really who wrote it but what it speaks to us.

†Okay, it was actually "worn," but the Tortured Poet in me loves a good proximate rhyme.

There's no doubt that's good. But I believe there's an entire story waiting to unravel itself here for us, tucked into the space of even fewer words. In fact... in just three.

You. Are. Here.

Welcome (back) to the base of the mountain.

Or, as one of my favorite roller coasters puts it, "Welcome back, riders! How was your RIDE?"

They always say it straight-faced and without an *ounce* of irony, as you come back looking just like Nick Nolte's mug shot, doing a postmortem on all the mosquitos you just picked out of your teeth, and making sure your C1 and C2 vertebrae are still firmly attached at the base of your skull. *Fantastic, thanks for asking.*

My point is, if you're just getting your footing after taking the long tumble down—here I can't help but picture the kind of cartoon fall where you land head over tail, *doink, doink, doink, doink*, all the way back down the mountainside—you may be feeling a little worse for the wear right now.

It's okay to be disoriented.

It's okay to feel like you might want to throw up.

It's okay to swear you're never going back up that mountain again.

But... you are here. *Here* is where you find yourself.

You're dazed and picking up the pieces of the dream you for so long held diligently in your shaking hands. There are hoodies and power bars, water bottles and trail maps, walkie-talkies and blister balm—these mountain-hiking survival supplies you once packed for the long road ahead—now strewn all around you on the ground like wreckage from the crash-and-burn heights you only recently learned how to climb. There is a ringing in your ears, the kind of shell-shocked disbelief you only get from an emergency landing. You quickly triage the damage, which at first glance appears to be nothing short of catastrophic, and you once again replay it all in your mind to find out just where, exactly, it all went upside down.

And what I know more than anything, from my own firsthand personal experience with the mountain, is that the thing you might be feeling most right now is... *grief.*

There is a grief that hits right around the time you blow out the candles on your fortieth birthday. Only I turned forty in the year of our Lord 2020, at the height of COVID-19, when the spring flowers and a raging pandemic were in full bloom. So, there was no breathing on anything, including the candles. *But I did make a wish.*

I wished that I could go back and tell half-my-age Mary some things she was about to get really wrong.

At this, I close my eyes and I see these unfurled threads upon the ground. The once tightly stitched seams that were forever dividing me into a before and an after, tight enough so that the light and other people could never get in, now burst forth from the pressure of holding it all together and rain down like confetti. It is at once a ticker-tape parade and a mourning processional, a long, slow march for all the mistakes I've made. These white-knuckle grips at last giving way in exhaustion to wide-open palms.

What they don't tell you is that the greatest gift of age and failure and starting over, even more so than the hard-won wisdom . . . is the *softening*. A soft heart born out of empathy. Soft voice born out of listening more than you talk. Soft judgment born out of the fact that you now realize just how much you've messed up too. And yes, even a soft belly. This too is a gift. For it pushes and rages back against a lifetime of being told to fit into these smaller containers.

And somewhere along the way, you learn how to breathe again.

Here at the bottom of the mountain, there is going to be a voice that will tell you how you need to try harder, get it together, that if you would just be better in *all the ways* then finally, *finally* life would be good.

It's going to tell you about your clutter, and how you keep forgetting that once again mildewed load of laundry waiting for you in the washer. It will remind you of your multiplying inbox and the twenty

> The greatest gift of failure, even more so than the hard-won wisdom . . . is the *softening*.

things that still didn't get done again today. In short, it's going to tell you how every day you're out here failing.

But what it's not going to tell you is how those words you spoke to a friend were a lifeline to them. How that gift you've been given changes lives. It will never show you how your face lights up when you see a dog or a sunset or a string of fireflies taking flight . . . or just how truly beautiful you are when you cry.

Instead, it's going to tell you how you're behind. It's going to show you every person doing better than you. It's going to whisper, "Why can't you be more like them?" It's going to tell you that you need to hurry, that you need to rush, that every second slipping away is already being wasted.

What it's not going to tell you is that there is a plan for your life. That the timing now unfolding was written into the very first tightly stitched celestial seam dividing day from night. And the same power that switched on the lights for the whole world to see isn't for a second worried about getting you where you're going right on time.

No, instead this voice is going to double down and tell you how you always take the long way around. How you always find a way to mess up what comes so easy to everyone else. It's going to say whatever you touch turns to fool's gold . . . shiny on the outside, worthless underneath.

What it's not going to tell you, but I WILL, is that there are people who look forward to you walking into a room. That they think about the words you speak for days afterward. That your laughter is one of their favorite sounds. And the whole world shines brighter with you in it.

What it's not going to tell you, but I will, is that this voice, the one that makes you doubt everything you do . . . *that voice is terrified of the day you finally realize that perfect records were never a prerequisite for purpose.*

You have spent a lifetime walking around as a patchwork of these tightly stitched seams. These compartmentalized versions of you that you think you can seal off, silence, surgically remove with precision anytime you want, anytime you find yourself walking into these very pretty rooms and believe the ugly parts of your story will never find belonging there. And then you're surprised when the stitches of all these missing parts leave you with extra scars.

We were not meant to be these paper dolls, a two-dimensional, paint-by-numbers, silent-screaming string of pretty maids all in a row.

We came out here to get our hands dirty, this two-part mixture of mud and blood caked under our cracked fingernails as we set about this hard, holy work of... unraveling. Coming apart at the seams. Coming undone to all the performing and pretending, this buttoned-up act of holding it all together and never once letting them see you stumble as you start again, *over and over and over*...

> **Perfect records were never a prerequisite for purpose.**

I close my eyes and I see these unfurled threads upon the ground.

Let us lean into the unraveling. It is an unbinding. An unshackling. An unfamiliar shimmering shore.

But it is not out there somewhere. This is no far-off moment of arrival. It is here and it is now. It is a daily undoing and an act of being made new.

You are here.

So, let's pull on that thread a little longer.

We Think Failure Is Wired Right into Our DNA

You don't get to forfeit the failure.

Even when we lay down these heavy things we were never meant to carry and begin a new kind of climb—this slow burn of a gentle rise, this scenic route of a road less traveled, a leisurely long way around born this time *not* out of a genesis of fear but one of curiosity—we will still inevitably be met with our first big failure along the way.

Failure looms large out here on the mountain.

It casts a long shadow over every inch of wide, spacious territory we have only just so recently reclaimed.

It's a ten-pound bag of marbles—at once glass and indestructible, capable of inflicting such deep, flinching pain—they are there to disabuse you of your newfound footing and do everything they can to trip you up along the way. Their swirl of intricate design is meant to distract you, this bright flash and flourish of color is there to keep you from seeing all the sheer damage they can contain. They come tossed and tumbling down the mountainside, a ball-bearing scattering that instantly sends you reeling, your cartoonish feet paddling beneath you as fast as they can while the firm foundation you were just standing on is now at once reduced to this sabotage of a slippery slope.

For some of us, we think failure is wired right into us, right down to our DNA.

We watched our parents struggle with money, so we believe we will always struggle with money. We watched a family business fail, so we tell ourselves maybe our lineage just didn't get the entrepreneurial gene. A ten-year marriage crumbled right in the midst of our most formative years and our young minds quickly got the message that maybe people in our family tree just aren't the staying kind.

FAILURE IS A TEN-POUND BAG OF MARBLES

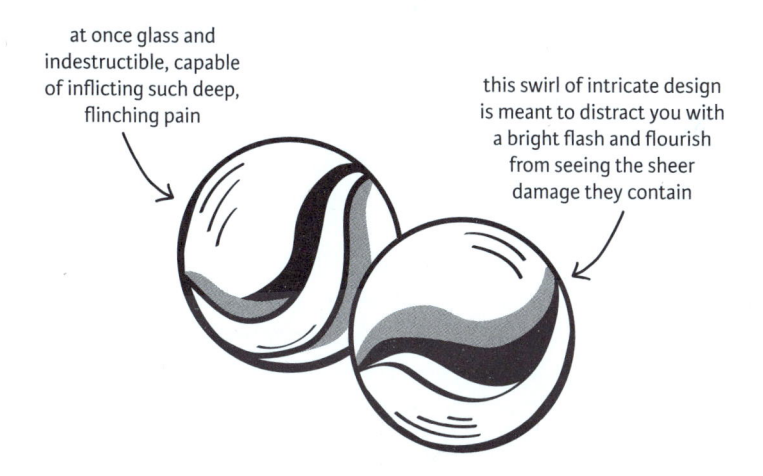

at once glass and indestructible, capable of inflicting such deep, flinching pain

this swirl of intricate design is meant to distract you with a bright flash and flourish from seeing the sheer damage they contain

We start to believe that we are carriers of a *regressive* gene—this aggressive, oppressive return to a worse state of being that absolutely refuses to ever skip a generation.

We carry the cumulative weight of every setback and disappointment and doubled-down mistake made by someone else well before our time. We burrow them down deep into our marrow, walk around with them at the very center of our bones.

But you and I are not a fatalistic outcome. We are not a foregone conclusion to this double-helix double jeopardy of a twice-indicted bloodline: A repeating, identical prosecution for these crimes we did not commit. A consecutive life sentence handed down long before we were born.

> You and I are not a fatalistic outcome.

We can't let the disappointments and the failures of the past become some unavoidable repeating pattern in our lives. Expecting to *always* fail is a habit. And you have no idea how much that expectation is creating your results. Pause right here, back down at the base of the mountain. What are the stories you keep telling as you find yourself once again staring down at the starting line?

Like I said, we think failure is wired right into our DNA.

Which really is to say . . . failure is an *identity thief*.

Hero Is a Journey, Not a Destination

One of the concepts I teach in my writing course is that of the Hero's Journey.

Made popular by Joseph Campbell, the Hero's Journey is a twelve-step process* that describes the different stages someone will go through when they are being called up from a place of ordinary—*obscurity*, even—to go out into the great unknown just to find their way back home a changed person. This is Dorothy in the *Wizard of Oz* clicking her ruby-red slippers together in the far-flung Emerald

---

*I teach it as twelve steps, but you can find versions of it anywhere from ten to seventeen steps.

City, found only by first journeying to the very end of the yellow brick road. She goes all this way to find everything she thought she was looking for, only to wind up whispering to herself, "There's no place like home."

Like I said, the Hero's Journey begins in obscurity, often called "The Ordinary World," until there is some sort of Call to Adventure that flings our would-be hero into the arc of the action by first disrupting the comfort and safety of what they have always known. And do you want to know what their immediate *reaction* almost always is? A response so repeatable and predictable you could practically set your watch by it. *"Annnnnnd . . . THERE it is."* A knee-jerk so universal that it was made into one of the official steps. It's called the Refusal of the Call. And it happens because the hero does not feel worthy of where they are being asked to go.

Sound familiar?

Our hero starts listing off all the ways they've gotten it wrong before, all the mistakes they have already made, the failures now unfailingly tattered and tethered to the rough-edged hem of their once good name. And they try to bow out now before they even begin. They would just rather remain in obscurity than journey out into the unknown and risk ever failing again.

But then, in step 4, something happens that changes everything. They meet a guide who points the way. (Remember: "Look for the guides. At the right time, a guide will be provided. So, if a guide has suddenly appeared, *maybe it's time*.") And then in step 5 they "Cross the Threshold" of what becomes their point of no return. At this point, our hero has gone far enough out into the unknown that they would rather commit to staying the course and see it all the way through . . . than to turn back now.

As the Hero's Journey proceeds, there are trials and failures and ordeals of many kinds. All of it is driving to one final moment—step 12, "Returning with the Elixir"—where the hero finds their way back home forever changed. Not only have *they* been transformed by what they have been through; they now return home with the ability to help others find healing in their stories too.

Somewhere among the fog of our own obscurity, a new picture is now taking shape.

Can't you see it?

Once you do, you can't look away.

This mountain standing in front of us, it was never about our uphill climb, this stratospheric trajectory we're on, or the breathtaking view we alone will get to see from the top. The places we are being called were never just about us.

It turns out this climb was never about our identity as a failure.

But it was never only about our identity as the *hero* either.

It was always about us making the true transformation to guide. So that we, in turn, can be the ones to point the way in someone else's story too.

And we don't get there by hiding out in obscurity.

We get there by walking right up to this threshold moment, this point of no return.

It is a place where from here on out we name the fear . . . and move forward anyway.

How to Fail at Failing: A Beginner's Guide

If you've ever been to London and taken a ride on the Tube (their version of a subway), you know that there is this repeating message in a posh lady's voice saying, "Mind the Gap," meaning don't get tripped up as you're exiting.

There is a similar feeling that comes up when you are living in the first-draft version of something you've been dreaming of for years, but you know it's still nowhere near where you want it to be. Ira Glass, host of *This American Life*, has this quote about what he calls "The Gap":

> All of us who do creative work, we get into it because we have good taste. But there is this gap. For the first couple years you make stuff, it's just not that good. It's trying to be good, it has potential, but it's not. But your taste, the thing that got you into the game, is still killer.

And your taste is why your work disappoints you. A lot of people never get past this phase, they quit. Most people I know who do interesting, creative work went through years of this.... And if you are just starting out or you are still in this phase, you gotta know it's normal and the most important thing you can do is do a lot of work. Put yourself on a deadline so that every week you will finish one story. It is only by going through a volume of work that you will close that gap, and your work will be as good as your ambitions. And I took longer to figure out how to do this than anyone I've ever met. It's gonna take a while. It's normal to take a while. You've just gotta fight your way through.[1]

In other words, DON'T mind the Gap... just acknowledge that it's part of the ride so you don't get tripped up too much on the way.

It's the same way with failure.

But most of us get in trouble with failure—we *fail* at failing, if you will—when we try to take it to one of two extremes.

1. Fear will try to tell us to ignore our failure altogether.

In an effort to minimize the intense sense of "embarrassment, anxiety, anger, sadness, and shame"[2] we feel when we fail at something that was important to us, our brains will often try to self-protect and escape that discomfort by convincing us we didn't really care about that goal to begin with. We'll say things like, "I used to have that dream, but I think I've grown out of it" or "I didn't really want to add that to my plate right now anyway."

But it turns out, the more we try to minimize that failure, the harder it is for us to process it and move on.

A study from the *Journal of Behavioral Decision Making* explains why: "You shouldn't try to slough off feeling bad after failure. Researchers discovered that thinking about your emotions—rather than the failure itself—is most helpful.... It can help you work harder to find better solutions so that you'll improve next time.... Label your emotions as you allow yourself to experience them."[3]

2. Fear will try to tell us that because we failed . . . we ARE a failure.

Or, on the other extreme, fear will tell us that ALL we should think about is how we failed and how that, therefore, makes *us* a failure. It makes it part of our very identity, so we think things like, "This is just who I am, someone who fails at things, someone who starts but never finishes, someone who everything I touch turns to waste." We think that if our dream didn't work out this go-around, it's because there is something broken in us right down to the wiring.

This can leave us living with regret or constantly relitigating the past to find out where it all went wrong. And most of all, it can leave us playing small with our goals moving forward out of a desire for control and certainty, as "I just never want it to feel that hard again" echoes in our minds.

Instead of either of these two extremes, we change our identity with failure when we are willing to adopt a beginner's mindset: Failure just means we were brave enough to try and fail at something new. Adopting this sort of resilient thinking really comes down to "approaching new challenges with curiosity and positive thinking rather than fear. Look at every situation as a learning experience and give yourself permission to not be a pro immediately. . . . If you're a perfectionist, you probably want to succeed in your first attempt. But this is an unrealistic expectation. You'll encounter roadblocks, and that's okay. Two small steps forward and one step back is still a net positive."[4]

But "beginner" is not the only new identity we'll want to adopt.

We Have to Become the Person Who Can Stand Inside These Goals

Do you want to know what's fun?

Starting is fun. Announcing is fun. Setting off bravely toward a brand-new horizon is fun.

Do you want to know what else is fun?

Finishing is fun. Launching is fun. Throwing the confetti is super fun.

Do you know what fear wants to convince you just ISN'T any fun at all?

Every other moment in between.

I heard an explanation once about the difference between setting goals versus intentions that really started to change all that for me. It said when you set a *goal*, you get to celebrate on one day: the day you actually reach that goal. But when you set daily *intentions* about who you have to show up as *today* in order to one day become the person who gets to stand in that goal, it means that every day you come one step closer is a cause for celebration.

In *Atomic Habits*, James Clear puts it this way:

> Every action you take is a vote for the type of person you wish to become. No single instance will transform your beliefs, but as the votes build up, so does the evidence of your new identity. This is one reason why meaningful change does not require radical change. Small habits can make a meaningful difference by providing evidence of a new identity. And if a change is meaningful, it actually is big. *That's the paradox of making small improvements.*[5]

Here are five meaningful changes we can make as we stop identifying with our failures.

1. Accept where you are.

The first step in this process is always going to be getting honest about where you are. It's allowing yourself space to grieve both the story you thought you would be living by now and all of your wide-eyed best efforts that have just met their most recent demise. Dealing with the reality of our situation is always one of the most important steps to building resilience. As Dr. Alison Cook writes, "You gaze unflinchingly at the truth. You start naming things honestly. You stop pretending. You stop trying to gaslight yourself into believing things aren't what they really are. You stop putting a whole lot of energy into manipulating yourself into feeling great."[6] Grief is a story not yet lived. So that means we are going to have to mourn this failure before we can move on from it.

2. Accept a healthy level of responsibility.

The tricky part about not allowing our failures to become a part of our identity is that it can become tempting to swing to the other extreme: to pretend like *none* of this was our fault. But we lose agency and ownership when we attempt to avoid shame at all costs that way. There is power in identifying how we contributed to this outcome; we just have to let it be a commentary on what we did and some character flaws we might want to clean up, versus a condemnation of the very core of *who we are*. As Amy Morin, psychotherapist and author of *13 Things Mentally Strong People Don't Do*, tells us, "It's important to accept an accurate level of responsibility for your failure.... Blaming other people or unfortunate circumstances [for] your failure will prevent you from learning from it. When you think about your failure, look for explanations, not excuses."[7]

3. Accept what this can teach you.

Here's our old friend "data" come back to bite us once again. I know that when you're still reeling from a disappointing result, the last thing in the world you want to do is dig into all the data—sixteen-column, color-coded spreadsheet in hand—to find out where exactly it all went wrong, right down to the decimal point. But this is where that separation—creating some breathing room between who we are as a person internally and the setback we've just experienced externally—becomes so crucial.

TED speaker and professor of astrophysics Erika Hamden knows something about that. She and her team spent a decade developing FIREBall, described as "a telescope designed to hang from a giant balloon 130,000 feet in the stratosphere." But upon launch, it suffered a catastrophic failure. "The balloon, it turns out, had a hole and crash-landed in the New Mexico desert."[8]

A decade of her life, just to watch it all *crash and burn*.

How did she bounce back from that very public, very perfect metaphor-in-the-making for how we *all* feel when something doesn't work out? "Hamden suggests taking a cue from the scientific method, which regards failure as an important—and necessary—step towards achieving progress. 'The whole premise of science is to prove that your hypothesis is wrong.... Failure is inevitable when you're pushing the limits of knowledge.'"[9]

She continues, "The point of doing something is being able to ask afterwards: 'What did you learn from it?' ... You learn more when things don't go correctly."[10]

So, when you inevitably meet failure along this new climb, I want you to ask yourself some important questions: What did I learn from this? What can I be proud of here? What am I *really* afraid of? What's the worst that could happen? What would make all of this worth it?

4. Accept how you've already grown from this.

My coaching client Brittany said something that I think is true for so many of us when it comes to being able to see our own progress clearly. She said, "The irony is that most other people would probably call us winners right now if they looked at everything we've done. Meanwhile we're over here feeling like we have *yet* to ever do anything right. We just can't see ourselves that way."

Above, I asked that question "What am I really afraid of?" For most of us what we're really afraid of is choosing wrong. Looking foolish. Wasting our time. Going too far down a wrong path only to have to start over once again. *We only see the failures.*

But what we don't realize is that *nothing is wasted*. We carry all of it with us. And even now, this disappointment is preparing us for what comes next.

A big part of accepting how you have *already* grown from this failure, even in real time as it's happening, is rejecting a fixed mindset for a growth mindset.

According to Harvard Business School, "Someone with a growth mindset views intelligence, abilities, and talents as learnable and capable of improvement through effort.... Someone with a fixed mindset views those same traits as inherently stable and unchangeable over time."[11]

The language of a growth mindset versus a fixed mindset was first put forth in *Mindset: The New Psychology of Success* by psychologist

Carol Dweck: "Her team analyzed students' brain activity while reviewing mistakes they made on a test. Those with a fixed mindset showed no brain activity when reviewing the mistakes, whereas the brains of those with a growth mindset showed processing activity.... *A fixed mindset can physically prevent you from learning from mistakes*, while a growth mindset can empower you to perceive mistakes as learning opportunities."[12]

A growth mindset is your once and for all rejecting this idea that you are a fatalistic outcome or that failure is wired right into your DNA. Instead, we return to our evidence to the contrary as proof of how our identity is growing every day.

5. *Accept where you go from here.*

One of my favorite things I tell myself often is "No Setback, No Story."

So before we move on from this failure, I want to leave you with just one more question to ask yourself:

Assume it all works out . . . how would you prepare then?

It can be hard to imagine, here when you're knee-deep in the mud of your most recent disappointment. But for just a second, pretend that this setback is just the setup for one incredible story. How would you show up then? What meaningful action would you start putting in every single day to prepare like you believe it?

I always tell my coaching clients, "Don't ask for rain and then not pack an umbrella." Show me the proof that you are actually preparing for what you asked for.

Here's what I need you to know: It ALWAYS doesn't work out . . . until it does.

Every great success story, if you turned it off in chapter 3, would sound like a great failure. But the story wasn't over. You just gave up when it was about to get really good.

Keep going. The plot thickens.

Our hero is just getting started.

the shift

Fear wants to use failure to confirm the worst lies you've already believed about yourself: that maybe you don't have what it takes, maybe you'll never amount to anything, maybe failing is wired right into your DNA. Instead, we have to adopt a new identity through daily intention: that of someone who is showing up every day and doing the work to become just a little bit more of the person who will one day stand in these goals.

12

criticism is an inside job

THE FIRST THING I LEARNED on the first day of law school was this: Good lawyers don't ask questions they don't *already* know the answers to.

On that very first morning, as we all nervously filed into one of the main lecture halls, a bow-tied professor stood at the front and presented us with a hypothetical scenario, complete with a limited set of facts and the imaginary defendant's mother on the stand.

"What would you ask her in your cross examination?"

Hands shot up all over the room.

Ask her where she was during the hours of the incident.
Ask her if she noticed anything strange about his demeanor that day.
Ask her if she bothered to search his room for any incriminating evidence.

The professor listened a long time as more and more suggestions were thrown out. He silently shook his head at every one until he finally said, "Enough."

We had apparently failed his first test.

"Based on this set of facts I've given, you have NO idea how she would respond to any of these questions. Burn this into your memory right now: More young lawyers have lost cases by underestimating a witness's ability to go rogue than they ever have because they were bested by the opposition."

He stared at us a long time. Based on this set of facts, there was clearly only one right question to ask.

"Mrs. Smith, I understand everything you've just told the courtroom about the events of that day, but just to clarify . . . you're the defendant's *mother*, correct? No further questions."

Don't ask questions you don't already know the answers to.

It was one of those very specific rules for a very specific set of circumstances that runs the very specific risk of being absorbed into the wide-open expanse of the rest of your once wild, untamed life.

As a guiding principle, "Don't ask questions you don't already know the answers to" leads us to a pretty fluorescent-lit existence.

We know this.

If there was a version of life that equated to sitting alone on a cold metal table in a paper gown, your bare feet dangling mere inches above the Clorox-streaked floor still wet from the mop, clutching at all these see-through seams now desperate for closure, all while trying in vain to keep your most vulnerable parts hidden . . . this would be it.

You sit very still and try not to move around too much, lest the crinkle of the paper be a bother to anybody. (Rule #2: Don't *ever* be a bother to anybody.) You sit straight up and plaster a too-big smile on your overly tired face at every hint of a footstep falling just outside the door, this absolute buffoonery of an "aw, shucks" good-girl sideshow act now gone hopelessly awry at the rote repetition and rehearsal of it all.

> "Don't ask questions you don't already know the answers to" leads us to a pretty fluorescent-lit existence.

As if they are secretly handing out gold stars for how well you waited your turn.

Meanwhile, a standard industrial tube light flickers overhead and casts a sickly green pall over everything that's meant to keep you safe.

Oh sure, it's a sanitary life. A bleak, antiseptic, paper-thin, neat and tidy life. It smells of freshly opened packages of sterile gauze and it's always ten degrees colder than it should be.

It is a life absolutely disinfected of anything that could ever get you into too much trouble.

But it's not where the magic happens.

Pretty soon, if we're not careful, "don't ask questions you don't already know the answers to" can turn into "you know what, just go ahead and don't do *anything* unless you know you can get it right the very first time." That first year of law school, I can't tell you how many times I found myself driving to class, the knot in my stomach feeling more and more like an ulcer every day, only to turn around and go back home before I got there out of fear that I would be called on in front of everyone . . . and I wouldn't know all the answers.

We do that, don't we? We avoid criticism at any and all costs. We get so afraid of what other people will think of us that we would rather never once raise our hands—we would rather never show up to our own lives at all, present and accounted for—than risk showing up and getting it wrong.

Once, when I was doing a summer internship at a big law firm in London, I was hauled into the managing partner's office and reprimanded for using too many exclamation points in my emails. In that, I had used *any*.

I have never had a metaphor served up to me so handily before.

Rule #1: Don't ask questions you don't already know the answers to.
Rule #2: Don't ever be a bother to anybody.
Rule #3: Live your life without exclamation points lest it offend all the people who are still stuck at a full stop.

If there was a *Robert's Rules of Order* for how to live a wholly uncreative life, these would surely top the list. Or, as the famous old adage goes, "To avoid all criticism, say nothing, do nothing, be nothing."*

But you and I are no longer in the business of safe, sanitized lives full of avoiding criticism at all costs, are we?

We're now about the messy, meaningful, liminal, sometimes meandering work of doing what we were most created to do.

And that starts by *first* being willing to raise our hand.

My Inner Critic's Name Is Dear John

I recently saw an interview between Deadpool and Wolverine.

Actually, it was a sit-down with actor Hugh Jackman as he asked his castmate Ryan Reynolds a question regarding how open he had been about having anxiety, and how that came into play with his work.

Ryan said something that immediately rang both true and familiar to me.

> My job benefits greatly from that. People who have anxiety are constantly thinking into the future. You're constantly [asking], "What if this happens? What if that happens?" You're always telling yourself stories. So, when you're working in movies . . . I'm not just shooting the movie, I'm also *sitting in the audience as its harshest critic* going, "I don't like that. I don't buy that." *So, anxiety creates that sort of ecosystem of awareness* that I wouldn't otherwise [have].[1]

Sitting in the audience as its harshest critic.

Yes. I play that game myself.

I know what it is to try to anticipate and preempt every grenade of criticism that could ever be lobbed your way—the ring pin still dangling from these imaginary bared teeth come back all at once to

---

*That is a quote often attributed to Aristotle, but recent studies say it more likely came from Elbert Hubbard in a volume of essays titled *Little Journeys to the Homes of American Statesmen* (1916).

bite you. These wolves in sheep's clothing, rows upon rows of newly sharpened canines left chomping at the bit to chew you up into tiny little pieces every chance they get, now left howling at the first hint of fresh blood. The sting of all these wide-open wounds once again making you a shell-shocked target for easy prey.

I know what it is to throw yourself on every perceived land mine as you tiptoe your way into uncharted territory, to test detonate what it would be like if the whole thing just blew up in your face. To sacrifice yourself on the altar of taking back this incendiary sacred ground, all these Bouncing Betties and #blessed broken roads now expertly camouflaged as peaceful green pastures. Sure, all this concealed weaponry scattered across the ever-changing landscape might just rip you to shreds in the process. But at least you will learn quickly how to never again step out of line.

And I know what it is to believe that all of it—the chewing yourself up into tiny little pieces on someone else's behalf, the ripping yourself to shreds before anyone else gets a chance to—is, in fact, responsible for all of your best work. That if you were to ever create from a place of love and not fear or, *God forbid*, actually speak kindly to yourself . . . then all of your excellence would disappear overnight.

Magical ritual thinking, indeed.

The truth is, we think that if we can just make a comprehensive enough cross-referenced running list of everything anyone could possibly say about us . . . then the criticism can't ever take us by surprise again. It will never again land like a sucker punch from somewhere in the cheap seats, never again come flying in from somewhere in our periphery like some sort of homemade concussion bomb. An explosive attack that now leaves us reeling. A cadence of criticism pounding in our heads we might never again recover from.

We bully ourselves for our own protection.

We browbeat our best work all in the name of perfection.

We dissect ourselves down into the sum of our worst parts and call it doing our due diligence.

Like I said, there is NO ONE harder on us . . . than *us*.

Me? I've gotten so good at getting in the head of my own worst critic that I've now officially given him a name: Dear John.

Dear John wears khaki pants. Or jeans freshly crisp and creased from the iron. His buttoned-up L.L.Bean wrinkle-free shirt comes in a pale plaid of crisscrossed colors. But nothing pastel or too bright or even bordering on the neighborhood of being too bold. None of that Vineyard Vines nonsense for him. Dear John only wears respectable shirt colors like tan and taupe and ecru. He wears tennis shoes with his dress pants—the quintessential "dad shoe," white with the navy trim—presumably so that he is always ready to run in and tell you what he thinks of you anytime you do anything that colors too brightly outside of his boring beige lines.

Dear John absolutely *hates* that I talked about Care Bears in a chapter about fear. "You MUST be joking. Are you *trying* to look like an amateur? No one will EVER take you seriously that way." He rolls his eyes so hard at me I'm afraid they may get stuck that way, permanently staring up at his precision-parted hair. The LA Looks gel forms his classic comb-over into a perfect plastic Ken doll mold and makes every strand feel crunchy. My critic is all hard lines and no soft edges. All IQ, no EQ. And he personally thinks my unfettered access to the full depth and range of my emotions makes me seem hysterical and weak.

Dear John deeply dislikes my wordplay, he finds my metaphors and pop culture references juvenile and banal (in that order, respectively). He couldn't care less about any of my personal stories and wishes I would just get to the point already. This whole thing could have been summed up in pamphlet form: Don't listen to fear. The End.

DJ (he also *hates* it when I call him DJ) likes to take minute-by-minute, time-stamped notes anytime I speak somewhere with detailed instructions on what I should do to get better. "Minute 13:02: Glanced back at the slides and temporarily broke eye contact. *Never, ever* break eye contact with me." He tears out the sheets of notebook paper—the rough-ripped spiral tabs still clinging to the edges like some sort of tortured confetti—and somehow figures out how to defy the laws of physics to fold the pages in on themselves at least a dozen times.* Dear John is nothing if not an expert at getting things to take up less space in this world. He places the tiny, serial-killer-worthy origami in the palm of my hand like a Rat Packer tipping a Vegas waiter. "Here, I hope you find this helpful," he breathily whispers into my ear, using just *way* too much saliva.†

Dear John is annoyed that I have opinions about the trajectory of my career and the worth I bring to the table. He would much prefer to mansplain to me about basic concepts I clearly already understand, interrupt me to make the same suggestion I was already in the process of making, and tell me again the way things have *always* been done. He finds it exasperating that I insist on having a voice. He finds it infuriating that I walk into a room with any shred of self-confidence at all. He carries a clipboard around with him and uses the handy attached pen he keeps chained up at all times to take note of all the rules he's written for me that I've clearly already broken.

But most of all, and true to his name, Dear John tries his best to get me to break up with all of my biggest dreams... *before* they become a bother to anyone else.

Here's the most important thing you need to know about Dear John, though.

I don't even like him.

He is not my ideal reader, my ideal friend, or even someone that I respect.

So, surely it's a *good* thing if he doesn't like my work, *right*?

And yet I continue to allow him to be the loudest voice in any room, doing everything I can to make him happy. Every time I sit down to write, he snarls up his lip in disgust and shouts at me how every word is "SO stupid! SO boring! SO derivative!" And for my part, I have dubbed myself the official head of the Dear John Complaint Department. Listening to every aired grievance. Doing my best

---

*Supposedly, mere mortals can only fold a sheet of paper in half seven times before it becomes impossible.

†I wish I was making this up. Truly, I do. I wish I was that creative. But sadly, this part actually happened to me in real life.

to calmly appease him. Offering up a litany of win-win-win solutions ... ones where I still somehow always end up the loser.

Remember what we talked about with positioning? When you know who you are and you aren't afraid to *own* it, the people who love you will love you without fail. And the people who don't? They were never going to get it anyway.

Now, here's the next piece of that puzzle.

It's what I call the "Lukewarm Litmus Test": Some people will love what you do and some people will hate what you do. And guess what? Either one is a win. The only way you get into trouble is if someone can look at the work you've created and think to themselves this lukewarm response of, "Meh ... *maybe*." That's because it means you've let the critics, both out in the world and in your own head, get so loud that you've now cut out everything that made you and your work interesting in the first place. You are now a mere tepid shell of the magic you once used to be.

The people who love you will love you without fail.

And the people who don't were never going to get it anyway.

Dear John is someone who was *never* going to get it anyway.

So why am I still fighting so hard to get him to love me?

You Can't Bubble-Wrap Purpose

You can't bubble-wrap purpose.

And there is no amount of *shrink*-wrap that will ever keep you safe. That means we have to stop acting like the biggest goal in life is to avoid the pain of criticism at all costs.

Yet, the very first thing most people tell me when I ask them what's keeping them from showing up and putting themselves out there is what other people are going to have to say about it.

They fear being judged.

They fear being misunderstood.

They fear that inevitable "Who Does She Think She Is?" moment.

They see the nasty comments racking up on other people's posts, how exposed they are to the worst things people could ever say

You can't bubble-wrap purpose.
And there's no amount of *shrink*-wrap
that'll ever keep you safe.

about them, and they are just terrified of bringing that on themselves too.

But you and I don't have to wonder and worry about that any longer. If you do work that matters, I *promise* you there will be pain.

There will be critics and doubters and backhanded compliments served up to you from the sidelines. They will be the first to notice each and every time you step out of line. The ones more than happy to point out every single one of your (double) faults.

There will be people committed to misunderstanding you. People who will always assume the worst about you before they even see the work you've done, the ones who are always more than willing to judge a book based solely on its cover. Trust me. If we ever end up face-to-face together over an overpriced coffee sometime, ask me about the Facebook thread I was never meant to see when *Dirt* first came out.

I know all about how *small* some people can be.

My point is this: There ARE people out there underestimating you and ready to criticize every move you make.

This is not some *Pollyanna* moment when I tell you that it's all in your head and other people aren't thinking about you nearly as much as you're thinking about yourself. Sure, that may be true in some random cocktail party full of strangers you're meeting for the very first time, where we're all just worried about the spinach stuck in our own teeth.

But this is *not* that. Let me be absolutely clear.

There *are* people you know right now who are hoping that you'll fail. That's not just all in your head.

We don't deal with criticism by pretending like it doesn't exist. We deal with it head-on by first acknowledging that if you do anything, *anything important at all*, people are going to have something to say about it.

Sometimes, it may even be the people closest to you.

Limiting Beliefs Are a Leaky Faucet

There is a form of water torture "in which cold water is slowly dripped onto [a person's] scalp . . . for a prolonged period of time." The process is said to produce "fear and mental deterioration" because "the cold sensation is jarring, which causes anxiety as a person tries to anticipate the next drip." The victims are "gradually driven frantic to the point of insanity, usually because they were led to believe that a hollow or severe [wound] would develop there."[2]

The TV show *MythBusters* did an episode where they tested this form of torture and found it to be very effective indeed. However, they also noted that, "The restraining equipment was providing most of the effect by itself, and when testing the dripping water alone on a relaxed, unrestrained subject, it was found almost negligible."[3]

The host of *MythBusters*, Adam Savage, went on to say, "The creepiest thing that happened after we did this episode was that I got an email from someone from a throwaway account [saying], 'We found that randomizing when the drops occurred was incredibly effective. That anything that happens on a regular periodicity can become a type of meditation, and you can then tune it out. [But] if you couldn't predict it,' he said, 'we found, we were able to induce a psychotic break within 20 hours.'"[4]

1. Slow drips over time can develop into deep wounds.
2. It is often that which keeps us restrained that has the worst effect of all.
3. Not being able to predict when the next one is coming is what we fear the most.

This sounds an awful lot like what I call "inherited limiting belief leaks."

I can still remember the exact curve in the road we were in—the turn-around-and-kiss-your-taillights one at the bottom of Fenwick Mountain—when Dad told me that I would never go to law school.

Well, specifically what he told me when I said I wanted to go to law school was, "*Yeah right.* You'll never stay in school that long."

Now, let me be clear right here. He has apologized for it at least a thousand times since. And there is NO one prouder of me and the fact that I went to Yale Law School than JR Bess. It's even something we can laugh about . . . *now*.

When he explains that moment he says, "I don't know, it just sorta slipped out before I even knew I was saying it. It really had nothing to do with you at all. I think it was just because I could never see *myself* staying in school that long. I mean, I barely graduated high school, you have to remember. So, I guess I put that on you too."

So often when people in our families of origin have their own internalized doubts about what they are capable of, they will unintentionally spill those limitations out onto us too, without even realizing they are doing it.

Limiting belief leaks.

For a lot of people, though, their inherited limiting belief leaks aren't nearly so benign. What they have experienced is far more methodical torture than accidental spill. More intentional wounding than a simple drip of the lip.

LIMITING BELIEFS ARE A LEAKY FAUCET

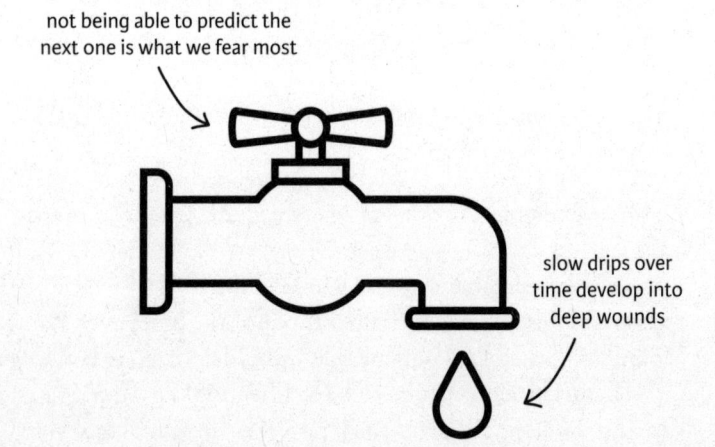

not being able to predict the next one is what we fear most

slow drips over time develop into deep wounds

What I hear from my coaching clients is that it is the random drips of the little side comments that hurt the worst because they never know when the next one is coming. Their families are constantly saying things like, "Oh, I guess somebody sure thinks a lot of themselves, don't they?" or "Don't quit your day job" or "Face it, people in our family just didn't get the (fill in the blank with your dream here) gene!"

They'll attack their appearance.
They'll attack their character.
They'll slap labels on them that do not belong.
Drip, drip, drip.
Forever leaving deep wounds in their wake.

It sort of reminds me of that jellyfish scene in the *Bridget Jones* sequel. Bridget runs into a woman she calls the "jellyfish" in a bar, and immediately the woman starts to zing her with insult after insult. At one point, we even see a little cartoon jellyfish appear in the corner that starts to rack up all the stings.

Maybe you've known someone like that too.

And if they were in your family growing up, chances are *theirs* is the voice that has now become your internal monologue. In fact,

> Most psychologists agree that *the roots of our inner critics are to be found in childhood.* The founding father of psychoanalysis, Sigmund Freud, explained the formation of our superegos as a process during which we internalize external views of ourselves—predominantly those of our parents. At the same time, we accept wider social expectations and ethical norms, and start to generate ego ideals—of which we then regularly tend to fall short. Freud's superego can be a cruel and self-flagellating force, which sadistically punishes and tyrannizes the ego. If our superego is in overdrive, *we spend most of our psychological energy on inner warfare and have little to give to the outside world. We may deem ourselves unworthy and despicable, and expect the world to see us that way, too.*[5]

That's us on our worst days.

On our best days, though—when we are operating as our most healed, highly evolved selves—we can remind ourselves that other people will often try to talk us out of the very work we were most created to do, because seeing us move forward on the dream is just a reminder to them that they AREN'T doing the work.

At the end of the day, it's not *really* about us. Steven Pressfield in *The War of Art* puts it this way:

> Resistance recruits allies. Resistance by definition is self-sabotage. But there's a parallel peril that must also be guarded against: sabotage by others. When a writer begins to overcome her Resistance... she may find that those close to her begin acting strange. They may become moody or sullen, they may get sick; they may accuse the awakening writer of "changing," of "not being the person she was." The closer these people are to the awakening writer, the more bizarrely they will act and the more emotion they will put behind their actions. They are trying to sabotage her. The reason is that they are struggling, consciously or unconsciously, against their own Resistance. The awakening writer's success becomes a reproach to them. If she can beat these demons, why can't they?[6]

My coaching client Kristen knows all about this. She told me, "No one around me in my family growing up was ever going to dream any bigger than what we had. So that was always up to me. But as soon as I start to get up that hill, I can feel them calling me back down to the bottom. So that's one reason I get stuck: I think of all the possible confrontations and relational hurt that could come from me trying for something more... and then I end up just trying to avoid it altogether."

In fact, avoiding relational hurt and confrontation with family is one of the biggest reasons I hear from most of my hard-story clients about why they play small.

They would rather just not try at all than bring on a fresh new round of their family's criticism. They *never* want to be responsible for hurting anyone (even those people who have *deeply* hurt them). They don't know how to reach for more without implying that there was something always lacking. Every step further up the mountain feels like a betrayal to the very people and places that once raised them.

So instead, they go on drifting year after year. Drowning in the *drip, drip, drip*.

Let's Stop Saying "Little"

A few years back, I was speaking at a conference.

I had just poured it all out on stage, given everything I had. And I had promptly removed myself to the bathroom to try to get myself together (aka, to wipe away the streaks of mascara now running down my face).

But as I stood there in front of the mirror, scratchy recycled bathroom paper towel poised perilously just above my cornea, I could see the door opening behind me in the reflection as someone from the audience came in.

We locked eyes in the mirror for one long, painfully awkward second.

I sort of sheepishly shrugged my arms, crumpled-up paper towel still in hand. And I felt her look me up and down in a once-over that would have given even Meryl Streep herself chills (she practically told me I wasn't *going to Paris*). That's when she said it.

"I liked your little talk in there."

Little? I thought to myself, "I can tell you right now, NOTHING about that felt little to me."

But instead of saying the thing I most wanted to say in the moment I most wanted to say it,* I just mumbled out a thank-you and stumbled out of the bathroom, mascara still running down my cheeks.

I've thought about that word "little" a lot since that moment in the bathroom.

Chances are, at some point in your life you've had someone say . . .

- "How's that little hobby of yours going?" (Where by "hobby" they mean your full-time business that now pays all of your bills.)

***You've Got Mail*, anybody?

- "Saw your little Instagram post . . ." (Oh, you mean the one where I poured my heart out about something really hard and brave to share? *Thanks for noticing.*)
- "How many people have signed up for that little workshop you're teaching?"
- "Saw that little talk you're giving at the conference—you must be so flattered they thought to invite you . . ."

But of all the times we've had someone else speak *little* over us, I think the hardest times are the ones when we speak it over *ourselves*.

It's when we talk ourselves out of raising our hand for that opportunity because we think there will always be someone better.

It's when we think we're not "there" yet to treat this business like a business, or to get started on the dream.

It's the times we let someone else steamroll all over us because we're afraid to tell anyone no or risk someone not liking us. It's all the *little* self-deprecating qualifiers we put on our most declarative sentences.

I don't know about you, but for all the critics out there . . .

It's the times when I've kept *myself* playing small that have, in hindsight, hurt the most.

At its core, "let's stop saying little" is both an act of rebellion and a reminder to us that *language matters*.

It's a call to remember that the way you speak about yourself and your highest-held dreams *trains* other people on how to think about you. *On how to treat you.*

It is a challenge extended to start catching yourself speaking small over your life midsentence in any way you can.

Something I started doing with my coaching clients is that every time I catch them using limiting language, I will actually do a Liz Lemon–worthy self high five right then and there.

Not because I want to celebrate it.

But because I want to *mark* it.

I want them to both see and hear exactly how often they speak *little* over their own lives.

Because it's the only way I can get them to replace it with *kindness*.

What If Kindness Is Actually Resilience?

What is that old saying about "If you don't have anything nice to say..."?

Oh, right.

"Then make sure you say *all* of it about yourself."

No? That's not how it goes? Okay. Try saying that to me with a straight face the next time you get started on the dream and you *immediately* start picking yourself apart all in the name of self-protection. I'll wait.

It sounds so obvious when we put it in singsongy nursery rhymes turned well-versed golden rules, doesn't it? Of course... *just don't say anything at all.* How hard is that?

But then the dream starts feeling a little too real. We remember that pretty soon there could be a lot of eyes (in that there will be *any* eyes at all) on what we're trying to do. And just like that, our magical ritual thinking kicks back in.

Every day it's out here to remind us.

We can't just *put* things out into the world without tearing ourselves to shreds first. What are we? Frat boys with a C- average turned corner office on the C-suite floor? Every mediocre boss we've ever had? That one dude on the weekly Zoom call who dominates every conversation?

We simply don't possess that level of unwarranted confidence.

Every day our magical ritual thinking tells us if we are going to have any kind of success at all, we're going to have to be willing to punch ourselves in the face first.

An article in *Psychology Today* calls this "the high performers paradox," noting that many high achievers have a heightened inner critic and are "driven by high standards through their relentless self-critical voice." This approach initially proves successful and can result in such qualities as "perseverance, ambition, and meticulous attention to detail."[7]

Check, check, check.

But here is the paradox: "They may turn to self-criticism as a strategy to amplify their efforts... convinced that their self-improving form of self-criticism contributes to their success. However, this approach backfires.... When not met with success, these individuals often face profound feelings of inadequacy and worthlessness."[8]

Let's just you and me get really honest here for a second.

The truth is, on some deep, dark level we don't really like to excavate down to let alone talk about, there is a very real part of us that thinks how *hard* we are on ourselves is one of the most *impressive* things about us.

It's the very proof that we are the hardest worker in the room.

It's the secret weapon behind all our most original ideas and unrelenting drive.

It's the very reason we are known as The One Who *Always* Comes Through.

For as long as I can remember, I've had the fear that if I were to start being *easy* on myself, then all that sudden self-acceptance would quickly snowball into full-blown apathy. I've thought for years that my superpower was my own self-abuse.

Science does not agree.

Study after study, in fact, has shown that kindness to ourselves—or what most studies refer to as *self-compassion*—is actually a key to resilience. And resilience, remember, is what keeps pushing us up this mountain we came out here to climb.

Dr. Kristin Neff and Dr. Pittman McGehee, in their seminal study on self-compassion and its positive effect on resilience, identified three major components—self-kindness, a sense of common humanity, and mindfulness—necessary for this result. They write:

> Put simply, self-compassion is compassion turned inward. Self-compassion refers to the ability to hold one's feelings of suffering with a sense of warmth, connection, and concern.... These components

> A very real part of us thinks that how *hard* we are on ourselves is one of the most *impressive* things about us.

combine and mutually interact to create a self-compassionate frame of mind.... Research suggests that self-compassion is strongly related to psychological wellbeing, including increased happiness, optimism, personal initiative, and connectedness, as well as decreased anxiety, depression, neurotic perfectionism, and rumination.[9]

Of course, we know all of this is easier said than done.

That's because some of us never learned how to speak kindly to ourselves, starting when we were little.

Neff and McGehee address this fact in their findings, saying a child "with a secure attachment bond, supportive mother, and functional family is likely to have more self-compassion than one with a problematic family environment, *given that care and compassion have been appropriately modeled by others*.... On the other hand, dysfunctional family relationships are likely to translate into self-criticism, negative self-attitudes and a lack of self-compassion.... Those raised in insecure, stressful, or threatening environments [might] be colder and more critical toward themselves."[10]

The truth is, we've been practicing being cruel to ourselves for as long as we can remember. For some of us, it's the only thing we've ever known.

But if we're going to do the work we were truly put here to do, we have to get our minds right first. The way we speak to ourselves, what we believe is possible, it all starts in our own heads. As Henry Ford famously said, "Whether you think you can or you think you can't... *you're right.*"

In other words, until *we* believe we can do it... it won't happen.

And that's going to require the introduction of a *different* voice.

The Inner Critic vs. The Experiencing Self

We treat criticism like it's fatal.

There is a reason we would rather become The Contortionist, twisting ourselves up into tiny, tethered knots, doing backbends until our back breaks.

It's because we actually believe that breaking ourselves in half like that is somehow *easier* than being criticized. Imagine how high our perceived pain of criticism must be in order for us to choose some sort of double-jointed double-down on disappearing altogether over the potential sting of someone else's words.

Sticks and stones, indeed.

Criticism feels so fatal to us in part because we see it as a threat to our very identity. If we don't have a strong enough sense of self, other people's words can feel devastating to the very core of who we are. We start to internalize the things they say about us as truth, even more so if the words they speak confirm some painful lie about ourselves we already believed.

I sat down recently and watched the film *Brats*, a documentary headlined and directed by Andrew McCarthy about a group of hot young actors in the 1980s who were on top of the world making hit movie after hit movie until one snarky news article dubbed them the "Brat Pack" . . . and the fallout of what that instantly did to all their careers.

I grew up watching movies like *The Breakfast Club*, *Pretty in Pink*, and *Sixteen Candles*. So I, like most of America at the time, had always thought being in the Brat Pack was actually a *good* thing. It was like being in the in-crowd. One of the "cool kids." But for McCarthy and many of the others it became a label they couldn't escape. As the tagline for the film put it, "In the 1980s, everybody wanted to be in the Brat Pack. Except them."[11]

Andrew, in particular, took the criticism hard. A classically trained theater actor turned reluctant 80s heartthrob, he felt it was some sort of reflection of him not taking his work or the craft of acting very seriously. He felt pigeonholed out of more serious roles. He felt like now the studios would all see him as a liability. All from that one simple word "brat," which by today's standards is not particularly biting criticism. But for thirty-five years Andrew has been carrying around this deep sting of pain at the unfairness of what someone else had to say about him, and in many ways it has defined the trajectory of both his career and his life.

This is what's at stake if we don't do the internal work: letting our whole lives be dictated and determined by what someone else has to say about us.

During the documentary, Andrew meets up with each of his fellow Brat Packers to get their take on the unfairness of the moniker. And at one point he sits down with Demi Moore, who said something I can't stop thinking about. She told Andrew that there was a belief he must have *already* held about himself that allowed what someone else said about him to *mean* more than it actually did. And that, in turn, created this lid—this upper *limitation*—on what he felt like he could create moving forward.

To which Andrew replied, "If it didn't touch on some fear we [already] harbored about ourselves, it wouldn't have mattered."

Demi continued, telling him that not only does he have a tendency to hold on to that feeling of being stabbed in the back—an experience Andrew acknowledges started for him at a very young age—but he will also have a tendency to *re-create* it in brand-new ways until he is finally ready to say "okay, I've had enough of that" and gets serious about actually healing it.

Chaos feels familiar.
We repeat the lesson until it is learned.
The boulder rolls all the way back down the mountain.

I have to be honest.

I thought about this documentary for *days* after watching it. It felt like a cautionary tale in the making. A full-frontal exhibition in futility. It's like one of those Guy de Maupassant short stories where someone works their entire life to pay off a debt it turns out they didn't actually owe.* It is a stark reminder of how quickly our days

---

*In *Dirt* I told how I once read a short story called "The Necklace" in Ms. Spencer's seventh grade English class. The basic plot goes something like this: A woman trying so desperately to belong borrows a fancy necklace from her wealthy friend only to later lose it at a party. Based on appearances that can be so deceiving, she assumes that her friend's necklace must be real diamonds. So she buys a replacement necklace on credit and spends the next ten years in poverty paying it off. When she runs into her friend all those years

can turn to decades. And how, if we're not careful, we'll look up one day thirty-five years from now and see that our entire life has been held captive by the words someone else once spoke over us.

Starting right now, we have to find a way to differentiate between our truest self and all the lies we've heard.

As you can imagine, that is all the more difficult to do when "the call is coming from somewhere inside the house" in the form of our inner critic.

Psychologists call this our "two conflicting sides," which is characterized by a "self-to-self relationship where different facets of the self engage in internal conflict." The dominant side, the inner critic, often bulldozes over the instincts of our other (truer) side, the "experiencing self." The inner critic tries to "adhere to established standards and norms" of society so it can achieve love and acceptance, even if we lose who we are along the way, while the experiencing self "instinctively knows what is right and desires to follow its [own] inclinations." They continue, "The interplay between the experiencing self and the inner critic is highlighted by expressions of struggle and coercion," which is why people will often say things like "I wish I could, but I can't."[12]

Self-criticism is considered to be among the most destructive stressors linked to psychological suffering.[13] So why do we continue to allow it to be the loudest voice in the room?

If we want to understand why the inner critic becomes the dominant voice in our own heads, we first have to understand how we, as humans, are wired for negativity. It's what's often referred to as the "negativity bias," a "positive-negative asymmetry," or even our "tricky brain."

> Negative self-talk is not evidence of something "wrong" with us that needs to be fixed; it is a feature of being human. *Our propensity to cause ourselves anguish is an evolved function of . . . our "tricky" brain.* Our complex cognitive system—able to imagine, anticipate and conceive of an objective "self"—is equally inclined to dwell on negative

---

later, just after the last payment has been made, in relief she confesses what happened and everything she's had to sacrifice in order to pay off that necklace. Through tears, her friend takes her by the hand and explains that all along the original had been a fake.

> thoughts such as "If only I'd . . ." and "I should have . . ." *This triggers the same fight-or-flight, physiological response as an external threat.*[14]

Scientists, in fact, tell us that our negativity bias is a holdover from our original survival mechanisms and locate the source of the inner critic to a very specific part of our brain: "A primitive 'survivor brain' that encompasses the brain stem . . . is highly attuned to danger. Hyper-vigilant, it is constantly on the lookout for threats."[15]

And what's even *more* interesting is how this negativity bias has been passed down.

> Our tendency to pay more attention to bad things and overlook good things is likely a result of evolution. Earlier in human history, paying attention to bad, dangerous, and negative threats in the world was literally a matter of life and death. Those who were more attuned to danger and who paid more attention to the bad things around them were more likely to survive. *This meant they were also more likely to hand down* the genes that made them more attentive to danger [in the first place].[16]

Ah, there it is. Humanity's first inherited limiting belief leak.

However, psychologists also tell us that this negativity bias was not just a function of our *physical survival*, it was also there to ensure our *internal survival* with what they call "psychological sense-making," where young children in particular will construct narratives about their hard stories to make them easier to bear. "For example, children who feel unloved, are constantly criticized, or the victims of abuse will tend to blame themselves rather than their parents. As the child depends completely on their parents for survival, the conscious acknowledgment of the parents' unfairness, cruelty, or incompetency is simply too devastating. It is much safer for the child to turn the criticism inward rather than outward."[17]

And now we start to see our inner critic in a brand-new light, that of the protector.

Inner critics are what Internal Family Systems (IFS) therapy calls *protective parts* who ultimately want us to be safe and loved. Although they can often be harsh, they are actually trying to "avoid future shaming by improving or hiding the vulnerable young parts of you."[18]

Deborah Lee, a clinical psychologist and the head of trauma services at Berkshire Healthcare, tells us we need to create a "knowledge landscape against which the pain can be recast," and that "in order for you to even see that you've got a self-critic, you've [first] got to become a wise observer." She also says, "Developing self-compassion is developing insight so that you can *see* yourself, rather than *be* yourself, as such."[19]

In other words, our inner critic wants us to *be* all the worst things that it has to say about us. Our experiencing self, on the other hand, wants us to *see*—to be a wise observer of what the inner critic has to tell us, to take what is helpful and leave what is not—without actually becoming the worst of what that inner critic believes about us.

Our first reaction as a wise observer when we realize all the things our inner critic has been saying to us may be one of anger. It's the same way I've been feeling about Dear John all along. But psychologists tell us this is actually the wrong response, as "responding to negativity with negativity" will only perpetuate that "inner conflict and strengthen the inner critic."[20]

Instead, the next time we hear that inner critic get loud, here are two steps for befriending it rather than fighting it, reminding ourselves that in its own messed up way it was always looking out for us.

1. *Ask your inner critic what it wants to tell you.*

Dr. Martha Sweezy, an expert on IFS therapy, tells us that we can actually ask our inner critic what it's trying to tell us, and the more "curiosity and kindness" we respond with, the "calmer and more responsive it will be."[21]

Our inner critic is an expert at seeing where we are vulnerable to criticism, rejection, or attack. It is always looking up ahead to see what might be coming. And while it is prone to catastrophizing, running things to the extremes, and asking us to change everything about who we are in order to belong . . . it *can occasionally* make a good point. Maybe we could work on being more on time. Maybe we could be more careful to keep our word and actually do what we say we're going to do. We don't have to listen to *everything* our inner critic has to say. The key is to let our experiencing self, our "wise observer," listen to what our inner critic has to say, and then decide for ourselves if it has merit. But in the listening, the noticing that our inner critic is trying to help, it will relax and calm down long enough for us to make that good decision.

2. Introduce your inner critic to the grown-up you.

According to Dr. Sweezy, our protective parts like the inner critic do what they do because they don't see any other option. They feel like no one else is stepping up to protect us so the burden has to fall on them. Sweezy tells us, "Your job is to interrupt this mindset by inviting them to . . . [notice] you. They are not alone, you exist, and you can help."[22]

She even suggests a script we can use to introduce our (grown-up) selves to our inner critic, and one of the most powerful moments she mentions is when we ask our inner critic how old it thinks we currently are. We may be shocked to find out *it likely still sees us as that littlest version of ourselves it was born to protect.* She advises, "Try it. See what happens. . . . As soon as the other parts are willing to step back, a different 'you' will be apparent." This version of us will feel "expansive, relaxed . . . *grown-up*." She tells us, "You are the one who remains when your parts make some *room* inside. . . . You are the one who can help."[23]

There it is.

I couldn't believe those words staring back at me.

I had to go back and read them twice.

There is a *grown-up* in the ROOM who can be trusted. That grown-up is you.

Confidence Is an Exercise in Excellence

Have you ever seen those national park posters they made using the worst of their one-star reviews?

"The only thing to do here is walk around the desert."—Joshua Tree National Park

"A hole. A very, very large hole."—Grand Canyon National Park

"Save yourself some money. Boil some water at home."—Yellowstone National Park

"No wow factor."—Olympic National Park

"Scenery is distant and impersonal."—Zion National Park

"Looks nothing like the license plate."—Arches National Park

I like to remind myself of these reviews any time my inner protectors get a little too loud and start trying to convince me there is actually a level of perfect I can reach that will insulate me from any and all criticism.

I'm here to tell you—*it doesn't exist.*

I sat once with Justin on the edge of the world at the Grand Canyon watching the sun rise. We found a ledge where we weren't afraid of falling, and we held on to one another as the light cast a thousand ruddy rainbows against a painted sky. I sat there in the great expanse—looked out at this great divide between where we were and where we wanted to be—and *I finally felt small enough, in the grand scheme of things, that I could actually get over myself.* I could stop making the greatest goal of my life to avoid pain at all costs.

And I could get on with this good work I was put here to do.

I'm telling you right now that if some of the grandest, most sweeping, majestic, painted places on this planet have their haters . . . then you and I don't stand a chance.

And that's the best news we could ever hear.

Because now we can finally give up on all this chasing perfect.

And we can get to work on what we were always meant to do instead: **Create with excellence.**

The truth is, you can be both a recovering perfectionist . . . *and* a person with an incredibly high standard of excellence. They are not mutually exclusive.

The trick is in knowing the difference.

Perfectionism = "hiding with better PR" and is driven by fear.

Excellence = "how you do anything is how you do everything" and is driven by love.

Love of the work. Love of the process. Love for the one person that it might help.

Excellence is the willingness to be honest with yourself. To keep going until you know in your gut that this represents the greatest, highest contribution* you had to make here. Or, as Kathy Bates's character Jo Bennett said to Michael Scott in *The Office*, "If you can put your name on this day and be proud of the work you've done, then by all means toodle on home."[24]

Whenever I'm working on a big project, there is always *this moment when it all finally snaps into place.* The best way I can describe it is that it feels like the final piece of a puzzle. When it at last snaps in just right, the whole big picture finally comes into shape. And somehow, you just know. This is what it was *always* meant to be. There is nothing missing. There is nothing lacking. You were faithful to the very end, not rushing any of these broken pieces. And the whole is now greater than the sum of its parts.

Before that, though, there is a whole lot of *"not yet, not yet, not yet."*

And *none* of it has to do with my perfectionism.

You will have to figure out for yourself what your own "snaps into place" moment feels like. But I can tell you this. I have never once created a perfect outcome. Not a perfect book, a perfect talk, or a perfect course. But I *have* created many things of excellence. And here's what it taught me: Excellence is the precursor to unshakable confidence.

> Excellence is the precursor to unshakable confidence.

Excellence is the internal conviction that you have done what you came to do. That you created with originality, integrity, character, and that you moved the conversation forward in a meaningful way. It's when you believe to

---

*Yep, that's an *Essentialism* reference. Greg McKeown, *Essentialism: The Disciplined Pursuit of Less* (Crown Business, 2014), 4.

the core of your very being that this thing you've just put out into the world will actually help people.

And when you know in your bones that these gifts of yours are going to help people, suddenly you don't really care that much any more what the critics have to say.

It is the moment when it finally stops being about you.

What other people might say about you.

How other people might *hurt* you.

And it instead becomes about acting like the work you are doing here *matters*.

We know the truth.

It turns out there is no perfect. Only delay.

And our days just keep getting shorter.

Let us not get to the very end and have to say . . .

In an effort to stay "safe," we traded it all for a life of playing small.

That's Okay, You'll Meet Them Later

They say it takes ten thousand hours to become a master at something.

But here's what they don't tell you: *most* people won't start watching until hour 9,999. And in that last hour, when you RISE to the places you were always being called and the world thinks you make it look easy, you alone will know all the people who underestimated you along the way.

The longer I live the more I realize this one thing that has the power to change everything. There is a type of person who can look at someone and see not just where they are but where they are headed. See not just who they are but who they are becoming. They can see it as clearly as if that final version is standing right in front of them. These are the visionaries, the teachers, the coaches, the fishers of men.

The problem is this group only makes up about 1 percent (according to my very *unofficial* math) of people in the world.

The other 99 percent can only see a thing once it is done.

Which means many times you often won't matter to them until it *is* done, until that ten-thousandth hour when you find your way to the top. At hour 9,999 they still act as if there is nothing special about you at all. *Because they do not have eyes to see.*

This is quickly becoming one of my favorite scripts I tell myself in moments like these:

That's okay. You'll meet them later.

We've spent so much of our lives chasing people.

We've carved off every one of our unfinished edges, ground down every extremity that could have made us different and interesting, and raced to the middle carrying our own buckets so we could water ourselves down.

We forget that anything that requires us to carve out and whittle away little pieces of us to belong was *never* meant for us anyway. And the work you are being asked to do is far more important than the worst of your critics.

Will there be pain? Yes.

Will it be worth it? Also yes.

Whether you go big or you go small, I promise you people ARE going to talk about it.

So, do the work *anyway*.

Write the words. Build the things. Say what needs to be said. Then watch the ripple effects of that work spread out far and wide around you.

While the critics are busy complaining ... do even more good work.*

Do not mistake other people not being able to *see* it for you not being *called* to it.

Their lack of vision has nothing to do with where you're headed.

Most people can only see what's right in front of them. They don't see what you see. And they don't understand a thing until it's already done. If you wait for the world's approval or co-signature before you do a thing, I promise you that you'll be waiting a very long time. Just smile when they snark. One day soon they'll be asking how you did it.

You have people out there doubting you right now?

That's okay. You'll meet them later.

---

*Inspired by Andy Warhol.

the shift

> Fear wants to keep you so terrified of criticism—both criticism from others and criticism from yourself—that you never once raise your hand. It wants those words to feel fatal. Instead, each time our inner critic gets loud, we can ask it what it wants to tell us. And then we can introduce it to a new voice—that of our wise observer: self-compassion. The more we turn the volume up on that voice, the more we will know our truest selves. And when we *know* who we are (and we aren't afraid to own it), other people's opinions just won't seem to matter that much anymore.

13

distraction is a clock that's ticking

DO YOU KNOW WHAT one of the most spoken lines in all of movie history is?

"Let's get out of here."

There is this great scene in the movie *Three to Tango*, where Matthew Perry and Neve Campbell are discussing this line.

Neve's character says, "Huh, it makes sense. It works for a lot of situations. 'They're shooting at us. *Let's get out of here.*' 'Aliens have landed. *Let's get out of here.*' 'I want to make mad passionate love to you. *Let's get out of here.*'"[1]

"Let's get out of here" is such a powerful movie line because it has become inherently hopeful. Do you know who says "let's get out of here"?

People who survive.

These are not the fools standing on the dock doing nothing, staring blankly ahead in shock as a giant barge carrying a T-Rex crashes into San Diego.

These are not the #ThatsSo90s twentysomethings partying in their overalls and choker necklaces on a rooftop holding up a "Make yourself at home" sign while the aliens prepare to vaporize them.

These are not the people who see a tornado back-building and decide to go ahead and drive straight into it full steam ahead, despite Helen Hunt's best warnings, just because they have some high-tech gadgets and fancy corporate sponsors.*

No, these are all people who do *not* survive.

And on some deep subconscious level as the audience . . . we're okay with that. "Serves them right," we think to ourselves. WE would have had the good sense to get out of there.

That's because "let's get out of here" taps into our most basic, primal instincts to bail the second it gets hard. To channel all our best self-preservationist main character energy. To run away and live to fight another day.

It's the same with distractions. We run to them when it gets hard.

I once heard this line that stuck with me: "Be willing to sit through the edginess."†

"Sit through the edginess" is the exact *opposite* energy of "let's get out of here."

It's a call to stay the course, even when the road ahead gets hard.

It reminds me of a saying that has commonly been attributed to Zig Ziglar: "F-E-A-R has two meanings: 'Forget Everything And Run' or 'Face Everything And Rise.' The choice is yours."

Here's the deal. When you finally sit down to get started on this dream, it's *going* to get uncomfortable. There is going to be this unbearable roaring in your ears at all the sudden silence settled in. The words aren't going to come. The ideas will all dry up. Your mind will just go . . . *blank*. Suddenly, none of the next steps will be clear.

And in that moment—when the roaring silence shouts at you, "See? Like I said, you just don't have what it takes, kid"—it's going to be so tempting to want to reach for an easy out.

---

*That's *Jurassic Park 2*, *Independence Day*, and *Twister*, respectively.
†Thanks to Anne Sage at the What If conference for this gem!

When you finally sit down
to get started on this dream,
it's *going* to get uncomfortable.

You'll look up and be amazed to find that—without even realizing it—you've yet again navigated away from what you were working on and are now somehow forty-two tabs deep into an internet rabbit hole you had absolutely no intentions of getting sucked into. Like what happens to bees when they're stuck in zero gravity space. Your thumb—like some sort of bewitched appendage in an Edgar Allan Poe story—will instinctively begin phantom scrolling motivational quotes that you stare at for hours without actually reading. The telltale sign you are avoiding your most important work.

Your laundry will suddenly need washing. The dog will want to go on another walk. You'll sit down to watch fifteen minutes of a true crime show and pretty soon you'll have a yarn stringboard on your wall with all your different theories of the case that would make even Charlie Day seem uncommitted.

Ah, distractions.

In my experience, Distractions show up in direct proportion to the presence of some other pretty insidious "D" words:

Disappointment: When the results are disappointing, when our work is not (yet) very good, when we try and we are not instantly an expert, we find that we would much rather distract ourselves than face the possibility that we might not have what it takes.

Defeatism: When it's taking too long, when it's happening for everyone else but us, when we suffer any kind of setback at all, we want to throw up our hands in defeat and use distractions to numb out the pain as we nurse these brand-new wounds.

Difficulty: As in, *level of*. When the work is hard, when the task is daunting, when the whole thing feels like it has too many steps and we're not sure how to even get started (much less stick the landing), we would just much rather distract ourselves with something that requires very little effort on our end.

Discomfort: When the words won't come, when the edginess gets thick, when the silence sizzles in our synapses and the weight of mediocrity makes us shift awkwardly in our chairs, we find we prefer the constant delay of distractions over the inevitable uncomfortable conclusion that this work *will*, in fact, be hard.

"Let's get out of here" has become our well-worn anthem to forget everything and run anytime the climb feels too difficult.

But then another year goes by. The clock goes on ticking. And the world is worse for our absence.

Be willing to disappear for a while. Be willing to shut out the noise. Be willing to take your time to get to an excellent end result you can be proud of, one that was always worth the wait. Be willing to turn down the volume on the whole world until you can recognize and trust the sound of your own voice again, the sound of your truest self.

Remember: Distracted work will never be your legacy.

Deep work will.

DEEP WORK > DISTRACTED WORK

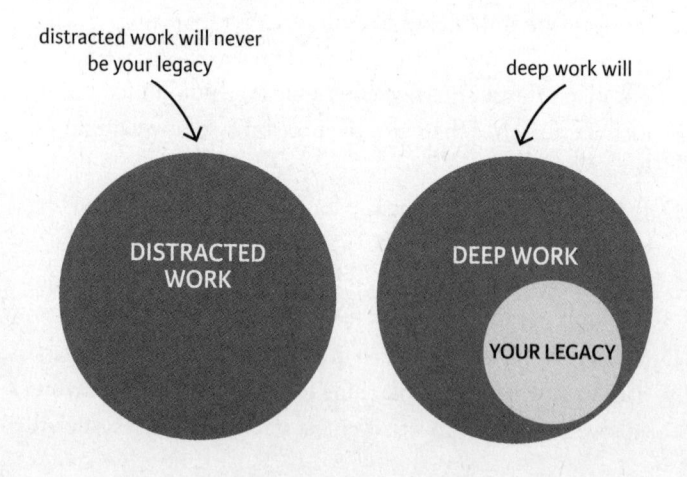

distracted work will never be your legacy → DISTRACTED WORK

deep work will → DEEP WORK (YOUR LEGACY)

Consistency Is an Econ 101 Class

I would be *horrible* at both horseshoes and hand grenades. That's because I've spent a lifetime believing that *close* doesn't really count.

When I was in college, I had to take an Econ 101 class as one of my final requirements for finishing out my degree, a double major in both political science and philosophy.

This particular Econ 101 class, though, had one very important loophole to all this *main requirement* energy: attendance was optional.

I had a very busy course load, not to mention a full schedule with both the debate team and my job in the undergrad recruitment office, so you could say I exercised that option . . . *freely*.

Let's put it this way.

The class grade was comprised of four equally weighted in-class exams.

And I attended that class exactly four times.

Coincidence? I think not.

Before each exam, I would just camp out in a booth at the local Eat'n Park—a restaurant chain with a dive diner feel that thankfully was open late. I'd order one open-faced turkey sandwich and endless refills of Pepsi. And then I'd pull an all-nighter as I opened up that section of the textbook for the very first time and taught myself everything I needed to know by morning. I'd roll into class at ten o'clock the next day, unshowered and unfazed, and start filling in little bubbles on the Scantron sheet like I'd been there all along.

I need you to know this next flex is going to be an eye-roll moment. *I know that, okay. I get it.* Don't worry, we're still going to be friends by the end.

I got a 100 percent on all four exams.*

By the third one, after my professor had caught on that he only ever saw me in class on exam day and yet I kept acing all his tests, he

---

*Please let it be known that if I was typing this on my phone I would for sure be using the red underlined 100 emoji. *Four* of them. *winky face*

legitimately chased me down on the sidewalk and tried to convince me to switch my major to econ. To which I replied, "Oh no, *philosophy* will surely open up far more lucrative job opportunities for me. Thanks, I think I'll just stay there."*

I tell you this story—partly because I've just been *dying* to work it into casual conversation—but more so because it stands for some hard and fast rules I believed for a long time about how the world should work.

1. I've spent a lifetime believing that talent should be enough. Excellence alone should win. The work should speak for itself. I didn't want to have to play this game of showing up over and over, checking a box, just for the sake of being seen.
2. And speaking of the work, I've also always believed that you should never, *ever* settle for a 99 percent when 100 percent is possible. Close only counts in horseshoes and hand grenades . . . and I wasn't playing around with either.

In other words, I've spent my whole life being an all-or-nothing kind of person, standing still or sprinting forward. But here's the thing they don't tell you about that kind of all-or-nothing thinking.

When you're not *all in* . . . it means you're doing *nothing*.

And you lose an untold amount of momentum in the nothing phase.

That Econ class told me that it was how good you are that matters; showing up was optional.

But that's not how the real world works.

The truth is, I've spent most of my life being frustrated that excellence doesn't always win the way I think it should. In fact, it *often* loses to people with far less talent, far less integrity, far less depth, far less substance, who offer far less value . . . just because they weren't afraid to show up.

---

*Just kidding. Nobody ever said that about philosophy. Ever.

Or, as Denzel Washington put it, "There are people less qualified than you doing the things you want to do, simply because they decided to believe in themselves. Period."

That infuriates me.

Because what it means is that the kind ones, the quiet ones, the ones so often overlooked who might actually have some *real talent* to share with the world... year after year they go on playing small and hiding in plain sight, afraid of being seen. And in doing so, they keep falling further and further behind.

Years after that Econ 101 class, I was sitting in the kitchen of a fellow photographer whose business had been blowing up in all the best ways, and I asked her (being the *super fun* girl I am at parties), "When you look back over the trajectory of your growth these last few years, what do you think is the *one* thing that has made the biggest difference?"

This is a delightful party trick I like to keep tucked in my back pocket that can be pulled out at any time. You think we're just sitting here making small talk over this simple plate of cheese and crackers. *Look at these adorable little gherkins. I wonder where this jam is from.* And then, BAM! You don't know it yet, but we're about to think about our whole lives before we leave this room.

She thought for a long minute and then said something about how it had to be consistency in the small things that added up over time. Every time she delivered a gallery faster than she said she would, it was like a drop in the bucket. Every time she answered an email and got back to people fast, that was another investment in her future that would pay out over time. She said anybody could do that once, but *consistency* allowed her to do it over and over with every single client, and that's why it *compounded* so much over time.

You know those moments where everything crystallizes in real time? Everything around you goes kind of blurry at the edges and starts moving in slow motion, but right in front of you everything within a two-foot radius suddenly becomes all superhero-sharp and starts moving in fast-forward, almost as if the blurry and the sharp are rotating in opposite orbits. *No? Just me? Okay then.*

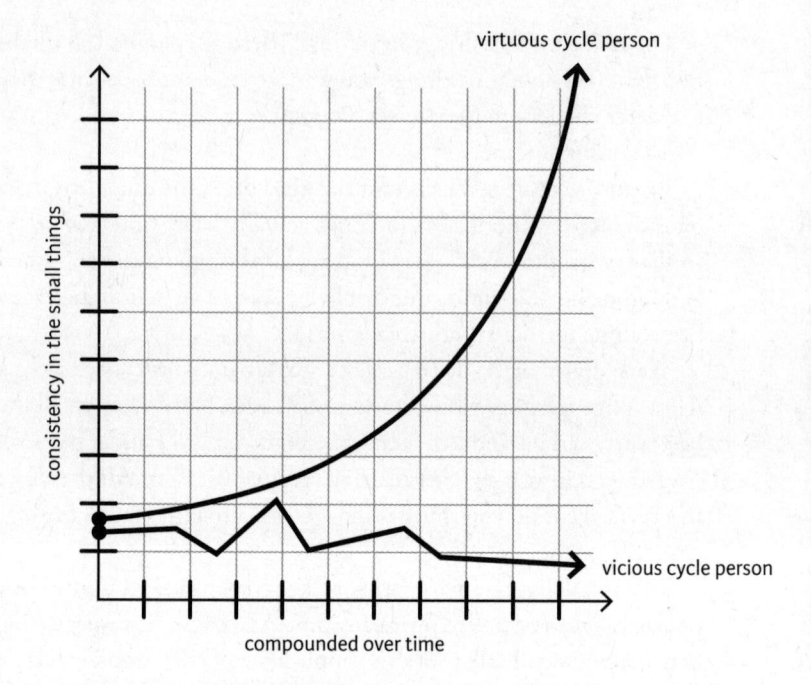

[Figure: A graph with y-axis labeled "consistency in the small things" and x-axis labeled "compounded over time." Two curves start from the same point: one labeled "virtuous cycle person" rises exponentially upward; the other labeled "vicious cycle person" fluctuates with small ups and downs before flattening out.]

    I swear to you, in that moment I felt like one of the keys to the universe had just been unlocked. My brain went all *Beautiful Mind*, and it was like I could see the charted graphs of two different trajectories—a virtuous and a vicious cycle—playing out right above her head. I saw two dots on the same starting line, and with every right decision—like a giant game of "choose your own adventure" where the stakes are only your entire life—the first dot pulled further and further away from the baseline. It was slow at first, but it quickly gathered steam when I added in the variable of time until it reached this exponential upward explosion into the stratosphere. Our other dot, on the other hand, was a series of starts and stutters and stops—this perpetual dance of two steps forward, three steps back—before eventually crashing and burning out back at zero.

    And I realized—right there over the cheese and crackers, the tiny gherkins, and the mystery jam—I am the second dot.

    The second dot is *me*.

I looked at her a long time, and then out of nowhere these words from that undergrad Econ 101 class resurrected themselves from somewhere in the deep recesses of my mind to put language to the epiphany moment before it dematerialized again before my very eyes.

"So what you're saying is . . . micro changes equal macro results."

Put another way: *Consistency wins.*

Consistency Compounds Over Time

Here's what successful people know that those of us who have been underestimating ourselves our entire lives don't: *consistency compounds over time.*

They know that the end results we see in their lives did not happen overnight. It was the diligence of daily inputs, those "small things on repeat" as my friend Hannah calls them. *And then you add in the variable of time.*

A lot of people credit Albert Einstein for saying "Compound interest is the eighth wonder of the world." But they miss the rest of that quote. He went on to say: "He who understands it, earns it. He who doesn't, pays it."

Anybody who has ever invested in their retirement or, conversely, tried to pay down credit card debt knows that's true.

Do you want to know why those two scenarios are such a good analogy to the compounding interest of consistency over time? It's *visibility*.

When you invest in your retirement, every month you get these big, bold statements complete with bar graphs that show you both where you are and how much you have grown over time. They show you how all of the inputs you've made have added up, contributed to, and compounded into this ever-growing return.

Credit cards don't do that.

Oh sure, they'll tell you the interest for that *month*. And the government has started making them tell you how long it will take to pay it off with just the minimum payment versus paying in a little bit more. You can probably even dig and find out how much interest you've paid year to date.

But I'm here to tell you, if credit card statements suddenly started arriving with a giant greeting at the top telling you how much *lifetime* interest you'd paid in to that company—*Greetings! You've now paid us $147,362 since we first bought your soul for a T-shirt freshman year. Have a nice day!*—there would be a lot more people performing what Dave Ramsey calls "plastic surgery," I can promise you that.[2]

But instead, just like sleeping on your dream for another year longer . . . you have NO idea how much it's costing you.

Visibility.

When we look at the people who feel the fear and move forward anyway, we see their results compounding on the surface. We see their outward success. But what we *don't* see is everything we're missing out on when yet another year goes by and we still haven't started.

And then we wonder why we have nothing to show for it.

We can thank the law of the harvest for that.

At its most basic, the law of the harvest tells us that we reap what we sow. The inverse, of course, is also true. We *do not* reap what we *did not* sow. Or as yet another power quote from Zig Ziglar puts it, "Don't be upset by the results you didn't get with the work you didn't do."

Ouch.

> Consistency compounds over time, so start counting the cost of not showing up.

The law of the harvest also tells us that we will reap in a different season than we sow, so we must be patient. But if we are willing to plant faithfully and patiently, adding in the variable of time, we will also reap far more than we sow.

A single planted acorn, for example, can grow into a mighty oak tree. And that single oak tree can then turn into ten thousand more acorns. Turn right around and plant all of *those* acorns and the numbers, of course, go up exponentially from there. Virtuous cycle, baby! Wins beget more wins. Momentum begets more momentum.

Consistency compounds over time.

So, I want you to start *counting the cost* of not showing up.

You can be the most beautiful writer in the world, but if you never show up and share your words, no one will ever see them. And you have no idea how many people just missed out on being helped.

You can be the smartest business owner in the world, but if you let your systems slide and stop delivering on your experience consistently, your clients will go from being your best word of mouth to your worst overnight. And all of that good ground you gained will be lost.

You can be the most talented person in the room, you could have the kind of gift that could actually *change* lives. But if you never take the risk of raising your hand out of fear of getting it wrong, then you stop being teachable. You stop growing in your craft. And you'll never get to see the kind of *excellence* you were truly capable of.

Consistency compounds over time.

The problem is, for most of us impatience kicks in long before consistency has a chance to.

Overnight Is Overrated

I'm not sure when "fast" became our highest definition of success.

I don't know about you, but I never want the most interesting thing about me to be how little time I've been at this work, how little thought or effort I've put in.

And yet, it's no secret that the world we're living in loves to worship at the altar of what I call this "fleeting currency of more"—how much, how many, how fast—until it can make it seem like if our success didn't happen overnight, then it doesn't really count at all.

But I actually think overnight success is a weakness, not a strength, a flaw in the very foundation of everything we are trying so hard to build.

Here are just five reasons why:

1. When we're just handed something overnight, we don't yet know how to steward it well. We don't yet have that *capacity*. You want to see an entire field of good fruit rot on the vine or be turned into scorched earth? Give it to someone who only showed up for the harvest.

2. Overnight is the enemy of resilience. It was easy once, so you expect it will always be this easy. And the first time that it's not, that disappointment becomes unbearable. That first failure feels fatal. Meanwhile, those of us who have been trying and failing all along, we know it's just the price of admission for building the dream. Building something over time builds up your grit muscle. It is not a one-time flex; it's waking up every single day and putting in your reps.
3. Ironically, *overnight*—this one-time windfall you couldn't possibly be responsible for—ends up making you think it's all about you. How good you are. How easy things come to you. Whereas slow growth—this work you diligently put in over the long haul—it soaks humility into your very bones. You realize the work you were doing was actually working on you all along.
4. Overnight will take you places fast ... but unfortunately it has no travel hubs to a place called "excellence." You want to master your craft? Slow down the work of your hands. Put in your ten thousand hours. Fall in love with the process and the practice and the work being done in hidden places. Stop to stare in wonder that you get to live this life of creation.
5. Ask any weed standing six feet tall on the surface and multiplying with dizzying speed what it stands for, and it will try to point to anything it can to distract you from the barely half an inch of roots that anchors it. It doesn't want you to see how easily it topples over with that first push. Meanwhile, it may take a hundred years for a redwood to finally walk among the giants. But just go ahead and ask it if it was always worth the wait.

Most of all, here is what I know about you and me: If tomorrow everything we ever dreamed of was just handed to us, just gifted to us in a quick windfall overnight ... *it wouldn't mean a thing*.

That's because you and I are the kind of people who don't want it unless we can get knee-deep and muddy building it with our own two hands.

We *want* to be people who did the work. We want the work to *work* on us.

And that's going to require us building up some calluses.

We're Building Up the Good Kind of Calluses

Do you want to know what lives rent-free in my head?

It's how many cars Mr. Miyagi got the Karate Kid to wax on, wax off for him before a young Ralph Macchio turned Daniel LaRusso finally said to him, "Hey, wait a minute . . . what does this have to do with karate?"

I mean, did he never read *Tom Sawyer* in school? Did he not *see* where this was going? Apparently not. Because Mr. Miyagi also got him to paint the fence.

And yet that moment where we, along with Daniel, finally find out what all of this was building to all along is still the stuff movie magic is made of.

Show me sand the floor.
Show me paint the fence.
Show me . . . wax on, wax off.

Muscle memory.

That's what we're really building here in this practice of showing up consistently.

We're just putting in our reps.

Leadership expert John Maxwell tells us, "The secret of your success is determined by your daily agenda. . . . You will never change your life until you change something you do daily."[3] Darren Hardy, author of *The Compound Effect*, puts it this way: "Since your outcomes are all a result of your moment-to-moment choices, you have incredible power to change your life by changing those choices. Step by step, day by day, your choices will shape your actions until they become habits, where practice makes them permanent."[4]

Choices → Actions → Habits → Practice Makes Permanent

That's another way of saying what we do *consistently* becomes a part of our very *identity*. Day by day, putting in the reps, we are *becoming* the person who can one day stand inside these goals.

It makes me think about the kind of calluses a guitar player gets from practicing.

The *good* kind of calluses.

This is not just about developing a thick skin, becoming so impermeable to criticism and what the world might have to say about you that you become numb to everything around you, including the work. No, this is the kind of toughening up that makes you better at what you do. It leaves its mark on you. It *alters* your identity right down to your fingerprints. And in the process, you become a person of endurance. Of faithfulness and excellence and perseverance too.

> When you actually show up and DO the work, the confidence will follow.

When you actually show up and DO the work, the confidence will follow.

Darren Hardy said it like this, "It's not the big things that add up in the end. It's the hundreds, thousands, or millions of little things that separate the ordinary from the extraordinary."[5]

You want the courage to show up when it counts?

Get busy putting in your reps.

If You Want to Trust Yourself, Stop Quitting

There is one final missing piece to all of this.

One of our favorite holiday traditions is to have some of our friends over around Christmastime to exchange presents, sit by a roaring fire . . . and work a puzzle together.

Like I said, I'm *super* fun at parties.

And one of the things I've noticed about putting a puzzle together is that it's *very slow* to start.

In the beginning you're just looking for things that *might* go together. Maybe you try to find all the edge and corner pieces first just so you have an outline, some borders and parameters of what this thing might eventually want to be. It can take what feels like an eternity just to get ONE piece to snap into place.

And then you have to do it *again and again*.

My point is, it's sort of like pulling teeth in the beginning.

And it's just not a lot of fun.

There comes a moment every single time we do this when we're already a couple *hours* into it and we don't seem to be making much progress at all. That initial "look how much FUN this is going to be" high has worn off, and we find ourselves right in the thick of the messy middle. My neck hurts. My back hurts. We've been sitting there for hours doing the WORK, and this one thought inevitably crosses my mind . . .

"THIS IS NEVER GOING TO COME TOGETHER IN TIME!"

We're going to have done all this work and spent all this time in the thick of the effort only for it to not actually come together like the picture-perfect outcome it's supposed to be. We're going to run out of time—our friends are *going* to have to head home eventually—and we're just going to wind up tearing up all this work we did and tucking it back in this neat and tidy little box. Hide it away and pretend like it never happened.

In other words, I think to myself, "This is ALL going to have been for NOTHING!"

But then something *magic* starts to happen.

Just at that moment where you start to think "I'm not even sure if these pieces are even *meant* to fit together, I'm not sure they go together at all. Are we sure we're even working on the *right* puzzle?"* something changes.

Just when you are *most* convinced these pieces are never going to come together, just at that moment when it's taking forever and

---

*FUN FACT: Two Christmases ago we did, in fact, realize part of the way through that they HAD put the wrong puzzle in our box. It was supposed to be this beautiful, serene beach scene. And instead it turned out to be . . . a BUNCH OF CHICKENS! We had to work that entire puzzle, with no guidance at all from the box lid. And, as it turns out, one missing piece. But hey, we got a great story out of it!

you're pretty sure you just want to quit and enjoy your life again . . . *the momentum starts to shift*.

The pieces start coming together faster. Entire sections snap into place. You can see what you couldn't see before about how this section leads into that one. And how this part right in front of you would have never made sense if you didn't spend all this time over here working on this other part first. The pieces are really flying into place now, and the BIG picture is becoming clear. Until, by the time you're finished snapping that final piece into place—that "there it is" moment—you are convinced this is the MOST fun you've ever had in your life.

It's like that with finally getting started on the dream once you know everything that goes into it.

When you first get that step-by-step blueprint, no matter how detailed it is, it's like someone has just dumped a 10,000-piece puzzle on the table in front of you. And the puzzle, by the way? It's called "Wheatfield in a Sandstorm." It's *going* to take a while.

It's going to be very slow to start.

You're not going to be sure exactly which piece to tackle first.

You're going to put in HOURS and still not have much to show for it.

You're not going to *feel* like doing the work.

But, as one of my favorite quotes says, "You will never always be motivated, so you must learn to be disciplined."

And just like that, a new "D" word has entered the chat.

Discipline.

Discipline > Motivated

Here's the secret: You have to have the discipline to be consistent even when you don't feel like it. But when you show up over and over with consistency, the momentum it builds starts to shift everything in the room. Until it *leaves* you feeling motivated.

Motivated is an *effect* of consistently putting in the work, not the cause.

Steven Pressfield says, "Momentum is forward motion. It's the groove you get into when you work every day. Momentum is cumulative. It builds and increases."[6] This is why the puzzle pieces really start flying into place there at the end. You remain a body in motion. With each small win, you pick up even more confidence and speed. The work you're doing now builds on all the (slow, small, hidden, messy) work you did before. The return on inputs becomes an off-the-charts exponential explosion there at the end. Until you're not even sure when it went from "This is never going to come together in time" to "I can't believe it's already done." I can tell you every single book I've written has followed this exact pattern. But it never would have gotten to that point if I turned tail and bailed every time it got hard.

If we want to trust ourselves, we *have* to stop quitting every time it gets uncomfortable.

Consistency is really the habit of keeping promises to yourself.

Show up when no one is listening, show up when you are overlooked, show up when it feels like nothing is working or that none of this will ever matter. Show up simply for the love of the work and the rest will follow.

Inch by inch, this work you're doing . . . it adds up.

It counts. It matters. It *changes* things.

One painfully slow, unseen, uncelebrated, unsatisfying input at a time.

Your life will not be transformed by what you do one day but by what you do every day. Consistency will become one of the most important habits of your life.

That's because, inch by inch, you are becoming a person who stays the course. Imperfect progress still adds up.

And all that momentum you've been building along the way?

You're going to need it as we once again near the top of this mountain.

It turns out there is one last ledge coming around.

And we're *going* to want to take a running leap at it.

the shift

When fear can't defeat you, it will instead try to distract and delay you. Distractions want to shout at you "Let's get out of here" anytime this work gets too hard. Instead, commit to the consistency of showing up, even when you don't feel like it. Sit through the edginess of putting in just a little bit of work every single day. And let the forward motion of that momentum add up. Let the promises you keep to yourself show you that you are becoming the person in the room who can be trusted to stand inside these goals.

14

success is a slippery slope

THE UNDERDOG is the role of a lifetime.

What I mean by that is, if you're not careful you could spend your whole life playing that part.

Have you ever noticed how Hollywood treats the underdog character? They spend two hours putting this poor unfortunate soul through the wringer with every kind of obstacle imaginable—every kind of disappointment, heartbreak, and humiliation they can throw at a person—only to finally relent and at last give them everything they ever wanted in the last thirty seconds. Roll the end credits. Cue the crescendo on the heart-swelling score. Our underdog then (quite *literally*) disappears from the scene, their storyline once again fading to black, usually never to be heard from again.

If you start to pay attention, you'll see that we don't get too many stories about someone who gets everything they ever wanted in those first few seconds of the film, and then the next two hours are just them stewarding that success well, being wildly generous, and spending the rest of their life living well-adjusted and happy.

Hollywood: *I mean, WHO wants to watch that?*

No, when I really started to think about it, I realized that about the only time Hollywood wants to give us a character who got everything they ever wanted early in their story is when twenty or thirty years have since passed. And they've now made a total and complete mess of their life.

They let all of that initial success go to their head. They've self-sabotaged and squandered. They've ruined relationships and radically mismanaged everything to the point that they are no longer recognizable. They are a mere shallow, empty shell of the person they once were. In other words, they're now *miserable*.

Hollywood: *Now, THAT'S the kind of story we can get behind!*

Ah, the oft-attempted, rarely well-executed Underdog Redux. (For point of reference: Deborah Vance in *Hacks* got it right. *Rocky V*, not so much.*)

Either way, the idea is that our main character has messed things up so bad—fallen so hard from grace and landed with a thud—that they are once again back in the position of being our unlikely hero. They have gloriously rejoined the ranks of those of us who keep finding ourselves back at the starting line. And we, as the audience, are HERE for it.

That's because Hollywood has trained us well. Years of movie magic have convinced us that unless someone is actively carrying the backbreaking weight of all the odds stacked against them—stumbling their way through their own "better and worse nature, proceeding sometimes nobly and sometimes ... foolishly"[1]—then their story doesn't really matter. We're here for the long, slow climb full of setbacks. We're here to watch them wrestle with being their own worst

---

*To be fair, in *Rocky V* it was Rocky's *accountant* who did all the mismanaging, but you get the point. *Rocky V* is still widely regarded as the worst film in the franchise, and in 1999 *Time* magazine even placed it on the list of the Top 100 worst *ideas* of the twentieth century. Brutal. Even Sylvester Stallone has reportedly publicly expressed hatred and regret for the film, giving it a zero out of ten. The Underdog Redux is a difficult landing to stick, indeed.

enemy. Heck, we're even here to cheer for the thirty seconds of glory. But the moment someone settles comfortably into a life filled with everything they ever wanted? We're out. And every reductive, repackaged, broken underdog script we know then tells us what comes next.

We won't get to care about them again—that is to say, no one will ever *love* them again—until they face some proverbial third-act problem.† Until that moment when they once again lose everything.

And we wonder why some of us struggle with MORE.

The truth is, we're afraid to let go of playing the Underdog. We're *addicted* to it, really. Everyone roots for the Underdog. The unlikely hero is the unmitigated darling of all the chanting masses. They love you so long as you struggle for it every single, *solitary* step of the way.

Do you want to know who doesn't have that kind of universal support? People who have already reached some level of success and kept it.

Oh, how quickly the crowds can turn on you then. "You had your moment, now let someone else have a chance." We're already on to the next unlikely story.

It is one thing to be the scrappy underdog, forever sliding back down this mountain.

It is quite another to have *arrived* . . . and find out just how *lonely* it can be at the top.

Most people won't start watching until hour 9,999. They'll tell everyone how they know you at hour 10,000. But the clock has already started ticking on who will turn on you by hour 10,001.

They say that leaders wear a bullseye on their back because they are always out in front. So, this final approach to the finish line makes us a moving target. We know this.

---

†A third-act problem is when the storyline doesn't properly resolve a character's development. But "third act" is also used to refer to the third and final part of a person's life, usually after retirement, when their own mortality takes center stage. So, our Underdog Redux hero usually finds themself facing both kinds of problems.

We know it. And it *terrifies* us.

Remember what my coaching client Liz said? "It honestly scares me to see myself as a 'winner,' someone who is successful like that."

This fear of success, it turns out, is a slippery slope.

And the only way we stop backsliding is to take *one giant leap*.

The Success to Significance Gap

You leaped the first time. But will you leap again the next time the ledge comes back around?

I had an aha moment a few years ago. It was a flash of insight, a picture that came to me as clear in my head as any I've ever seen before. It was a quick advance of a slide deck—a Don Draper-worthy Kodak Carousel shining a light on what really matters and making me ache with nostalgia for a far-off summit I had not yet seen. And then just as quickly, it was gone again. But not before changing the entire narrative. It told me everything I need to know about why this boulder of ours keeps rolling back down the mountain.

Business experts will often talk about the survival to significance hierarchy. In entrepreneurship terms, it is a series of five stages that anyone who is trying to make a life and a living doing this thing they love will have to ascend through if they ever want to build something that truly lasts. But really, when you zoom out just a little, you see that it's this same journey up the mountain that all of us are out here trying to climb.

In the beginning, when you are first getting started, you are just trying to **survive**, barely making ends meet as you work to build out this dream. Once things get going and the bills are being paid, you then move into **stability**. From there, as you start to have a little bit more than enough, you reach the **security** stage. And beyond that is when people start calling you a **success**.

The way I always understood this climb was that if you just stick with it long enough—if you'll just keep *pushing* harder—eventually you'll arrive at **significance**.

And as someone who has spent her whole life feeling underestimated, there was no place I wanted to arrive more... than *significant*.

In *Slow Growth* I wrote:

> "Will I ever matter?"
> You might be shocked if you knew how many times those words have spilled from my lips....
> Sometimes I feel like I might disappear altogether....
> On those days when the approval doesn't come, when I disappear into the background noise of a thousand shouting voices, I feel like I may just disintegrate altogether. Dematerialize. A billion atomized molecules floating quietly into the roaring void.[2]

We are the kind ones, the quiet ones, the ones so often overlooked.

And a lifetime of being underestimated has told us we will only ever matter when we finally show everyone just how far we've come. When we finally reach the top and there is no more mountain left for us to climb.

Enter the aha moment.

We've been assuming all along that the road to significance is a series of consecutive steps, a well-worn, repeatable path where if you just keep climbing long enough and never once step out of line... you will inevitably reach the top. Most people spend their whole lives pushing and pushing just trying to get up that hill.

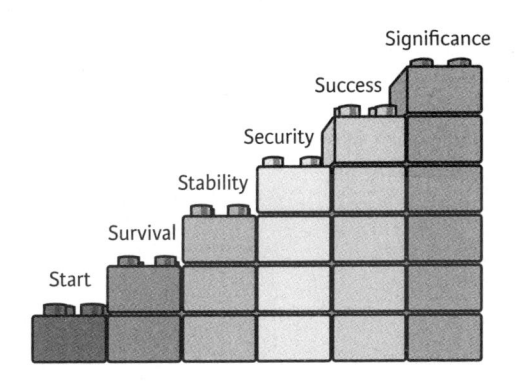

Start → Survival → Stability → Security → Success → Significance

But the picture that came to me so clearly in that moment—the one that slid into my mind with a flash of light and changed the entire narrative—is that the graph should *actually* look something more like this:

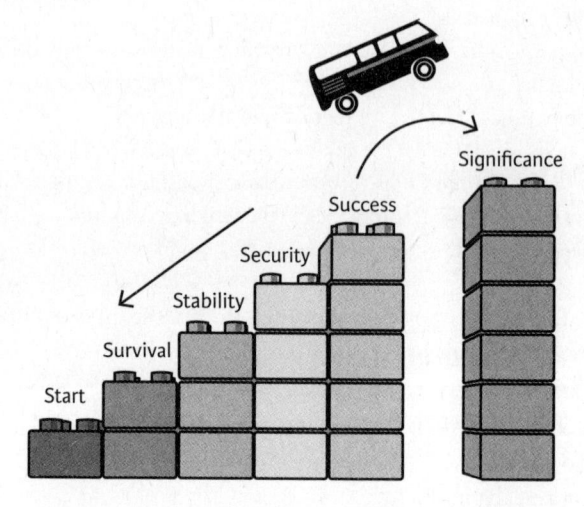

It turns out there is this *Speed*-worthy "it's finished on the map" gap at the top between success and significance.

Look closer.

Once you see it, it changes everything.

This was NEVER just a mountain we were out here climbing... but a ledge come back around that we now have to *leap*.

And the name of that leap is, "It's finally about something bigger than you."

See, all of those other steps... that's really focused on us. It's about *our* survival, *our* stability, *our* security, and yes, even eventually *our* success.

But we don't stop there.

That's because we make our successes about us.

But we make our *scarcity* about us too. *Our* fears, *our* failures, *our* disappointment, *our* being embarrassed, the criticism that might eventually come *our* way.

We climb all the way up this mountain. And then, just at that last second—just as we reach this threshold point where we might actually make a significant difference with all these gifts we've been given—we flinch at the ledge once again come back around.

We take our eyes off of where we are headed. We make eye contact with everyone suddenly watching at home. And for just one split second, we self-consciously glance down.

We put our eyes back on ourselves.

And *that* is the moment when we blink.

We stutter-step and stumble backward. We lose our newfound footing. We get tripped up over all our old excuses already laid out there behind us in a familiar bright-orange line, as we once again quickly back ourselves away from the brink. And in the process, we lose every inch of this only-recently reclaimed ground.

We lose our grip.

We lose our way.

And the boulder rolls all the way back down the mountain.

Now here's what should *really* scare us.

Most people will spend their whole lives in this perpetual survival-to-success loop, forever starting back over from the bottom, without ever once making that leap. We'll gain a little bit of ground, gain a little bit of traction, maybe even gain a little bit of success along the way. But at some point in our lives, this self-preservationist switch got flipped in us. And now we don't know how to stop making everything we do ultimately be about keeping ourselves safe.

We'll go on simultaneously self-sabotaging and self-protecting like that for years, *until we realize that taken to extremes they are, in fact, the same thing.*

And either way, it sends us running right back into survival mode every time.

> This was NEVER just a mountain
> we were out here climbing . . .
> but a ledge come back around.

The only way forward is to make this leap from self-preserving to serving the world, realizing that this work we are doing was *always* about something much bigger than us.

It's the moment when we stop asking, "What might go wrong?" and we *start* asking ourselves, "Yeah, but who might it help?"

Proving People Wrong Is a Powder Keg

You want to blow up your entire life? Internally self-combust?

Make proving people wrong your favorite form of jet fuel.

On February 7, 2008, at around 7:00 p.m. local time, fourteen people were killed and thirty-six people injured in a horrifying accident when the Imperial Sugar refinery in Port Wentworth, Georgia, exploded. Rescuers on the scene described it as "walking into hell."

The cause?

Sugar dust.

"The origin of the explosion was narrowed down to the center of the factory, in a basement located beneath storage silos. Large accumulations of sugar dust due to poor housekeeping became airborne . . . leading to a series of massive secondary explosions spreading throughout the factory. . . . According to Imperial Sugar CEO John Sheptor, the accumulated sugar dust likely acted like gunpowder."[3]

This is the kind of chain reaction of destruction that happens when you are dealing with an unstable accelerant . . . no matter how *sweet* it may be.

I have known what it is to stall out hard at the success level, to become so addicted to the saccharine satisfaction of winning that I make my entire purpose revolve around proving other people wrong. I have known what it is to act like there is no form of revenge that could ever be sweeter than showing up and showing everyone just exactly how far I've come. And I've known what it is to wind up a hollow, burned-out shell of myself as a result.

In *Dirt*, I described this feeling from my first year at Yale: "I think at the time, I just wanted God to keep the wins coming, like some sort of never-ending Pez dispenser doling out success. A daily hit of the good stuff, this concentrated sugary-sweet high of getting everything you ever wanted. . . . *Just keep the candy coming.*"[4]

Achieving to prove your worth is a lot like eating marshmallows for every meal and wondering why you're still starving. Sure, you'll get a quick boost of energy when that sugary high hits . . . but somehow it only leaves you feeling *emptier* every time. If we are going to make it up this mountain, we're going to need a more sustainable fuel source.

To carry us up this hill we're going to need *purpose*, not proving other people wrong.

I can't tell you how many hard-story people I know who have managed to reach some real, impressive level of outward success . . . only to wind up losing it all because none of it ever made them feel any different on the inside like they thought it would.

They learned the hard way that there is no amount of MORE that can ever make you stop feeling LESS than. That work has always been an *inside* job.

It took me a while to learn that lesson myself. In *Dirt* I wrote, "I suppose when I look back at it now, that's really what I was trying to do. Trying to stuff my life so full of things and achievements, of capes and costumes and masks, that they would pile up and accumulate and somehow backfill that hole. Like a landfill of gold stars and brand-name labels, the temporary hits of my preferred drug of choice that seemed to numb but never satisfy."[5]

I let it all pile up and accumulate, every sweet success that somehow never satisfied.

But I never bothered to clean up that mess before it all went airborne.

All those days when the approval never came.

Every empty win that made me feel like I may just dematerialize altogether.

A billion atomized molecules floating quietly into the roaring void.

"Will I ever matter?"

This sugar dust turned into a powder keg.

Desperation Is the Enemy of Creation

There is a saying Justin and I came up with that I repeat to myself often:
Desperation is the enemy of creation.

Oh sure, there's that old adage that necessity is the mother of invention. And it can be true that tough times will lead you to places that easy ones never would. In the short term.

But in the *long* term, survival mode is never where true significance is built.

The data backs this up. Research tells us that people stuck in a desperate survival-to-success loop never feel like they have the capacity to handle more. When you are so busy focusing on just surviving, it consumes every free brain cell you have just to make it through another day.

In a 2013 study, in fact, researchers discovered an important link between experiencing a scarcity of resources and a significantly diminished cognitive function, saying it "consume[s] mental resources, leaving less for other tasks."[6] "A scarcity mentality affects your ability to solve problems, retain information, and reason logically. It also impacts your brain's decision-making process. A scarcity mindset limits your ability to plan, focus, and start a project or task. Your brain is too busy thinking about something you don't have."[7]

This survival mentality tells us, "Forget about ever having more than enough. That doesn't happen for people like you. Just focus on not losing what you already have."

Scarcity tells us to isolate and self-protect. It sends us racing back into hiding. When we're so consumed with just surviving, we can't even think about building or growing beyond where we are. Every day becomes an exercise in just trying to get by. And every little bit of ground we gain quickly resets back to zero.

Yes, desperation is the enemy of creation.

And the antidote to all this Scarcity, it turns out, was always Generosity.

This is where true significance begins.

One of my favorite books of all time is *The Go-Giver* by Bob Burg and John David Mann. In it, they talk about two universal laws that will shape our way forward.

The Law of Value says, "Your true worth is determined by how much more you give in value than you take in payment."[8]

The Law of Influence says, "Your influence is determined by how abundantly you place other people's interests first."[9]

In other words, as Burg and Mann say, "If you want more success, find a way to serve more people. It's that simple."[10]

I've spent a lot of time unscientifically observing this. And every Virtuous Cycle person I know in real life, the ones whose stock is always rising up and up and up . . . they seem to do these three things on repeat:

1. They show up with CONSISTENCY. They fall in love with the work.
2. They REINVEST TO GROW. They understand the law of the harvest.
3. They pour into their people with GENEROSITY. They give more than they take.

It's that simple. Whenever you feel stuck, come back to these three things. On repeat.

The Go-Giver book tells us that people who are generous are *magnetic*. And if you've ever met someone like this, you know it's true.

But more than any outward success that being generous can give you, it's the work that's being done on the inside that really matters. With every small act of generosity, you are prying back scarcity's death grip on your life. Every act of giving is actually an act of rebellion against your own survival mode. You are proving to yourself over and over that you are becoming a person who has more than enough.

And it's safe now for you to rest.

You want to start trusting yourself more? Stop making everything you do be about getting yourself to some mountaintop moment. And start making it about who you can help along the way.

That work is going to require us to do at least four important things.

Clean Up Your Mess

Desperation can take on a lot of different forms. The most common, of course, is financial. But it can also be desperation for other people's approval so that you lose your true sense of self, desperation to cut corners so you get there faster at the sacrifice of your excellence, desperation that makes you so laser-focused on reaching your own level of success that you stop seeing other people along the way. Anytime you give in to your desperation at the expense of your character and integrity, you are forfeiting true significance. Spend some time now doing all the housekeeping for whatever has accumulated. Deal with the sugar dust before it becomes a powder keg.

Redefine Your Safe

Part of our perpetual return to survival mode is due to that self-preservationist switch that got flipped in us. It is the voice of the Big Bad Wolf ripping at our heels, telling us to run and not stop running, that it will never be safe to stop. We shift out of that constant return to chaos and expand our capacity for peace when we redefine what it means for us to have enough. When we redefine what it means for us to finally be safe.

Maintenance and Margin

One of the worst-kept secrets among truly successful turned significant people is that they get really good at being faithful with the boring stuff. They consistently build in time for maintenance and margin. They not only successfully acquire good things, but they also successfully steward them well by maintaining them. They also regularly build in margin with both their time and their money. As the old saying goes, "Show me your checkbook and your calendar, and I'll show you what's important to you." By never living on the edge with either, they have the breathing room to show up and give more.

Reinvest to Grow

But do you want to know the most important thing that people who want to make the leap to significance AREN'T doing? It's spending every dollar they make trying to look impressive enough on the outside to show other people just how far they've come. Nothing will kill your momentum faster. Instead, they are doubling down on the law of the harvest. They are consistently reinvesting to grow, whether that is by growing their email list, signing up for coaching, taking a course, investing in a new website, or by some other means. And even more importantly, they are reinvesting their time and generosity into other people. They are consistently showing up and pouring into their community long before they ever come to them with an "ask." They understand the value of planting long before the harvest. As Burg and Mann tell us in *The Go-Giver* book, "Most people just laugh when they hear that the secret to success is giving. . . . Then again, most people are nowhere near as successful as they wish they were."[11]

The Handbook for HERE

You are HERE.

Here at the ledge come back around, staring out together at this very edge of significance, I feel the need to tell you a few things about who you are . . . and who you are *becoming*.

You have always been the kind one, the quiet one, the one so often overlooked.

But I, for one, now look at you and only see the pure *magic* you hold inside.

You have been out here doing the *work*. It's just that yours is the kind of work that is going to change generations. You're not weak, you're not fragile, you're not delicate.

For some of us . . . it just takes a little longer.

We rumble and reckon with our family tree right down to the very root. We put our own DNA under a microscope looking for every weakened bond where failure might already be wired right in. We hold up a mirror to our own lives and we see those who came before staring right back at us. And empathy becomes the stranger in the room that we meet in the second act.

Elisabeth Kübler-Ross said, "Beautiful people do not just happen,"[12] and I could not love that more.

See, I have this very (un)scientific theory that pain like progressively finer grits of sandpaper rounds off the hard edges we're all born with and makes hard-story people a safe, soft place to land for others.

Because of this, the people with some mud in their stories are *exactly* the ones we need out there lighting up this world. But because of their kind, tender hearts . . . they can't believe their story will ever matter.

Fear with all its boring scripts has been loud in your life for far too long. So, from here on out, let these words be louder:

Actually, perfect isn't keeping you safe. Hiding in plain sight doesn't prevent disappointment. Creating nothing isn't preferable to creating failure. And apologizing for taking up any space at all was never a requirement to be loved. While we're at it, your story does matter. It hasn't all been done. You're not disqualified. It isn't too late. The world does need your voice.

And some of us think how long you've been at this work is one of the most interesting things about you.

I also need you to know, here before we take this leap . . .

It always feels hardest just before the breakthrough.

They say *transition*, that moment just before something new and beautiful is birthed into the world, is the hardest part of labor.

It's the same with your gifts.

Just as you are about to hold everything you've been working so hard for, that is the exact moment when you are going to MOST want to give up.

In those moments, I remind myself of this one line people say before the final push.

Fight for your baby.

Fight for what you are trying so hard to get out into the world.

I am convinced the greatest work of our life will come about little by little with "just one more" when everything in us wants to quit.

Just one more sentence.
Just one more small idea.
Just one more time showing up.

These small but important commitments on repeat. Showing ourselves over and over, we are the grown-up in the room. And this time, we *can* be trusted.

You might have wanted to quit again this very morning. To go running back into the familiar comfort of your survival mode. But instead try seeing what happens . . . *with just one more.*

the shift

The broken Underdog scripts in your mind have been telling you that if you ever get everything you ever wanted, that is the exact moment when people will stop loving you. Success feels like a moving target on your back. So, you slide back down this mountain, forever stuck in a survival loop. Instead, try getting a running start at this ledge come back around. There is a gap between success and significance. And the name of that gap is "it's finally about something bigger than you."

the summit

finish lines are a full-circle moment

Hello from the other side.

We took this running leap at the ledge come back around. And *this time* we finally stuck the landing.

The first thing we did was to lay these heavy things down, this junk we were never meant to carry. This curse of a rolling boulder at last come to rest in wide-open, spacious ground.

The slippery slope is now behind us. And we'll linger here a little longer to take in a new kind of view.

It may take a while for your eyes to adjust here. The landscape floods with golden light and makes glittering, gilded flecks out of all this dust we just kicked up that still hasn't had a chance to settle. But somewhere just a few feet in front of us, a new small, wooden, staked sign in the ground is already taking shape.

This time it doesn't speak of arrival points. It does not tell you the elevation of the most recent heights you've climbed. Instead, it tells an entire story—changes the entire narrative, in fact—as it points our way forward with just three simple words:

RETURN TO BASE.

See, we didn't come out here to climb this mountain just so that we could plant our flag in the ground, make the leap to significance just so that WE could be the ones who matter. You don't summit a dizzying height like this and not come back a guide for someone else. A hero transformed who can now point the way for others. Can't you see it? It is now dawning on us with each new day.

This mountain was never a one-way trip.

It was *always* a full-circle moment.

And it turns out, your strength never depended on proving yourself, showing other people just how far you've come, or convincing everyone who ever said you'd never amount to anything that they were wrong.

Your *true* strength is in your gentle spirit, the way you make other people feel known, your ability to look at a person and speak life into who they are and who they are becoming, to take them by the hand and say, "We have to GO. We can't stay here."

A lifetime of being overlooked ... has now turned you into someone who sees.

FINISH LINES ARE A FULL-CIRCLE MOMENT

Return to base

a new kind of small, wooden, staked sign in the ground

base camp, where in a full-circle moment you return to where you started, now as a guide for others

acknowledgments

WRITING A BOOK IS A TEAM SPORT, and there is NO ONE I would rather have on my team than Justin Marantz. Justin, you saw these words before *anyone* else did. You saw them in the "pacing, curled up in the fetal position, staring up at the ceiling, existential crises (plural), questioning man's search for meaning, lizard brain, I CAN'T DO THIS" phase... and you saw them in the "I can't wait to run downstairs and read you these new words, *wait, is this book actually *gasp*... GOOD!*" phase. You have been my champion, my cheerleader, my first editor, my co-comedy writer, the first one to tell me when it wasn't there yet, and even my footnotes formatter. But most of all, when the voice of fear got LOUD... yours was the voice in my head that was even louder, telling me everything this book could be (which is amazing, since everyone knows you are *such* a low-talker). I love you more with every breath you take (every move you make). It is the honor of my life to be your wife.

    A huge thank-you also goes out to a few of our best friends—Erin and Peter, Kristin and Justin—for being some of the first people in the world to know this title, hear this concept, see this book cover. Your feedback and love helped shape this book from the very beginning. We love doing life with you!

To the formidable, inimitable, AUDACIOUS Sharon McMahon ... THANK YOU for putting your name on this cover alongside mine. Thank you for writing such a beautiful foreword and thank you for shouting this book from the rooftops. You are truly one of the most generous people I know, an absolute national treasure, and your friendship is one of the greatest gifts of my life.

To Jon Acuff, Steven Pressfield, Dr. Alison Cook, Christy Wright, Jess Ekstrom, Mattie Jackson, Laura Tremaine, Jason VanRuler, and Graham Cochrane ... thank you for believing in these words and endorsing them. Each of you has been a longtime hero of mine. And I'm grateful to now call you friend!

To my incredible coaching clients who shared their stories of fear and being underestimated with such honesty, grace, and courage ... and allowed me the privilege of sharing them with the world. To Brittany Bruce, Kristen Hallinan, Heather Mrva, Liz Bagwell, Jessica Boarman, Ashlee Ilg, Tracy Riccio, Jennifer Woodward, Stacey Ritter, and all the "Underestimated Girls" of the world ... I see both who you are and who you are *becoming*. You are generation changers, each and every one of you. The leaders this world has been waiting for.

To the entire team at Revell—Kelsey Bowen, Amy Nemecek, Eileen Hanson, Olivia Peitsch, Laura Klynstra—from the bottom of my heart, thank you for seeing this book for what it was ... *and* for everything it could be. For pushing back in just the right places, and not giving up until this book reached its highest version of itself. I'm a better writer (and person!) because of each of you. And to my agent Jenni Burke for your infinite wisdom, guidance, and kindness every step of the way. Thank you all for being compasses in a stopwatch world.

Finally, to you the reader. Thank you for coming out here to this mountain with me and having the audacity to once again climb. It takes courage to chase a dream. It takes heart and grit and fortitude to change your family tree. Let this be your final reminder: *You're not weak, you're not fragile, you're not delicate.* You are out here doing work that matters.

I hope tomorrow you rise, turn your tired face to the sun, and say to a world all too willing to overlook you, uninvite you, count you out before you're done...

Go ahead. Underestimate me... That'll be fun.

notes

Chapter 1 Starting Over Is a Rolling Boulder

1. Mary Marantz, *Dirt: Growing Strong Roots in What Makes the Broken Beautiful* (Revell, 2020), 27.
2. Julie Harris, "Hope: Unraveling the Last Evil in Pandora's Box," Medium, May 21, 2023, https://jhwordsmith.medium.com/hope-unraveling-the-last-evil-in-pandoras-box-22f96b1d4245.
3. Harris, "Hope."
4. Marantz, *Dirt*, 236–37, emphasis added.

Chapter 2 Fear Is a Broken Script

1. *The Shawshank Redemption*, directed by Frank Darabont (Castle Rock Entertainment, 1994).
2. Steven Pressfield, *The War of Art: Break Through the Blocks and Win Your Inner Creative Battles* (Black Irish Entertainment, 2002), 21.

Chapter 3 Self-Sabotage Is a Shot Glass

1. Generally attributed to Jim Collins, *Good to Great: Why Some Companies Make the Leap . . . And Others Don't* (Harper Business, 2001).
2. Lindsay C. Gibson, *Adult Children of Emotionally Immature Parents: How to Heal from Distant, Rejecting, or Self-Involved Parents* (New Harbinger Publications, 2015), 11–12, emphasis added.
3. Annie Tanasugarn, "4 Ways We Get Conditioned to Chaos," Medium, August 7, 2023, https://medium.com/invisible-illness/4-ways-we-get-conditioned-to-chaos-c9fc3493ff1d.
4. Alison Cook, *The Best of You: Break Free from Painful Patterns, Mend Your Past, and Discover Your True Self in God* (Thomas Nelson, 2022), 25.

5. Cook, *The Best of You*, 25.
6. Stephen R. Covey, *The 7 Habits of Highly Effective People: Powerful Lessons in Personal Change* (Free Press, 1989).
7. Cook, *The Best of You*, 23.
8. Mary Marantz, host, *The Mary Marantz Show*, "The Selfless Move Toward Healing with Dr. Alison Cook," October 4, 2022, https://podcasts.apple.com/us/podcast/the-selfless-move-toward-healing-with-dr-alison-cook/id1478272407?i=1000581519623.
9. Cook, *The Best of You*, 124–25.
10. Marantz, *Dirt*, 138–39.
11. Eric Nelson, "The Secret to Coming Up With Ideas People Can Get Excited About," LinkedIn, September 19, 2017, https://www.linkedin.com/pulse/secret-coming-up-ideas-people-can-get-excited-eric-nelson/.

Chapter 4 Second-Guessing Is a Missing Handbook

1. *Bird Box*, directed by Susanne Bier (Netflix, 2018).
2. Jennifer Guttman, clinical psychologist and author of *A Path to Sustainable Life Satisfaction*, quoted in Vivian Manning-Schaffel, "Here's How to Stop Second-Guessing Yourself All the Time," Better by TODAY, February 4, 2020, https://www.nbcnews.com/better/lifestyle/here-s-how-stop-second-guessing-yourself-all-time-ncna1128681.
3. As quoted in Manning-Schaffel, "Here's How to Stop Second-Guessing Yourself All the Time."
4. As quoted in Manning-Schaffel, "Here's How to Stop Second-Guessing Yourself All the Time."
5. Rizza Bermio-Gonzalez, "When Anxiety Makes You Second-Guess Every Decision," Healthy Place, March 1, 2022, https://www.healthyplace.com/blogs/treatinganxiety/2022/3/when-anxiety-makes-you-second-guess-every-decision, emphasis added.
6. Amy Chua and Jed Rubenfeld, *The Triple Package: How Three Unlikely Traits Explain the Rise and Fall of Cultural Groups in America* (Penguin Books, 2014), 1.

Chapter 5 "Not Enough" Is a Blank Space

1. Marantz, *Dirt*, 172–74.
2. Mary Marantz, *Slow Growth Equals Strong Roots: Finding Grace, Freedom, and Purpose in an Overachieving World* (Revell, 2022), 43.
3. Vladas Griskevicius et al., "When the Economy Falters, Do People Spend or Save? Responses to Resource Scarcity Depend on Childhood Environments," *Psychological Science* 24, no. 2 (February 2013), https://journals.sagepub.com/doi/abs/10.1177/0956797612451471.
4. Kelly Berry, "How Growing Up Poor Impacts Future Spending Habits," One Cent at a Time, August 5, 2018, https://onecentatatime.com/how-growing-up-poor-impacts-future-spending-habits/.
5. Marantz, *Slow Growth*, 145.

6. "Enneagram Type Four: The Individualist," The Enneagram Institute, accessed July 1, 2024, https://www.enneagraminstitute.com/type-4/, emphasis added.

7. Mary Marantz, host, *The Mary Marantz Show*, "Get Past Your Past: Why Your Story Does Not Disqualify You with Jason VanRuler," October 3, 2023, https://podcasts.apple.com/us/podcast/get-past-your-past-why-your-story-does-not-disqualify/id1478272407?i=1000630016332.

8. Jason VanRuler, *Get Past Your Past: How Facing Your Broken Places Leads to True Connection* (Zondervan, 2023), 22, emphasis added.

9. Adapted from Marantz, *Slow Growth*, 106–7.

10. *A League of Their Own,* directed by Penny Marshall (Columbia Pictures, 1992).

Chapter 6 Impostor Syndrome Is a Sheet of Thin Ice

1. Margie Warrell, "Afraid of Being 'Found Out'? How to Overcome Impostor Syndrome," *Forbes*, April 3, 2014, https://www.forbes.com/sites/margiewarrell/2014/04/03/impostor-syndrome.

2. Warrell, "Afraid of Being 'Found Out'?"

3. Pauline Clance and Suzanne Imes, "The Impostor Phenomenon in High Achieving Women: Dynamics and Therapeutic Intervention," *Psychotherapy: Theory, Research, and Practice* 15, no. 3 (1978): 241.

4. Quoted in "18 Famous 'Imposters,'" Phoenix Performance Partners, accessed August 23, 2024, https://www.phoenixperform.com/single-post/18-famous-imposters.

5. Quoted in "18 Famous 'Imposters.'"

6. Quoted in "18 Famous 'Imposters.'"

7. Warrell, "Afraid of Being 'Found Out'?"

8. Carl Richards, "Learning to Deal With the Impostor Syndrome," *New York Times*, October 26, 2015, https://www.nytimes.com/2015/10/26/your-money/learning-to-deal-with-the-impostor-syndrome.html.

9. Alicia Liu, "Overcoming Impostor Syndrome," Medium, July 10, 2013, https://medium.com/counter-intuition/overcoming-impostor-syndrome-bdae04e46ec5.

10. Clance and Imes, "Impostor Phenomenon."

11. Clance and Imes, "Impostor Phenomenon," 241, emphasis added.

12. Marantz, *Dirt*, 163–64.

13. Clance and Imes, "Impostor Phenomenon," 244, emphasis added.

14. Marantz, *Slow Growth*, 172.

15. Warrell, "Afraid of Being 'Found Out'?"

16. Jon Acuff, *Finish: Give Yourself the Gift of Done* (Portfolio, 2017), 124.

17. Hannah Brencher, *If You Find This Letter: My Journey to Find Purpose Through Hundreds of Letters to Strangers* (Howard Books, 2016), 247.

18. Clance and Imes, "Impostor Phenomenon," 242.

19. Clance and Imes, "Impostor Phenomenon," 241.

20. Clance and Imes, "Impostor Phenomenon," 245.

21. Clance and Imes, "Impostor Phenomenon," 245–46.

Chapter 7 Overthinking Is an Orange Safety Cone

1. H. Bottemanne et al., "The Predictive Mind: An Introduction to Bayesian Brain Theory," National Library of Medicine, August 2022, https://pubmed.ncbi.nlm.nih.gov/35012898.

2. University of Oxford, "The Brain Is a Prediction Machine: It Knows How Well We Are Doing Something Before We Even Try," Experimental Psychology Medical Sciences Division, March 16, 2021, https://www.psy.ox.ac.uk/news/the-brain-is-a-prediction-machine-it-knows-how-good-we-are-doing-something-before-we-even-try.

3. University of Oxford, "The Brain Is a Prediction Machine."

4. Sian Ferguson and Olivia Walters, "Catastrophizing: What You Need to Know to Stop Worrying," Healthline, April 10, 2023, https://www.healthline.com/health/anxiety/catastrophizing#causes.

5. Christopher Bergland, "New Research Explains Why Overthinking Can Hinder Creativity," *Psychology Today*, June 8, 2017, https://www.psychologytoday.com/us/blog/the-athletes-way/201706/new-research-explains-why-overthinking-can-hinder-creativity.

6. Bergland, "New Research Explains."

7. Bergland, "New Research Explains."

8. Allison Fallon, *The Power of Writing It Down: A Simple Habit to Unlock Your Brain and Reimagine Your Life* (Zondervan, 2021), 54–55.

9. Shi Baoguo et al., "Different Brain Structures Associated with Artistic and Scientific Creativity: A Voxel-Based Morphometry Study," *Scientific Reports* 7 (February 21, 2017), https://www.nature.com/articles/srep42911.

10. Emma Proud, "Your Brain on Innovation," Medium, November 8, 2021, https://medium.com/hellobrink-co/your-brain-on-innovation-40a8770895aa.

11. Proud, "Your Brain on Innovation."

12. Estanislao Bachrach, *The Agile Mind: How Your Brain Makes Creativity Happen* (Virgin Books, 2017), chap. 1, Kindle.

13. Bachrach, *The Agile Mind*, chap. 3.

14. Proud, "Your Brain on Innovation."

15. Mary Marantz, host, *The Mary Marantz Show*, "The Power of Writing It Down: 6 Ways to Get Unstuck and Unlock Your Brain with Allison Fallon," February 2, 2021, https://podcasts.apple.com/us/podcast/power-writing-it-down-6-ways-to-get-unstuck-unlock/id1478272407?i=1000507419533.

16. *The Sandlot*, directed by David Mickey Evans (20th Century Fox, 1993).

17. *Walk Hard: The Dewey Cox Story*, directed by Jake Kasdan (Columbia Pictures, 2007).

18. Kristopher Benke, "Why Thinking Hard Makes You Tired," *Neuroscience News*, August 11, 2022, https://neurosciencenews.com/cognitive-fatigue-21226/.

19. Benke, "Why Thinking Hard Makes You Tired."

20. Benke, "Why Thinking Hard Makes You Tired."

Chapter 8 Procrastination Is a Double-Edged Sword

1. James Clear, "Procrastination: A Scientific Guide on How to Stop Procrastinating," JamesClear.com, accessed May 21, 2024, https://jamesclear.com/procrastination.

2. Clear, "Procrastination."

3. Joy Emeh, "Stress: Can It Cause Flu-Like Symptoms?," Medical News Today, September 6, 2023, https://www.medicalnewstoday.com/articles/can-stress-cause-flu-like-symptoms#can-stress-cause-flu.

4. Jennifer N. Morey et al., "Current Directions in Stress and Human Immune Function," National Library of Medicine, October 1, 2015, https://www.ncbi.nlm.nih.gov/pmc/articles/PMC4465119/.

5. Anne Lamott, *Bird by Bird: Some Instructions on Writing and Life* (Anchor Books, 1995), 21.

6. *The Office*, season 4, episode 4, "Money," directed by Paul Lieberstein, aired October 18, 2007, on NBC.

7. Psychology Today, "Procrastination," PsychologyToday.com, accessed May 21, 2024, https://www.psychologytoday.com/us/basics/procrastination, emphasis added.

8. Georgia Griffiths, "The Science Behind Procrastination," Arc UNSW, accessed May 21, 2024, https://www.arc.unsw.edu.au/blitz/read/The-Science-Behind-Procrastination.

9. James Surowiecki, "Later," *The New Yorker*, October 4, 2010, https://www.newyorker.com/magazine/2010/10/11/later.

10. Lakshmi Mani, "Hyperbolic Discounting: Why You Make Terrible Life Choices," Nir and Far, accessed April 26, 2023, https://www.nirandfar.com/hyperbolic-discounting-why-you-make-terrible-life-choices.

11. Zawn Villines, "What Is Cognitive Dissonance?," Medical News Today, January 15, 2024, https://www.medicalnewstoday.com/articles/326738.

12. Dr. Alison Cook, *I Shouldn't Feel This Way: Name What's Hard, Tame Your Guilt, and Transform Self-Sabotage into Brave Action* (Thomas Nelson, 2024), 81.

13. *Mom*, season 4, episode 17, "Black Mold and an Old Hot Dog," directed by Anthony Rich, aired March 30, 2017, on CBS.

14. Eric Jaffe, "Why Wait? The Science Behind Procrastination," *Observer* 26, no. 4 (April 2013), https://www.psychologicalscience.org/observer/why-wait-the-science-behind-procrastination.

15. Jaffe, "Why Wait?"

16. Quoted in Jaffe, "Why Wait?"

17. Jaffe, "Why Wait?"

18. Psychology Today, "Procrastination."

19. Kendra Cherry, "What Is the Fear of Success?," Very Well Mind, January 20, 2023, https://www.verywellmind.com/what-is-the-fear-of-success-5179184.

20. "The Science Behind Causes of Procrastination," UPMC Health Beat Mental Health, February 28, 2024, https://share.upmc.com/2024/02/causes-of-procrastination/.

21. Drew C. Appleby, "The First Step to Overcoming Procrastination: Know Thyself," American Psychological Association, January 2017, https://www.apa.org/ed/precollege/psn/2017/01/overcoming-procrastination.

22. "The Science Behind Causes of Procrastination."

23. Ada Zohar et al., "Active and Passive Procrastination in Terms of Temperament and Character," *PeerJ* 7:e6988 (May 29, 2019), https://doi.org/10.7717/peerj.6988.
24. Kendra Cherry, "What Is Procrastination?," Very Well Mind, updated July 7, 2024, https://www.verywellmind.com/the-psychology-of-procrastination-2795944.
25. Zohar et al., "Active and Passive Procrastination."
26. Zohar et al., "Active and Passive Procrastination."
27. Anne-Laure Le Cunff, "The Neuroscience of Procrastination: A Short Primer," Ness Labs, accessed April 25, 2024, https://nesslabs.com/neuroscience-of-procrastination.
28. Charlotte Lieberman, "Why You Procrastinate (It Has Nothing to Do with Self-Control)," *New York Times*, March 25, 2019, https://www.nytimes.com/2019/03/25/smarter-living/why-you-procrastinate-it-has-nothing-to-do-with-self-control.html.
29. Britt Frank, "Feeling Stuck? 2 Types of Procrastination," *Psychology Today*, January 15, 2023, https://www.psychologytoday.com/us/blog/the-science-of-stuck/202301/feeling-stuck-2-types-of-procrastination.
30. Le Cunff, "The Neuroscience of Procrastination."
31. Griffiths, "The Science Behind Procrastination."
32. Le Cunff, "The Neuroscience of Procrastination."
33. Griffiths, "The Science Behind Procrastination."
34. Frank, "Feeling Stuck?"
35. Lieberman, "Why You Procrastinate."
36. Frank, "Feeling Stuck?"
37. "The Habit Poem," author unknown.
38. Quoted in Amy Spencer, "Want to Train Your Brain to Stop Procrastinating? Read These Tips From a Neuroscientist," *Real Simple*, updated May 1, 2023, https://www.realsimple.com/work-life/life-strategies/time-management/procrastination.
39. Spencer, "Want to Train Your Brain to Stop Procrastinating?"
40. Spencer, "Want to Train Your Brain to Stop Procrastinating?"
41. Quoted in Spencer, "Want to Train Your Brain to Stop Procrastinating?"
42. Mary Marantz, host, *The Mary Marantz Show*, "The 4 Tendencies: The Secret Way Expectations Can Shape Happier Habits with Gretchen Rubin," April 27, 2021, https://podcasts.apple.com/us/podcast/4-tendencies-secret-way-expectations-can-shape-happier/id1478272407?i=1000520010772.
43. Jeffrey Bernstein, "Try This Simple Trick to Overcome Procrastination," *Psychology Today*, March 2, 2024, https://www.psychologytoday.com/us/blog/liking-the-child-you-love/202402/try-this-simple-trick-to-overcome-procrastination.
44. American Psychological Association, "Psychology of Procrastination: Why People Put Off Important Tasks Until the Last Minute" (press release), April 5, 2010, https://www.apa.org/news/press/releases/2010/04/procrastination.

Chapter 9 People-Pleasing Is a Lonely Intersection

1. The Film Bandit, "Lost and Found: The Ending of 'Cast Away' Explained," TheFilmBandit.com, accessed April 29, 2024, https://thefilmbandit.com/lost-and-found-the-meaning-behind-cast-aways-ending.

2. Marantz, *Slow Growth*, 109–10.
3. Victoria Albina, "Root Causes of Why We People Please," VictoriaAlbina.com, May 28, 2020, https://victoriaalbina.com/root-causes-of-why-we-people-please/.
4. Kendra Cherry, "How to Stop People-Pleasing: Are You a People-Pleaser?," Very Well Mind, updated May 19, 2024, https://www.verywellmind.com/how-to-stop-being-a-people-pleaser-5184412.
5. Cherry, "How to Stop People-Pleasing."
6. Albina, "Root Causes of Why We People Please."
7. Brain Aware Training, "The Brain Science Behind Belonging: Why 'Fitting In' Matters to Humans," LinkedIn, February 22, 2024, https://www.linkedin.com/pulse/brain-science-behind-belonging-why-fitting-matters-9fzec/.
8. Brain Aware Training, "The Brain Science Behind Belonging," emphasis added.
9. Albina, "Root Causes of Why We People Please."
10. Zawn Villines, "People Pleaser: What It Means and How to Stop," Medical News Today, March 1, 2023, https://www.medicalnewstoday.com/articles/people-pleaser.
11. Netplanet, "The Downside of People-Pleasing—Fawning," New Directions Psychology, accessed April 29, 2024, https://ndpsych.com.au/the-downside-of-people-pleasing-fawning.
12. Albina, "Root Causes of Why We People Please."
13. Marantz, *Dirt*, 222.
14. Samanee Mahbub, "The Permission Gap: Why Do We Seek Permission To Do the Things We Always Wanted To Do?," Medium, August 26, 2016, https://medium.com/conscious-career/the-permission-gap-e3155b37651b.
15. "People-Pleasing," PsychologyToday.com, accessed April 29, 2024, https://www.psychologytoday.com/us/basics/people-pleasing.
16. Albina, "Root Causes of Why We People Please."
17. Simon Sinek, *Start with Why: How Great Leaders Inspire Everyone to Take Action* (Portfolio, 2009), 47.
18. Billie Wade, "Self Matters: Stop Asking Permission To Be You," Create Write Now, November 16, 2020, https://www.createwritenow.com/life-matters-blog/self-matters-stop-asking-permission-to-be-you.
19. Sian Ferguson, "Approval-Seeking Behavior: Signs, Causes, and How to Heal," Psych Central, updated October 27, 2022, https://psychcentral.com/blog/what-drives-our-need-for-approval.

Chapter 10 Perfectionism Is Hiding with Better PR

1. Ian Morgan Cron and Suzanne Stabile, *The Road Back to You: An Enneagram Journey to Self-Discovery* (InterVarsity, 2016), 134.
2. Cron and Stabile, *The Road Back to You*, 143.
3. Mary Marantz, host, *The Mary Marantz Show*, "The Enneagram Journey: How to Take Off the Mask and Live Your Truest Self with Ian Cron," June 23, 2020, https://podcasts.apple.com/us/podcast/enneagram-journey-how-to-take-off-mask-live-your-truest/id1478272407?i=1000479239561.

4. Beatrice Chestnut, *The Complete Enneagram: 27 Paths to Greater Self-Knowledge* (She Writes Press, 2013), 287.
5. Chestnut, *The Complete Enneagram*, 285, emphasis added.
6. Chestnut, *The Complete Enneagram*, 287, emphasis added.
7. Marantz, *Dirt*, 110–11.
8. Marantz, *Slow Growth*, 109.

Chapter 11 Failure Is a Bankrupt Identity

1. Ira Glass, host, *This American Life*, "The Gap," January 25, 2014, https://www.thisamericanlife.org/extras/the-gap.
2. Amy Morin, "10 Healthy Ways to Cope With Failure," Verywell Mind, updated November 29, 2022, https://www.verywellmind.com/healthy-ways-to-cope-with-failure-4163968.
3. Morin, "10 Healthy Ways to Cope With Failure."
4. Elizabeth Perry, "7 Ways to Overcome Fear of Failure and Move Forward in Life," BetterUp, October 11, 2022, https://www.betterup.com/blog/how-to-overcome-fear-of-failure.
5. James Clear, *Atomic Habits* (Avery, 2018), 38, emphasis added.
6. Alison Cook, *I Shouldn't Feel This Way: Name What's Hard, Tame Your Guilt, and Transform Self-Sabotage into Brave Action* (Thomas Nelson, 2024), 13.
7. Morin, "10 Healthy Ways to Cope With Failure."
8. Kara Cutruzzula, "How to Move On After Failure—And Rebuild Your Confidence," Ideas.Ted.Com, December 21, 2020, https://ideas.ted.com/how-to-move-on-after-failure-and-rebuild-confidence-erika-hamden/.
9. Cutruzzula, "How to Move On After Failure."
10. Cutruzzula, "How to Move On After Failure."
11. Catherine Cote, "Growth Mindset vs. Fixed Mindset: What's The Difference?," Harvard Business School, March 10, 2022, https://online.hbs.edu/blog/post/growth-mindset-vs-fixed-mindset.
12. Cote, "Growth Mindset vs. Fixed Mindset," emphasis added.

Chapter 12 Criticism Is an Inside Job

1. Ryan Reynolds (@vancityreynolds), Instagram, May 30, 2024, https://www.instagram.com/p/C7leiEzM9uY/?hl=en.
2. Wikipedia, "Chinese Water Torture," last modified June 11, 2024, https://en.wikipedia.org/wiki/Chinese_water_torture.
3. *Mythbusters*, season 2, episode 25, "Brown Note," developed by Peter Rees, aired February 16, 2005, on Discovery Channel.
4. *Mind Field*, season 2, episode 3, "Interrogation," created by Michael Stevens, aired December 6, 2017, on YouTube Premium.
5. Anna Katharina Schaffner, "Living With the Inner Critic: 8 Helpful Worksheets (+PDF)," Positive Psychology, October 15, 2020, https://positivepsychology.com/inner-critic-worksheets/, emphasis added.

6. I can 100 percent attest that all of this is true. Steven Pressfield, *The War of Art: Break Through the Blocks and Win Your Inner Creative Battles* (Black Irish Entertainment, 2002), 19.

7. Nelda Andersone, "Understanding the Inner Critic," *Psychology Today*, December 15, 2023, https://www.psychologytoday.com/us/blog/human-inner-dynamics/202312/understanding-the-inner-critic.

8. Andersone, "Understanding the Inner Critic."

9. Kristin D. Neff and Pittman McGehee, "Self-Compassion and Psychological Resilience Among Adolescents and Young Adults," *Self and Identity* 9, no. 3 (2009): 226.

10. Neff and McGehee, "Self-Compassion and Psychological Resilience," 227–28, emphasis added.

11. *Brats*, directed by Andrew McCarthy (Hulu, 2024).

12. Andersone, "Understanding the Inner Critic."

13. Andersone, "Understanding the Inner Critic."

14. Elle Hunt, "Silence Your Inner Critic: A Guide to Self-Compassion in the Toughest Times," *The Guardian*, January 6, 2021, https://www.theguardian.com/lifeandstyle/2021/jan/06/silence-your-inner-critic-a-guide-to-self-compassion-in-the-toughest-times, emphasis added.

15. Schaffner, "Living With the Inner Critic."

16. Kendra Cherry, "What Is the Negativity Bias?," VeryWellMind, updated November 13, 2023, https://www.verywellmind.com/negative-bias-4589618, emphasis added.

17. Schaffner, "Living With the Inner Critic."

18. Martha Sweezy, "The Inner Critic: An Internal Family Systems Perspective," *Psychology Today*, updated September 1, 2023, https://www.psychologytoday.com/us/blog/internal-family-systems-therapy-for-shame-and-guilt/202308/the-inner-critic-an-internal-family.

19. Quoted in Hunt, "Silence Your Inner Critic."

20. Schaffner, "Living With the Inner Critic."

21. Sweezy, "The Inner Critic."

22. Sweezy, "The Inner Critic."

23. Sweezy, "The Inner Critic."

24. *The Office*, season 6, episode 19, "St. Patrick's Day," directed by Randall Einhorn, aired March 11, 2010, on NBC.

Chapter 13 Distraction Is a Clock That's Ticking

1. *Three to Tango*, directed by Damon Santostefano (Warner Bros., 1999).

2. Dave Ramsey, *The Total Money Makeover: A Proven Plan for Financial Fitness* (Thomas Nelson, 2003), 114.

3. "5 Leadership Thoughts from John C. Maxwell," Leadr, May 10, 2019, https://blog.leadr.com/5-leadership-thoughts-from-john-c-maxwell.

4. Darren Hardy, *The Compound Effect: Jumpstart Your Income, Your Life, Your Success* (Vanguard Press, 2010), 53.

5. Hardy, *The Compound Effect*, 44.
6. Steven Pressfield (@steven_pressfield), Instagram post, June 19, 2024, https://www.instagram.com/p/C8ZlMXnSo8y/?img_index=2.

Chapter 14 Success Is a Slippery Slope

1. Will Boast, "5 Tips for Writing a Memoir," Publications Unltd, December 5, 2014, https://publicationsunltd.com/2014/12/06/5-tips-for-writing-a-memoir/.
2. Marantz, *Slow Growth*, 121–22.
3. Wikipedia, "2008 Georgia Imperial Sugar Refinery Explosion," last edited July 27, 2024, https://en.wikipedia.org/wiki/2008_Georgia_Imperial_Sugar_refinery_explosion.
4. Marantz, *Dirt*, 175.
5. Marantz, *Dirt*, 175.
6. Anandi Mani et al., "Poverty Impedes Cognitive Function," *Science*, August 30, 2013, https://scholar.harvard.edu/files/sendhil/files/976.full_.pdf.
7. Allison Torres Burtka, "What Is Scarcity Mentality?," WebMD, February 25, 2024, https://www.webmd.com/mental-health/what-is-scarcity-mentality.
8. Bob Burg and John David Mann, *The Go-Giver, Expanded Edition: A Little Story About a Powerful Business Idea* (Portfolio, 2007), 31.
9. Burg and Mann, *The Go-Giver*, 63.
10. Burg and Mann, *The Go-Giver*, 43.
11. Burg and Mann, *The Go-Giver*, 11.
12. Elisabeth Kübler-Ross, *Death: The Final Stage of Growth* (Simon & Schuster, 1975), 96.

MARY MARANTZ is the bestselling author of *Dirt* and *Slow Growth Equals Strong Roots*, as well as the host of the popular podcast *The Mary Marantz Show*. She grew up in a trailer in rural West Virginia and was the first in her family to go to college before going on to Yale for law school. Her work has been featured on CNN, MSN, Business Insider, Bustle, Thrive Global, *Southern Living*, Hallmark Home & Family, and more. She and her husband Justin live in an 1880s fixer-upper by the sea in New Haven, Connecticut, with their two very fluffy golden retrievers, Goodspeed and Atticus. Learn more at MaryMarantz.com.

CONNECT WITH MARY

MaryMarantz.com
TheMaryMarantzShow.com

🅕 🅞 @MaryMarantz

Take the Achiever Quiz at MaryMarantz.com/quiz

A Note from the Publisher

Dear Reader,

Thank you for selecting a Revell book! We're so happy to be part of your life through this work.

Revell's mission is to publish books that offer hope and help for meeting life's challenges, and that bring comfort and inspiration. We know that the right words at the right time can make all the difference; it is our goal with every title to provide just the words you need.

We believe in building lasting relationships with readers, and we'd love to get to know you better. If you have any feedback, questions, or just want to chat about your experience reading this book, please email us directly at publisher@revellbooks.com. Your insights are incredibly important to us, and it would be our pleasure to hear how we can better serve you.

We look forward to hearing from you and having the chance to enhance your experience with Revell Books.

The Publishing Team at Revell Books
A Division of Baker Publishing Group
publisher@revellbooks.com

Revell